British

‘. . . indispensable . . . the ideal complement to introductory texts on Britain.’ *Professor Dr Jürgen Kramer, Dortmund University*

‘. . . a valuable introduction to many aspects of British life.’ *Dr Ovidi Carbonell, University of Salamanca*

‘. . . well organised, and gives consideration to a variety of relevant factors in the formation of identity . . . eminently readable.’ *Dr Ian Inglis, University of Northumbria*

British Cultural Identities analyses the various and constantly changing ways in which people who live in the UK position themselves and are positioned by their culture today. Each chapter covers one of the seven intersecting themes:

- Places and peoples
- Education, work and leisure
- Gender, sex and the family
- Youth culture and style
- Class and politics
- Ethnicity and language
- Religion and heritage

The second edition of this invaluable book brings it right up to date to cover such ‘phenomena’ as Posh and Becks, Jamie Oliver, *Big Brother*, the Millennium Dome, and Harry Potter.

Mike Storry was Senior Lecturer in English at Liverpool John Moores University and is now retired. He co-edited *The Encyclopaedia of Contemporary British Culture* (Routledge, 1999) with Peter Childs. **Peter Childs** is Principal Lecturer in English at the University of Gloucestershire and author of *Modernism* (Routledge, 2000) and editor of *Post-Colonial Theory and English Literature* (Edinburgh University Press, 1999).

British Cultural Identities

SECOND EDITION

■ Edited by Mike Storry and Peter Childs

Routledge
Taylor & Francis Group

LONDON AND NEW YORK

First edition published in 1997 by Routledge
Second edition published in 2002 by Routledge
2 Park Square, Milton Park, Abingdon, Oxon, OX14 4RN

Simultaneously published in the USA and Canada
by Routledge
270 Madison Ave, New York, NY 10016

Reprinted 2005

Routledge is an imprint of Taylor & Francis Group

© 1997, 2002 selection and editorial matter, Mike Storry and Peter Childs
© 1997, 2002 individual chapters, their authors

Typeset in Sabon and Futura by Florence Production Ltd
Printed and bound in Great Britain by TJ International Ltd, Padstow, Cornwall

British Library Cataloguing in Publication Data
A catalogue record for this book is available from the British Library

Library of Congress Cataloging in Publication Data
has been applied for

ISBN 0–415–27860–0 (hbk)
ISBN 0–415–27861–9 (pbk)

Contents

List of figures   ix
List of tables   xi
List of contributors   xii
Preface   xiii

Introduction: Britain in the modern world   1

Institutional Britain   8
Popular culture   9
Schooling   9
Methodology   10
Politics   11
Society   12
Culture   12
Sport   13
Xenophobia   14
Postmodernism   15
Media   15
Language   16
The *Sunday Times* Rich List   16
The Observer: Britain Uncovered   17
Channel 5: *An A-Z of Britishness*   18
England, England   19
Individualism   21
Heroes   22
Princess Diana   22
The Beckhams   24
Media celebrities   25
Business   26
Reality television   26

Dumbing down   27
British Cultural Identities structure   29
Exercises   31
Reading   32
Cultural examples   33
Websites   34

1 Places and peoples: nation and region   35

Nation   43
Country   44
Region   48
County   52
City   55
Town   59
Village   61
Conclusion   64
Exercises   69
Reading   70
Cultural examples   70
Websites   71

2 Education, work, and leisure   73

Schools   75
Colleges and universities   78
Educational changes and trends   79
Employment   83
Unemployment and economic change   87
Leisure around the home   90
Public entertainment   92
New patterns in leisure   100
Trends in entertainment   103
Conclusion   107
Exercises   108
Reading   109
Cultural examples   109
Websites   110

3 Gender, sex, and the family   111

The family unit   114
Gender and British institutions   117
Women and employment   120

Marriage and divorce   123
Parenting   126
Sexuality and identity   128
Conclusion   134
Exercises   135
Reading   136
Cultural examples   136
Websites   137

4 Youth culture and style   139

Youth, teenagers, and adolescents   143
Going out: 'dressing up and dressing down'   145
Staying in: young people and the media   151
Sex and drugs and rock'n'roll   156
Conclusion   163
Exercises   170
Reading   171
Cultural examples   172
Websites   173

5 Class and politics   175

The upper class   179
The middle class   183
The working class   187
Social change   191
The nature of politics   192
Party politics   195
Voting behaviour   199
Conclusion   203
Exercises   205
Reading   205
Cultural examples   205
Websites   207

6 Ethnicity and language   209

Varieties of English   213
Gaelic, Scots, Welsh   217
New languages, new identities   223
Conclusion   232
Exercises   236
Reading   236

Cultural examples	237
Websites	238

7 Religion and heritage 239

The established church	245
Background religion	249
Other world religions in Britain	251
Religious festivals	255
The New Age	258
Religious differences: age and sex	262
The heritage industry	264
Conclusion	268
Exercises	269
Reading	270
Cultural examples	270
Websites	271

Conclusion: Britain towards the future 273

Europe	276
Multiethnic Britain	281
New technology	286
Conclusion	288
Exercises	289
Reading	289
Cultural examples	289
Websites	290
Glossary	293
Index	299

Figures

0.1	Shops or stalls selling national goods and souvenirs from (a) England, (b) Scotland, (c) Wales or (d) Ireland	6
0.2	Floral tributes outside Kensington Palace immediately after Princess Diana's death	23
0.3	David and Victoria Beckham	25
1.1	Map of the British Isles	38
1.2	Big Ben	39
1.3	The lion and the unicorn, symbolising England and Scotland, on Queen Elizabeth Gate, London	42
1.4	Edinburgh Festival fringe 2001	45
1.5	Rolling English countryside of the shires (Gloucestershire)	49
1.6	Typical English rural scene	53
1.7	Boats waiting for the tide to come in on the north Wales coast	54
1.8	Boats and houseboats on the Thames at Richmond	56
1.9	'Save the Countryside'	62
2.1	A trip to the seaside	100
2.2	English samba band	102
2.3	Shopping	103
2.4	The Millennium Eye	105
2.5	Strawberry picking	107
3.1	Margaret Thatcher	118
3.2	A woman building worker	121
3.3	Traditional wedding	124
3.4	The Gay Pride Mardi Gras	131
4.1	Black London punk	147
4.2	Female London punk	148
4.3	Haçienda clubbers	151
4.4	Crowd at U2 concert	161

4.5	Boot store in Camden market	165
4.6	Goth and punk clothes store in Camden market	168
5.1	Labour Party poster	178
5.2	Houses of Parliament	182
5.3	May Day protest against consumer capitalism	186
5.4	Legalise cannabis	190
5.5	The government's 'war on drugs'	195
5.6	Political party fliers	200
5.7	Driving Britain into Europe	203
6.1	Bagpipe player in Edinburgh	220
6.2	Mosque in Edinburgh	225
6.3	Distribution of ethnic groups in Britain, 1993	227
6.4	Notting Hill Carnival 2001	231
6.5	Black street vendors selling British flags	234
7.1	Westminster Abbey	247
7.2	The Alpha Course	250
7.3	Community-built mosque in Hounslow, West London	253
7.4	Last night of the Proms	256
7.5	The Globe	260
7.6	Horse Guard and street performer guardsman	263
7.7	Buckingham Palace	265
7.8	Shakespeare's Head Pub, Carnaby Street	266
7.9	Brighton Royal Pavilion	267
7.10	Prince Charles sups a pint of beer	269
8.1	Twinning	277
8.2	Britain's ethnic mix	281

Tables

0.1	Subjects of conversation with friends and family, 1991	4
0.2	An A–Z of Britishness	18
0.3	Quintessences of Englishness	20
1.1	Resident populations of UK countries, 1981 and 1994 and 1999	40
1.2	Resident populations of largest urban districts, 1994 and 2001	51
2.1	The workforce in Britain, 2001	85
2.2	Unemployment in Britain, 1980–2000	85
2.3	Most popular television soap operas, series and quizzes, 2001	92
2.4	Readership of selected newspapers and magazines, 2000	93
2.5	Most popular magazines read by men, 1980–2000	93
2.6	Most popular types of books bought	94
3.1	Divorces in the UK, 1971 and 1992	115
3.2	UK employment status by sex	121
5.1	The *Sunday Times* rich list, 2001	180
5.2	Membership of selected major unions, 2001	189
5.3	General Elections, 1992–2001	199
6.1	Comparison of ethnic populations	212
7.1	Attendance at religious ceremonies, 1992 and 1998	243
7.2	Church members by country, 1985 and 1992	244

Contributors

Peter Childs is Principal Lecturer in English at the University of Gloucestershire. He has edited, with Mike Storry, *The Routledge Encyclopaedia of Contemporary British Culture*.

Jo Croft is Lecturer in Literary Studies at Liverpool John Moores University.

Edmund Cusick is Senior Lecturer in Imaginative Writing at Liverpool John Moores University.

Gerry Smyth is Reader in Cultural History at Liverpool John Moores University.

Frank McDonough is Senior Lecturer in Modern Political History at Liverpool John Moores University.

Roberta Garrett is Lecturer in Literature and Cultural Studies at the University of East London.

Mike Storry was Senior Lecturer in English at Liverpool John Moores University. He has taught widely in Britain and abroad. He has published fiction and poetry and edited, with Peter Childs, *The Routledge Encyclopaedia of Contemporary British Culture*.

Preface

A book about British cultural identities immediately raises a number of questions: Whose Britain? Whose culture? Whose identity? Do a majority of people in the UK any more think of themselves in terms of being British anyway?

British Cultural Identities is aimed at people interested in these questions. It approaches the idea of British identities through contemporary practices and activities: not through institutions or economics, but through culture. The book is written in a clear, accessible style, making it especially useful to the student, at home or overseas, who wishes to be introduced to the variety of British experiences at and after the year 2000. In both the first and the second editions, it has aimed to be a different kind of book about the contemporary UK: one which looks at Britain in not sociological or historical but cultural terms. Each chapter is clearly structured around key themes, has a timeline of important dates, a list of recent cultural examples, and a section of questions and exercises. The book is illustrated with photographs and tables throughout.

All the contributors to this collection outline the plurality of identities found across the UK at the start of the twenty-first century. The essays begin from the belief that identities are the names we give to the different ways we all are placed by, and place ourselves within, our culture. The contributors have been asked to think of culture as the practices and beliefs that people encounter and share – events, ideas, and images that shape their lives everywhere and every day. The introductory chapter deals with 'Britain now': with the issues being discussed in Britain at the start of 2002. The remaining seven chapters cover intersecting areas: gender and the family; religion and heritage; places and peoples; youth culture and age; class and politics; language and ethnicity; education, work, and leisure.

The chapters are organised in the following way. At the beginning of each one you will find a timeline, usually of the most significant dates for the area covered. There follows a structured discussion of ways in which that area can be understood in different ways and at different levels. The conclusions drawn by each chapter are open because all the contributors believe there are many Britains and many British cultural identities. You will find many opinions expressed, but all the writers aim to outline current debates, key moments, and speculative questions rather than to supply definitive answers. Consequently, our collective aim is to explore the face of British culture today, while at the same time suggesting that it will have changed tomorrow.

At the end of each chapter, you will find some questions and exercises, preliminary answers to most of which will be contained in the text. However, some of the questions are designed to stimulate your thoughts and to encourage you to go to libraries where necessary to conduct research or to test our suggestions by looking at the numerous cultural products that supply a way into an understanding of cultural identity in contemporary Britain. The further reading shows you where to go next for more detailed study. Some of the books suggested will also have been chosen because they cover aspects which the chapter itself has not been able to treat at length. In an introductory text such as this we cannot cover the minutiae of all social, ethnic, or even regional groupings; however, we intend to sensitise readers, particularly those outside the UK, to Britain's cultural diversity. Lastly, we have also listed at the end of each chapter some recent cultural examples which we feel will give you an insight into concerns, anxieties and tensions within contemporary British culture. These novels, films, and television programmes are of great importance because they provide specific British cultural representations relevant to the issues under discussion. We have chosen to select books, movies, and programmes that are both current and particularly helpful or are widely available in print or on video.

Introduction: Britain in the modern world

Mike Storry and Peter Childs

- Institutional Britain 8
- Popular culture 9
- Schooling 9
- Methodology 10
- Politics 11
- Society 12
- Culture 12
- Sport 13
- Xenophobia 14
- Postmodernism 15
- Media 15
- Language 16
- The *Sunday Times* Rich List 16
- *The Observer*: Britain Uncovered 17
- Channel 5: *An A–Z of Britishness* 18

- *England, England* 19
- Individualism 21
- Heroes 22
- Princess Diana 22
- The Beckhams 24
- Media celebrities 25
- Business 26
- Reality television 26
- Dumbing down 27
- *British Cultural Identities* structure 29
- *Exercises* 31
- *Reading* 32
- *Cultural examples* 33
- *Websites* 34

Timeline

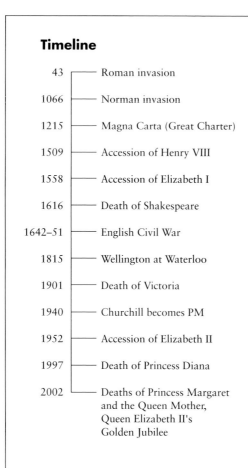

43	Roman invasion
1066	Norman invasion
1215	Magna Carta (Great Charter)
1509	Accession of Henry VIII
1558	Accession of Elizabeth I
1616	Death of Shakespeare
1642–51	English Civil War
1815	Wellington at Waterloo
1901	Death of Victoria
1940	Churchill becomes PM
1952	Accession of Elizabeth II
1997	Death of Princess Diana
2002	Deaths of Princess Margaret and the Queen Mother, Queen Elizabeth II's Golden Jubilee

THIS IS A BOOK ABOUT contemporary Britain and British people. On the one hand, Britain is a country with defined boundaries, a recognisable landscape, a long history, and a position in the various international economic, social, and political league tables. On the other hand, British people are much harder to describe. To begin with, some British people do not live in Britain. Also, many people living in Britain do not think of themselves as British. Nationality is a matter of allegiance and cultural affiliation. Some people say that your nationality is indicated by where you choose to live or by the team you support at sports events; others say that it is a question of whom you would fight for. It has also been argued that nationality is no longer a powerful force in Britain, that it is simply a matter of circumstance, and that today it is far less significant than local or global identities: relatives, friends, and communities are more important to us and so is transnational culture.

Above all, nationality is a question of identity and so is crossed by other kinds of identity, such as ethnicity, gender, sexuality, religion, age, and occupation. This book aims to outline some of the kinds of identity found at those intersections in Britain at the beginning of the twenty-first century. As such, it will be implicitly questioning the difference between British cultural identities and cultural identities in Britain. Fifty years ago, T. S. Eliot famously said that 'culture' was something that included 'all the characteristic activities and interests of a people'. He thought that this meant for England: 'Derby Day, Henley Regatta, Cowes, the twelfth of August, a cup final, the dog races, the pin table, the dart board, Wensleydale cheese, boiled cabbage cut into sections, beetroot in vinegar, nineteenth-century Gothic churches, and the music of Elgar'. Fifty years on, conceptions of English and British identity have changed enormously and, for example, few people would attribute any significance to the twelfth of August, the opening day of the grouse-shooting season. Moreover television, which didn't feature for Eliot, would appear from Table 0.1 to be the main cultural bonding agent between British people.

The term 'British' is itself contentious. In recent years, partly as a response to the devolution of political power to Scotland, Wales, and Ireland, there has been much questioning of what it means to be British.

TABLE 0.1   Subjects of conversation with friends and family, 1991

Subject	Percentage of people who ever talk about subject
Advertising	2
Big business	2
Bringing up children	26
Clothes and fashion	19
Cost of living	43
Education	20
Gardening	16
Law and order	16
Neighbours or workmates	21
Politicians	8
Religion	6
Sport	25
Television programmes	48
The government	19
Trade unions	1
Newspaper articles	19
Health and welfare services	18
Unemployment	16
Personal health	21
None of the above/don't know	3

Source: TOM *Attitudes to Advertising Survey*, 1991

If we are all British, then why should people feel a need to revert to their previous 'nationalities'? And if others in the UK have power devolved to them, what becomes of the formerly dominant English?

In examining nationality we should add the caveat that Britishness is often used instead of Englishness. On William Gladstone's tombstone, he is described as 'Prime Minister of England' – ignoring Wales, Scotland, and Ireland! People from Wales, Scotland, and Northern Ireland believe that making Englishness synonymous with Britishness erases their identity. If British and English are the same, there is no room within the term for other nationalities who live in the British Isles. R. S. Thomas, the Welsh poet and clergyman, said 'Britain does not exist for me. It is an abstraction forced on the Welsh people.' For him it was just an aspect of imperialist domination and he wanted no part of it.

The debate has broadened out into questioning whether we are anyway determined by nation any longer. Some commentators suggest that it is easier to define British cultural identity by looking outside than inside. The argument goes that Britain is just another constituent of Marshall McLuhan's 'Global Village' – the product of various world influences, rather than the outcome of home-grown social developments. Doubtless there is some truth in this. One has only to see the popularity of McDonald's, American branded clothing, or the prevalence of overseas restaurant cuisines. (Britain has eight thousands Indian restaurants.) This view should certainly be borne in mind. Don't we live in a global culture, don't we enjoy influences from many geographical areas and isn't identity different for everyone? Some people are influenced by the fact of their age, by the fact that they live in a big city, are well or badly off financially. In short hasn't nationality been overridden by 'cultural' identity? This book seeks to address those questions.

Cultural identity is something which is partly imposed by one's background and partly chosen by people. All people have a number of influences bearing on them, from both Nature and Nurture. That is, they inherit their ethnicity, physical abilities, intelligence and so on, in large measure from parents. But many other 'environmental' factors affect their development: for example family, region, schooling, religion, music, etc. determine their experience. To a degree they form their own cultural identities by selection from a range of options. So for example they are Beatles fans or Manchester United supporters, or go to opera or watch films. They conform with or react against the values of their parents and accept or reject society's expectations of them. These influences, absorbed wittingly or unwittingly, determine identity.

We have used the plural 'identities' in our title to make the point that no single mould fits British people. The population is diverse in all sorts of ways and this is one of the strengths of the culture which has evolved over the past two thousands years. Many races and continents have contributed to its development. For example most people don't know that in Roman Britain a garrison of African soldiers, under Septimus Servius, guarded Hadrian's Wall. Modern Britain contains numerous elements, often in tension with one another, but more usually complementary. For example many people who elsewhere have come to blows – Hindus and Muslims; Protestants and Catholics; Greeks and Turks – in Britain have for the most part found ways of working together in peaceful co-existence. Their liking for stability, good-quality education, healthcare and robust economic conditions has overridden their ideological differences. One of the aims of our study is to identify elements of British culture which have brought about this benign effect.

British Cultural Identities describes how people in Britain see themselves. It is concerned with the culture they generate and are in turn formed

(a)

(b)

(c)

(d)

FIGURE 0.1   Shops or stalls selling national goods and souvenirs from
(a) England, (b) Scotland, (c) Wales or (d) Ireland

by. 'Culture' is meant in its broad sense as shared experience – that which comes out of a dynamic mix of ages, races, regions, sexes, income levels and interests. The identities which are produced by this culture are personally and collectively fluid. Because what we are examining is complex and changing, our conclusions will be tentative and general. Our constant is the fact that the people who live on the islands are the way they are, partly because they live there.

In conducting our study, we will look at specific current political, social, and cultural events. This will enable us to give basic background information on Britain: who is in power, what is the racial mix, the size of the population, the key institutions, the main sports, religions and so on. We will include some succinct contrasts with the past to fill out that background. Recent events chosen for examination reveal some basic truths about Britain in the political, social, and cultural arenas and lead us to emphasise the complexity of British society and the need for careful analysis.

Institutional Britain

A list of traditional pillars of mainstream Britain would identify the key 'official' institutions as Parliament; a legal system which enforces the rule of law; an educational system of good quality; the Anglican Church; the Bank of England; the Stock Exchange; the BBC. These are all elements of a stable society, but examination of them doesn't really begin to tell the story of the culture, for which they are prerequisites. There are several other 'institutions' which are equally or even more influential in people's lives, and whose influence, though 'unofficial', is widespread. There is Henley Royal Regatta (rowing); cricket at Lords in London; Badminton Horse Trials; yachting at Cowes; rugby at Twickenham; the Glastonbury pop festival; the Edinburgh Festival; the Notting Hill Carnival. None of these events is 'institutional' but each figures largely on individuals' psychological calendars and forms part of the cultural menu from which some British identities are chosen. They are supplemented with numerous other sporting and social entertainments: soccer matches, greyhound and horse racing, darts tournaments, snooker matches, Townswomen's Guilds. These are all seen by their fans as indispensable to their individual cultural landscapes.

This 'semi-official' British cultural scene has a further supporting infrastructure of self-regulating organisations which serve to channel the talent which in another culture would not find an outlet. These include the Football and Amateur Athletic Associations, private art galleries promoting the likes of Damien Hirst, Tracey Emin and Martin Creed with their sheep in formaldehyde, bed with used condoms, or *The Lights Going On and*

Off; publishing houses making the Harry Potter phenomenon possible; film and video production companies, which create soaps such as *Brookside* and *Hollyoaks*; the advertising and design industries; the music industry, from small recording studios to major artist recruiting houses such as EMI and HMV. These are part of Britain's cultural fabric yet they have no official status and no state funding.

Popular culture

One consequence of examining the nation through its official institutions is that large cultural areas will always be unexplored. Ethnic communities will have no place. Teenage fashions, clubbing, comics, pubs, around which many people's lives revolve, won't get a look in. The Britain covered in the myriad special-interest magazines will not feature. A more comprehensive picture of contemporary British culture is likely to emerge if we examine the experience of the man or woman in the street. By and large, he or she is exposed to the culture which has welled up from below. This experience may be read through elements of popular culture such as music, magazines, television and film, examples of which are offered throughout this book.

Popular culture, which comes from below (soaps, tabloids, 'reality television' such as *Big Brother*), can be more useful for our analysis than high culture (opera, theatre), because it reflects widespread, particularly youthful, public taste and thus enables us to explore Britons' psychology, motivation and aspirations. High culture, on the other hand, is imposed from above via school curricula, and deliberately ignores life as lived experience, and contemporary social trends. The most vibrant cultural development in Britain comes from the margins not from the centre. The following for example have become incorporated into the mainstream: in music, hip hop and rap; in fashion, saris and kimonos; in style, dreadlocks, body-piercing and tattooing; in literature, novels by Hanif Kureishi or Zadie Smith, poems by Benjamin Zephaniah.

Schooling

Concentration on popular culture also enables us to keep pace more easily with the rapid changes in society. For example there have been significant shifts in patterns of education. The fee-paying private schools have always had a disproportionately significant influence throughout British society largely through their reinforcement of class structures. Ambitious members of ethnic minorities see Britain as a place where 'the old school tie' matters and, faced with latent racial prejudice, see their way forward as through private education. This is leading to profound cultural changes in one of Britain's dominant media for social advancement. There has always been an ethnic-minority presence in such schools, but pupils were usually sons of powerful overseas dynasties. For example, in Billy Bunter's school Greyfriars, in the 1930s *Magnet* comic, there was an Indian boy, Hurree Jamset Ram Singh, who was the Nabob of Bhanipur. The featuring in popular culture of such figures has undoubtedly contributed to the mystique of the great public schools, such as Eton and Harrow, whose prevailing ethos was nevertheless predominantly white, Anglo-Saxon, Protestant, Establishment. Today, however, the private sector contains a much higher ethnic element than state schools. This element is 'domestic' rather than overseas and leads to the greater integration into the corridors of power of British society for some ethnic Britons.

Other factors in the current cultural transformation are: the renegotiation of the whole concept of the family; the new technology: computers, mobile phones, the internet, DVDs. People's daily lives are adapting to shifts in career patterns, new skills requirements from employers and new entertainments. The majority of those who attend university today for example are taking courses which didn't exist ten years ago. There are degree courses in fashion, tourism, nursing, film, media, football, and pop music studies, to name a few. For a conservative country such as Britain that is a fundamental change.

Methodology

In this period of flux, where the only constant is change, what it means to be British today is markedly different from what it meant ten years ago. Enduring stereotypes are not a great deal of help. For example a 1999 poll of young Europeans associated five elements with Britain: Shakespeare, London, the BBC, The Beatles, and the Royal Family. This is very out of date. Any single snapshot of British identity will also be blurred. So what we have chosen to do is to look at a number of recent studies of the way people live, and to see how helpful they are in explaining the way our society works. A number of sources have recently offered their particular take on areas which they think are important. We shall look later at four specific examples. Firstly, every year *The Sunday Times* publishes a list of the thousand richest people in Britain. This is one way of making a judgement about the people who live here. It assumes that their wealth reflects not only their commitment and work but also their aspirations, their values, and their outlook. Secondly, in March 2001 *The Observer* Sunday newspaper published a study 'Britain Uncovered' dealing with 'the way we live now: Money, work, love, sex, crime, youth, race, religion, education and ignorance'. It contains an eclectic mix of things happening on the cultural scene which represent significant trends. Thirdly, Channel 5 produced *An A–Z of Britishness* which was another attempt to pin down the essence of contemporary British culture. We will, fourthly, look at a list of 'Quintessences of Englishness' offered in Julian Barnes's 1998 novel *England, England*. We will examine each of the above attempts to describe the moving target of British culture and will see how useful their various approaches can be, but first a look at a number of political, social, cultural, and sporting events and incidents will let us see how people reflect and inform the culture around them.

Politics

The General Election of June 2001 gave Labour a second term of office with 413 MPs to the Conservatives' 166. This is an astonishing majority. It is 31 per cent greater than Margaret Thatcher's landslide second victory in 1983. So today, ostensibly, 'New' Labour, which came into power in 1997 on a wave of euphoria, appears to be very firmly in control and to have the broad support of the people. However, a better indication of how people feel about their country and their politicians might be the fact that in both the 2001 and the 1997 elections, two single-issue mavericks, standing as Independents, were elected without the benefit of any elaborate party machine. These were: in 1997 Martin Bell; in 2001 Richard Taylor. Bell, a former war correspondent, stood as an Independent on a 'decency' manifesto, and defeated the sitting Tory MP Neil Hamilton, who had become embroiled in accusations of sleaze. Taylor, a retired hospital consultant standing on the single issue of the downsizing of his local Kidderminster hospital, unseated a Labour junior minister by 17,630 votes! Both Bell and Taylor countered elaborate, sophisticated and expensive political machines, during electoral landslides. Meanwhile young voters are so disaffected from the whole political process that, to try to secure their votes, the parties resorted to texting them on their mobile phones during the last election.

Conclusions we can draw from this are that, although Labour is in power, and although Parliament is sovereign and elected by the people, British voters are still wary of having their lives determined by professional politicians and are prepared to drop them instantly when opportunity knocks. This signals a long-standing distrust, by British people, of professionals (Disraeli was Britain's first full-time Prime Minister, only in as late as 1868) and professionalism (Rugby Union retained its amateurs-status only, until the 1990s). People have in the past preferred to be governed by the 'gifted amateur' or the aristocrat whose inherited wealth made him (rarely her) less likely to be corruptible. Now, when professionalism is more accepted, they are still prepared to elect people who operate without the benefits and constraints of a party machine.

Society

In the social arena, when the Queen Mother celebrated her 101st birthday in 2001, the Royal Family gathered around for the happy occasion. The Queen Mother was personally popular with all social classes. Hitherto Buckingham Palace has not handled public relations well, but now, trying to be 'user-friendly', the Royals organised a photo opportunity for the benefit of the media. However an unplanned outcome of the event was that newspapers took the Royal Family to task for literally wheeling out Princess Margaret, the Queen's sister, in an invalid chair. She was clearly seriously ill and it was seen as inhumane – a violation of her rights as an individual, to display her to the masses. So what was meant to be an orchestrated moment of celebration became an opportunity for anti-monarchists to express their reservations about royalty and the Royal Family.

Here we can conclude that once again characteristic British individualism kicked in. People do not like their emotions and responses to be stage-managed. One of the effects of Britain's Protestant Reformation was that the individual retains his or her right to a personal view. This Protestant tradition of independence is linked to ideas of egalitarianism and fair play. It favours the views and behaviour of the individual over those of the herd. Consequently people resent attempts to manipulate and orchestrate their private views. They want to accord themselves and others freedom, and that includes the freedom of privacy when necessary.

Culture

The building of the Millennium Dome at Greenwich was an attempt by the government to showcase aspects of Britain which it felt were important. It was also undoubtedly meant to lend authority to the government which produced it – a precedent set by the Great Exhibition of 1851 at the Crystal Palace in London's Hyde Park. Tony Blair called the Dome 'a triumph of confidence over cynicism'. The government spent £1 billion of taxpayers' money erecting a tent at Greenwich and filling it with amusements. There were several 'zones' including a 'Faith Zone' and a 'Body Zone' which were meant to inform and to entertain.

However, from the beginning the project was a disaster. It was intended to represent Britain, but the people weren't consulted and didn't feel they had any stake in it. Target visitor figures of 12 million material-ized as 5.4 million. People contrast the Dome with the Eden Project in Cornwall (a huge biodiversity project under geodesic domes), which thrives and which started as a community project. People saw the Dome as a further example of money being syphoned from the regions to be spent in London. They didn't like being managed into visiting it, and, the more they were hectored by government ministers to attend, the more reluctant they were to go.

The low attendance figures illustrate two things: firstly, the mixture of elements chosen to be celebrated was awry (the Faith Zone was partly financed by the subsequently disgraced Hinduja brothers), secondly, people do not like to be told, least of all by government, what they should like, or what they should do. This rejection of the authority of government is a major aspect of British cultural identity. People will not be bullied. (The song 'Rule Britannia' contains the line: 'Britons never never never shall be slaves'.) The failure of the Dome project illustrated the powerlessness of government in a democracy.

Sport

Taking pride in the sporting achievements of one's nation is clearly a significant indicator of one's attachment to one's homeland. That this persists, and even increases, despite political devolution to the regions and Britain's integration within Europe, is a conundrum which will be examined later on. (The *Daily Telegraph* still reports Europe under 'Foreign News' three decades after Britain became a member of the European Economic Community.)

Britain is a country where interest in sport has always flourished. Traditionally its sports stars have been lionised: W. G. Grace the nineteenth-century cricketer; Roger Bannister, the first four-minute miler; Linford Christie, the sprinter, and so on. Britons particularly welcome the success of sporting heroes in football, or soccer, as it is known. The game of soccer is central to Britain's view of itself and is supported fanatically by people of both sexes, from all social classes, ages, and regions, so for example any soccer match between England and Germany assumes more than sporting importance. There is national glee in remembering England's 4–2 defeat of Germany in 1966. The commentator's 'They think it's all over . . . it is now' became a famous *Sun* newspaper headline after that match (and is the name of a popular BBC sports quiz programme). After England's 5–1 victory over Germany in 2001 (following a 1–0 defeat at Wembley nine months earlier) all sorts of genies good and bad came out of the bottle. Even people who don't normally follow football were exultant. This was reflected on television and radio where newsreaders, male and female, did not even try to appear dispassionate. The so-called 'black-edged voice', reserved for describing the normal disasters of the news, disappeared in the reporting. Sport here proved cohesive and positive. The fact that one section of British society, rampaging English hooligans, went round Munich after the match chanting 'there's only one Bomber Harris' went largely unnoticed in the British media. Overnight there was a shift from middle-class apprehension about the prospective behaviour of British hooligan-fans overseas, to a display of triumphalism where 'a few hotheads' must not be allowed to detract from the very real victory which took place.

Xenophobia

The way in which news is reported reveals much about British readers and viewers. The coverage of refugees and asylum seekers for example has revealed sharp differences in British attitudes to foreigners and in generally accepted notions of what it means to be British. Former Tory Party leader William Hague applied the phrase 'bogus asylum seekers' to refugees, presumably in the belief that it would endear him to his followers. In practice it raised the anger of opponents and supporters alike. For the former it was evidence of Tory racism, for the latter it failed to distance him from the lack of compassion of his predecessor-but-one, Margaret Thatcher.

Events like this can enable a latent nationalism to arise. This happens instantly, and newspapers can rally support against an 'enemy' overnight. In 1981 the *Sun* orchestrated hatred for 'the Argies' over the Falklands conflict. Most *Sun* readers were unaware where the Falkland Islands were, but they rose to the invitation to be xenophobic anyway. That Iraqi leader Saddam Hussein, the Serb Slobodan Milosevic, or Zimbabwean Prime Minister Robert Mugabe could equally be vilified at a moment's notice indicates a xenophobia always ready to be ignited in certain sections of the British public. Even the 2001 Royal Variety Performance featured a comedian who centred his act around the British hatred of the French! Dislike of other nationalities is not far beneath the psyche particularly of some of the older generation. Meanwhile the young and the educated look for their values towards Europe and the USA.

The above examples from current affairs show how complex a country Britain is. It is difficult to make generalisations about because Britain is an amalgam of paradoxes. It is generally conformist and conservative but is also in a constant state of change. It is governed by Parliament, but the people's voice is strong. It has a monarch but many people are republicans. It generates a lot of popular and much 'high' culture, but also philistinism and hooliganism. Constituency of its population also is in flux. The majority of the population is Caucasian, but 6.8 per cent of people are now from ethnic minorities – predominantly from the Caribbean, Africa, and the Indian subcontinent. It is hard to embrace such contradictions and tensions. It is much easier to talk about 'Britains', or for that matter the 'Identities' of our title.

Postmodernism

It might also be argued that modern Britain is no different from any other developed state. In a postmodern world of surfaces, public relations, stylistic fusions, and so on, new urban developments are the same everywhere. Manchester's Trafford Centre shopping mall, for example, is a collage of global culture. It has *trompe l'oueil* artwork, Greek statuary, Art Deco mouldings, Whistleresque murals, Venetian frescos, a mock-up of the deck, deck-furniture, and lifeboats of the *Titanic* (presumably designed to dredge up images of upper-class travel, as well as of the teenage, heart-throb film *Titanic*, from shoppers' unconscious). There is also a fibreglass statue of Sammy Davis Jr! This shopping mall and others like it, steeped in global 'culture' (or kitsch?), are now firmly entrenched on the cultural map for British young and old alike. Are these people 'consumers' defined by the products they are made to buy, or Britons who assert their multicultural identities and individuate themselves by shopping? That is where our debate lies.

Media

More important perhaps than global influences is the role played in British life by home-grown media. Everything is now played out on television. Moral and ethical dilemmas, from gay rights and cosmetic surgery to euthanasia and abortion, are illustrated and aired in soap operas. Everyone in the public eye, all organisations, and corporate Britain have P(ublic) R(elations) people to help to manage information flow. Politicians are forced to resign in time for *The Six O'clock News*. Ministers must act quickly in order to seem decisive, rather than wisely, having considered in depth. The medium dominates the message. Nobody in Britain can claim to be unaffected by the barrage of noise coming from these external influences. However, people do discriminate between what they tolerate, what they accept, and what elements of the culture (or counterculture) they choose for themselves as a buffer against the outside world.

Language

We should also be careful with language. In any discussion of nationalism, identity, or current affairs, language is never 'innocent'. The choice of words reveals the underlying outlook of the speaker. So for example the word 'foreign' in English is much more hostile than the *étranger/estrangeiro* found in most romance languages or than the German *ausländer*. Latent British xenophobia is revealed in the offensive tabloid expression 'Johnny Foreigner'. Our chapter 'Language and Ethnicity' says a lot more about this, but for now think about the impact on national relations and culture of the following uses of language: To welsh is to cheat or renege; to scotch is to thwart, to squash, to prevent; an Irish lanyard is an untidy rope. In other words the names of the three 'subsidiary' nations in the British Isles have negative connotations in the language of the dominant one. Thus national prejudice is encoded in the English language.

Bearing these points in mind, we will now turn to examine the approaches of the four recent studies referred to earlier, each of which uses a list or key words to identify salient characteristics of British people.

The *Sunday Times* rich list

Financial status is clearly one determinant of cultural outlook. The *Sunday Times* evidently believes that, as F. Scott Fitzgerald, said: 'the rich are different'. Wealth affects culture because, even if they are philistines individually, the rich collectively tend to be patrons of the arts. For decades Maurice Saatchi has been buying the work of contemporary British artists. As often as not the rich are distinguished by the flamboyant garishness of their taste, rather than by their discernment. Ruby Wax conducted viewers around the Duchess of York's 'distinctive' home in a famous television programme. Their sense of identity is determined by the fact that they *are* rich and therefore insulated from the constraints and inconveniences of the poor – which is the rest of the country. Many of the latter will be public servants – teachers, social workers, postal employees, workers in the civil service – people defined by their usefulness. However the rich, as a group, would rarely claim that their chief aim is public service. So, in the *Sunday Times* richest thousand list we see forty-one people who made their money in fashion companies, including familiar high-street names such as Joseph, French Connection (now FCUK) and Russell & Bromley. The aim of these companies is the continued creation of wealth for the benefit of the families which own them and of wages for the people who work for them, rather than public service.

In 2001, after the dotcom bubble burst, old money continued to do rather well. The land-owning Duke of Westminster (300 acres of Mayfair and Belgravia) was the richest man in Britain. But that does not mean that the rise of Britain's meritocracy is faltering. In 2001 there was another drop in the proportion on the list of those who inherited their wealth. Only 241 of the thousand in the list inherited their fortunes. This is the smallest proportion since the list was first drawn up in 1988. Then about 70 per cent of the two hundred entries had inherited their money. This represents a significant shift in a culture in which inherited wealth plays such a major part. Financial change fuels the process of social and cultural change. The *Sunday Times*'s focus on money reveals very little about the rich people profiled or the lives of the mass of the population however, the fact that most of those on the list are 'household names' indicates that they are part of a social community, as well as a purely financial British hierarchy.

The Observer: Britain uncovered

Whereas the *Sunday Times*'s list offers a snapshot of a segment of British society whose primary motivation and identity is fiscal, *The Observer*'s 'Britain Uncovered' supplement takes a 'sociological' approach to contemporary culture and covers a broader spectrum. It contains a survey of public attitudes (69 per cent are against same-sex marriage; the most popular European country is Spain; only 19 per cent of people would not take out private healthcare or educate their children privately, if they had plenty of money) and behaviour (37 per cent would keep a wallet they found with £200 in it). It also looks at people's activities across the age range from deprived teenagers to pensioners; attitudes to work; drug culture; education and finally eccentricity. Two sections deal with the spiritual state of the nation – broadly speaking, the decline of institutional religion in favour of 'house churches' and the appeal to young Muslims of traditional Islam.

As a barometer of 'the health of the nation,' the supplement is quite hopeful. Society is changing, but the fixed standards from which people are straying hover in the background. For example the journalist Burhan Wazir complains about the severity of his own upbringing in Pakistan, but reports that young British Muslims are managing to combine the practice of their religion with the freedom to go clubbing if they want to. The film *East Is East* (1999) highlights similar dilemmas. The section on eccentricity suggests the impossibility of pigeonholing people. Miranda Sawyer, author of a book on suburbia, *Park and Ride* (2001), meets a pensioner who is feeling wobbly 'because he'd taken two Es' (Ecstasy tablets). In her view, eccentricity is what keeps the culture vibrant and makes Britain interesting, because unpredictable.

The Observer's approach is trying to present a snapshot of the real Britain as opposed to that of the tourist brochures. It is partly limited by factors surrounding any inquiry based on questionnaires. Questions and the scope for replying to them can be limited. Respondents do not always tell the truth. The funky and the bizarre sell newspapers etc. and hence figure larger than life. But by and large we are given a dispassionate overview, within the constraints of *The Observer*'s liberal, left-wing leanings.

Channel 5 An A–Z of Britishness

In 2001, Ian Russell produced a programme called *An A–Z of Britishness* for Channel 5. Using twenty-six headings, the programme-makers looked at various aspects of contemporary Britain. Their list of topics was random and eclectic, and the tone flippant, with, for example, taxi drivers from the North and South voicing prejudices about either side of the divide. However, most viewers of a programme intended for home consumption could relate to the items raised. The list is reproduced in Table 0.2 and might be used for a classroom brainstorming exercise. Many of these items are obvious, but a few require explanation. Deep-fried Mars Bars and fluorescent green peas are northern food delicacies; Britons are evidently the highest *per capita* consumers of jigsaw puzzles; there is an attempt to introduce the kilt as a fashion garment for men; the pedestal water-closet was

TABLE 0.2   An A–Z of Britishness

Alcohol	North–South divide
Bingo	Older people
Cockney	Pantomime
Dome	Queue
Eccentricity	Routemaster
Food – peas, Mars Bars	Saucy postcards
Gnomes	Thatcher
Housing crisis	Union Flag
Inventors	Victory
Jigsaw	Weather
Kilt	X-rated
Lavatory	Yobs
Manners	Zebra crossings

Source: *An A–Z of Britishness*, Channel 5, March 2001

pioneered in Britain, by Thomas Crapper in the nineteenth century; Routemasters are red London buses; 16 million saucy postcards were sold in 1963 – the company is now defunct; the rating 'X' for films, which gave them a forbidden-fruit status, was abandoned in 1981; yobs are thugs – the cartoonist Tony Husband got his own back on his muggers by drawing 'Yobs' cartoons for *Private Eye* for fifteen years; the idea of black-and-white zebra street crossings was exported around the world.

The programme was a lighthearted venture, but made some telling points. For example it interviewed three people, Scottish, Irish, and English respectively. The two former knew the dates of their respective national saint's days (St Andrew: 30 November, St Patrick: 17 March), but the English person did not know that St George's Day is on 23 April. This tends to support the idea that it is English people who are least aware of their nationality and whose sense of identity is now most in crisis.

The programme included a comment from the writer Ross Benson that Britons have good manners in order to mask their underlying violence. He said that during the Falklands conflict the Argentines found it very difficult to deal with the good manners of British diplomats. 'They subject you to their charm, and if you don't agree with them, they kill you.' The programme concentrated on some of the more outrageous elements of Britain. Many of the people featured were 'oddballs' – a Cockney Pearly King; a garden gnome collector; a man who walked the length of the country barefoot, and lived in a cave.

The limitations of the approach in this case are: programme time constraints; the appeal of the bizarre rather than the ordinary – presenting a wackier Britain than the norm; the absence of all the 'ordinary' features of British life – work, sport, family, landscape and perhaps the most dominant element of British culture: television itself. However, largely because of its idiosyncratic approach, this was a successful programme bearing a message, broadly speaking celebrating eccentricity, which British people wanted to hear about themselves.

England, England

In Julian Barnes's 1998 novel *England, England*, a powerful businessman plans to turn the Isle of Wight into a theme park, so that tourists will not have to traipse from Buckingham Palace to Stratford-upon-Avon to Chester and so on. His business blueprint lists the following 'Fifty Quintessences of Englishness'. Some of these items are tongue-in-cheek, and one could argue about the order in which they are prioritised, but they represent some common perceptions and will be familiar to many within and outside the United Kingdom.

TABLE 0.3 Quintessences of Englishness

Royal Family	London taxis
Big Ben / Houses of Parliament	Bowler hat
Manchester United FC	TV classic serials
Class system	Oxford / Cambridge
Pubs	Harrods
A robin in the snow	Double-decker buses / red buses
Robin Hood & Merrie Men	Hypocrisy
Cricket	Gardening
White cliffs of Dover	Perfidy / untrustworthiness
Imperialism	Half-timbering
Union Jack	Homosexuality
Snobbery	Alice in Wonderland
God Save the King / Queen	Winston Churchill
BBC	Marks & Spencer
West End	Battle of Britain
Times newspaper	Francis Drake
Shakespeare	Trooping the Colour
Thatched cottages	Whingeing
Cup of tea / Devonshire cream tea	Queen Victoria
Stonehenge	Breakfast
Phlegm / stiff upper lip	Beer / warm beer
Shopping	Emotional frigidity
Marmalade	Wembley Stadium
Beefeaters / Tower of London	Flagellation / Public schools
	Not washing / bad underwear
	Magna Carta

Source: Julian Barnes, *England, England* (1998)

Examining the list we can see that it contains some physical monuments, some historical figures, some works of the imagination, some
ceremonials. Most people can easily relate to these elements of Englishness
even if they don't apply them to themselves.

The monarchy, for example, is a common topic of conversation,
though most Britons have never seen the Queen in person. Members of all
social classes, and older people especially, support the monarchy but draw
the line at the minor royals who they see as contributing nothing to the
welfare of Britain. They point for example to the moral lead meant to come

from royalty. The marital breakdown rate of the present Queen's children, at three out of four, is worse than the national average of one in three. Despite this disillusionment, 70 per cent of Britons say they prefer to live as subjects under a monarch rather than as citizens in a republic. However, 68 per cent of them believe that we will not have a monarchy fifty years from now.

As regards the classic serials category listed above, most people could name *The Forsyte Saga*, or Jane Austen adaptations, but they would be just as likely to include preferred television sitcoms such as *Blackadder*, *Fawlty Towers*, or *Rising Damp*, as well as detective series such as *Inspector Morse* and *Midsomer Murders*. Much of British culture is based on the supposed essential rurality of the country. John Major refered to 'warm beer, cricket and ladies cycling' as essences of Englishness. These are country pursuits. television series such as those above trade on this rural myth. Set in beautiful locations, they are essentially about restoring order and calm to an idyllic place whose waters have been ruffled by the odd murder or two.

Partly because of its context in a nostalgic novel, Barnes's checklist has an historical bias. Past glories overshadow such present-day banalities as 'whingeing', 'emotional frigidity', and 'shopping', and this list, more than the others, records the traditional British vices of snobbery, hypocrisy, and perfidy. There is a dated feel to such an approach. The tenor of the items is before the past half-century. It is Britain in aspic, disabled by its past, and really has little relevance for the contemporary British student population for example, who are more tuned in to travelling through Europe, music, and the drink and drugs culture.

Individualism

One thing all these studies have in common is their admiration for British individualism. They praise British people's dissent, scepticism, lack of conformity, the ability to set rather than follow fashion trends, and individuality over the herd instinct. Eccentricity is one stage further on from this and is admired even more. Undoubtedly for a country of eccentrics to thrive, fundamental tolerance of dissent or difference is necessary, and clearly this exists in Britain. Environmental protesters such as Swampy become national heroes, through media exposure. Ken Livingstone was elected mayor of London despite the government's best efforts to thwart him. It would be nice to think that Britain supplies a model of diversity which could be exported to other post-industrial democracies. However, many people ask the question: how long can Britain remain an oasis of diversity and tolerance of difference in the face of the homogenising forces of globalisation?

Heroes

A pragmatic way of looking at British identity and of examining the aspirations of ordinary people is to look at the kind of contemporary heroes they have created. These heroes reveal a lot about the people who have created them. They reflect how people would like to be themselves, or what they see as admirable in others. As a group, heroes represent the values of their culture. Significantly this cynical age has thrown up many *anti*-heroes or stage villains, such as 'Nasty' Nick Bateman from *Big Brother*, and Anne Robinson from *The Weakest Link*. Previous generations tended to admire Establishment figures or politicians, such as Churchill or Macmillan, but today sports people tend to predominate. For example Sally Gunnell, the hurdler, is also well known outside her sport. Others well known enough outside their sports to appear in television advertisements are: Frank Bruno the boxer, Gary Lineker and Vinnie Jones the footballers, Steve Redgrave the Olympic rower and Steve Davis the snooker player. Steve Redgrave won five Olympic medals for rowing at successive Olympic games. In 2001 it took him around six hours to run the London Marathon because so many well-wishers impeded his progress. As a national hero he embodied virtues of doggedness and determination, good humour and stability which even the MTV generation of slackers can evidently relate to.

Heroes of the day are decided much more by the young than they were hitherto, and consequently television and media personalities such as Carol Vorderman and Chris Evans tend to feature, as well as those from sports, business, and commerce. So nowadays the range of heroes is much wider. In order to examine this phenomenon, we will consider in more detail a small number of select prominent examples.

Princess Diana

An unlikely hero – or heroine – was Princess Diana. She was born into privilege, the daughter of Earl Spencer and, after her fairy-tale marriage to Prince Charles, had several palaces to choose from. She became a fashion icon and her appearance was widely imitated. The other side to her was her compassion for people with Aids and her opposition to land mines – a product of the military-industrial complex of which she herself was arguably a part. Perhaps for this reason, people saw the latter as a particularly principled stand.

She was a paradoxical heroine in that her wealth could have separated her from people in the street, but it didn't. She was genuinely liked by her future subjects: so much so that Tony Blair could make political capital by calling her 'the People's Princess' – at her funeral. The arrival of

FIGURE 0.2   Floral tributes outside Kensington Palace immediately after Princess Diana's death

Princess Diana was a watershed in attitudes to the monarchy. Buckingham Palace completely misread the public mood with their reaction when she was killed with her lover in a car crash in Paris in 1997.

People already knew from a television interview with Martin Bashir that Diana was at odds with the palace, and, when the latter appeared to be prepared to give her a low-key funeral, they were outraged. There was a national outpouring of grief. It was a moment when the nation came together in sorrow because Diana represented values which were theirs as well as hers: compassion for the sick in an uncaring Thatcherite world; frustration at restrictions in a society hidebound by hierarchy; open-mindedness in a Britain needing to become multicultural; an evident belief in the need for women to break out from the stultifying conventions of marriage and assert their sexual freedom – although arguably the latter was just the continuation of an upper-class practice made much harder to hide nowadays from paparazzi. Her funeral was one of the periodic, unscripted moments in current affairs which unleash genuine feelings of solidarity among British people. It is as if they wake up from their traditional passive conservatism and realise how much they really care about certain issues. There is a subtle shift in the public mood and in people's relations with one another.

It should also be said that many other Britons were totally non-plussed by this public display of grief. They speculated bemusedly on the spiritual bankruptcy of those whose emotional lives were driven by the need to hero-worship public figures. They were astonished by the uncharacteristically British public expression of emotion. We can conclude that Britain contains many opposites, and also note that some British heroes are more unequivocally revered abroad than at home. So, Diana's saint-like media image was drawn on by the 2001 French film *Amélie* (directed by Jean-Pierre Jeunet), in which the heroine's life as a do-gooder is inaugurated at the moment she is watching the news report on Diana's death in Paris.

The Beckhams

Two contemporary heroes for young people are David Beckham, the Manchester United footballer and England captain, and his wife Victoria. Posh and Becks, as they are called, are style icons and are observed minutely by the media, their fans, and detractors. In *Burchill on Beckham* (2001), for example, Julie Burchill said that David displays 'Diana-faced *gravitas* . . . [and] seems so aristocratic', while [Victoria] is 'so delightfully common'. The couple feature as key characters in *Alistair McGowan's Big Impressions* on BBC1. Posh was so called when formerly a member of the manufactured group the Spice Girls. Today they are very real trend-setters – parents worry that teenage pop fans will copy Posh's wearing of a lip ring. Boys copy Becks's haircuts.

They both have jobs to do, and theoretically the intense media interest which surrounds them 'just happens'. Although what is reported is made to seem spontaneous and natural, it is in fact the product of an elaborate public relations campaign. In August 2001 the British national press contained 450 stories about Victoria Beckham. This cannot have been accidental. Becks has his child Brooklyn's name tattooed in gothic script on his lower back, where press photographers can see it. As an ambitious young couple they have realised that for them life in the media is money in the bank. So they set about cultivating their public personas.

In a sense the 'Posh and Becks' phenomenon is too closely orchestrated to be genuine popular culture, despite its dependence on mass support. Whereas most youth culture is about iconoclasm, rebellion, and anarchy, their fame is orchestrated by PR firms. Posh and Becks are part of a process of the transfer of wealth and power from a previous generation to a new one. In 2001, they went by helicopter from their Cheshire mansion to the home of Lord Leverhulme for the dispersal auction sale of its contents. They spent £2.1 million on purchases of antique furniture. The effect of this was to strengthen the position of Establishment antique-collectors; to spread the message to their own fans that the past contains items of value; and to transfer the proceeds of other people's consumerism into wealth for their own future generations. Hence they consolidate the

FIGURE 0.3 David and Victoria Beckham are the most reported-on individuals in Britain, having completely eclipsed royalty in terms of media interest (© Popperfoto/Reuters)

wealth of Britain past, while engaging in processes (pop music and football) which are seen as transitory and ephemeral.

Media celebrities

Another young contemporary hero whose career has risen on the strength of media publicity is the television chef Jamie Oliver. He is young. He does everything in the eye of the media. He writes for The *Times Magazine*. He travels to New York. He gets married. He entertains his friends. He appears in advertisements. He is a talented individual but more important than that is the publicity machine which sells him. He is a 'media hero' who is mainly valued for his appearance, style, and presentation. He lives his life in public and never seems to have private moments. All his T-shirts are ones the audience would like to own. They are never crumpled. Their owner looks confident. He never appears depressed or having moments of introspection. He is forever cheerful and cuddly. In reality such people don't exist. He has abilities in cooking undoubtedly, but his main skills are in self-promotion. He is the subject of complaints and controversy in liberal organs such as the *Guardian*, but meanwhile he is laughing all the way to the bank, and is evidently the twenty-first-century version of the renaissance man the people want to admire.

Business

Young people today particularly esteem achievers in business, commerce, and finance. The businessman Richard Branson is the most admired figure. He is self-made, rich, zany and takes part in dangerous sports such as ballooning, and powerboat-racing. He has dealt in elements of youth culture such as CDs, videos, and DVDs through his Virgin Megastores. Young people admire the megalomania of his ambition – he has also owned an airline and a train company – as much as the City distrusts him for his lack of focus.

Anita Roddick, who founded the Body Shop, is also admired for the stances which she takes on matters such as the testing of cosmetics on animals. As a female entrepreneur she is mould-breaking and serves as a role model for a younger generation of women who want to make power and principles a part of their identities.

Finally, a most unlikely 2000 overnight heroine, at the age of twenty-four, was Derbyshire-born Ellen MacArthur. The yachtswoman came second in the *Vendée Globe* single-handed round-the-world race. It was a phenomenal achievement, and what struck a chord with people from all walks of life was the fact that she was not well connected nor well-heeled and was not a particularly media-savvy person. In demeanour she was modest and didn't seem particularly confident. However she was obviously extremely self-sufficient and competent, and had worked single-mindedly for her fame. She had started as a sailing instructor in Hull, had lived in a container in France, and gained her achievement on her merits. For these reasons, including also the nautical connection for an island people, she appealed to young and old.

Reality television

Such is the power of television in Britain, that some heroes can be blatantly manufactured and presented to the audience, rather than chosen by the population at large. This is done in a semi-documentary format. The public are voyeurs who see behind the scenes of auditions etc. People collude with the pretence that they are a part of the programme-making and delude themselves into believing it is all real. The sense of empowerment they are thus given makes them more likely consumers of the eventual product. In 2001 an ITV series *Pop Stars* set about auditioning young hopefuls from all over the British Isles to form a band. The programme masqueraded as a talent competition, and the band which was produced, called Hear'Say, was presented as something that rose commercially on its own merits. The audience was expected to ignore the paraphernalia of the production process (editing, promotion, stage-management). The group was put together in front of the viewers' eyes week by week on television, and yet spectators were quite happy to be hoodwinked by a process which they were bankrolling.

The series was very like 'reality television', where people's lives are turned into soap opera. Successful candidates' families were interviewed. We vicariously experienced emotions with them. And yet the whole system of heats and talentspotting was a sham in the sense that it pretended to replace a haphazard system where talented singers sink or swim, depending on their luck, with one where merit is all. So for example Claire Freeland, a Glasgow call centre supervisor, was widely considered the most talented singer. However the verdict of the programme producer Nigel Lythgoe was Voice: 10. Looks: 3. So she was dropped from the group.

The show was really about generating interest to fuel a market for a product which it was creating. This will ultimately sell CDs, make the pop group stars and the programme producers rich, and subvert the previous norm, under which it was consumers, not manufacturers, who decided what they wanted to consume. A slot was even found for Hear'Say for the Royal Variety Show in 2001. The formula is commercially successful and promoter Simon Cowell then did a series *Pop Idol* for ITV seeking a solo performer.

Dumbing down

Many people are made anxious by the loss of quality in television, Britain's dominant information medium, illustrated above. They see standards of all sorts being lowered in the media generally, and call it 'dumbing down'. They attribute this decline of British cultural standards to deficiencies in the educational system. For years it has been suggested that the median level at which television is beamed is the third form at secondary school (age: fourteen). If that link is retained, media standards will fall even further, so the argument goes.

Every year GCSE and A level results are greeted with complaints from the newspapers that the exams are getting easier. There is a ritual denial of this from teachers and teaching unions, who say that people should give credit to the young for their hard work and achievement instead of under-mining their morale. The government supports the examiners' line that standards have not in fact declined, but the government would say that, wouldn't it?

Editorials complain that skills shortages have arisen because students have all done undemanding 'new' courses such as media studies and sports science. Nobody really wants to hear or address complaints about the erosion of standards of quality in education. Students are the last people who will complain about so called grade-inflation in schools or universities. Why should they? *Private Eye* runs a column called 'Dumb Britain'. Sample recent extracts include:

> Steve Wright Radio 2
> Wright: What is the Italian word for motorway?
> Contestant: Expresso

> Grant Stott Show, Radio Forth
> Stott: Who is the leader of the Ulster Unionist Party?
> Contestant: Geri Halliwell

> *The Weakest Link*, BBC1
> Anne Robinson: In science, what is botany the study of?
> Caroline O'Shea (*Big Brother* contestant): Bottoms.

It is tempting to suggest that this anxiety about dumbing down is a result of Britain's diminished economic and military significance in the world. Or again, it is one of the effects of devolving power to regions hitherto controlled by England. A former Chief Scientific Adviser to the Government said in 2001 that universities are under-funded and must not be seen 'simply as a substitute for National Service to keep youngsters off the dole queue'. Whatever the reason, fears about dumbing down of radio and television programmes, turning ideas into sound bites that can be assimilated by a not-very-well-educated audience is rife, and we will see later whether there is just cause for this view, or whether it is a symptom of a moral panic.

The debate about standards is like an annual game which is never satisfactorily resolved and which mirrors other social and cultural divides and anxieties. People who have themselves been to grammar schools and attended the old universities feel that they worked harder than the present generation and were more competent. Progressives on the other hand welcome the new ways, applaud the sloughing off of Britain's imperialist past and attribute complaints to traditional British snobbery and conservatism.

Pessimists suggest that the undereducated young, having lost interest in the pursuit of knowledge, are politically unconcerned and merely dissipate their energies in drugs, sex, and pointless consumerism. This is not so. One has only to point to the Canadian writer, Naomi Klein's anti-globalisation book *No Logo*, which sold forty thousand copies to eighteen-to-thirty-year-olds in less than a year in Britain in 2000.

British Cultural Identities structure

Having reviewed a number of potential approaches to the question of British cultural identity, we have chosen to structure our book into seven chapters. We have headed each chapter with a timeline because one needs to be aware of 'public' events which shape people's private experiences. After each of the chapters we have included review exercises which allow the development of discussion on issues which British people themselves debate. In order to inform discussion we have included some 'cultural examples'. These are items, mainly from popular culture, which people value. They include films, television, drama, novels, social commentaries and other artefacts which illustrate the cultural state of the nation. They are not academic references, but signposts towards cultural understanding.

Our first chapter, 'Places and Peoples', deals with the cultural geography of Britain. People are products of their biology and environment (Nature and Nurture) and we try to determine what they have in common – what the British 'system' produces. The chapter considers how far people pride themselves on being from a particular area. There is a well known North–South divide but there is also a continuing historic rivalry between Lancashire and Yorkshire. People from Cornwall and Devon (the West Country) feel they are different from those in London, which is three hundred miles away and yet rules them. Londoners see themselves as at the authentic heart of Britain, and so on.

'Education, Work, and Leisure' deals with the formal and recreational aspects of living in Britain. It assesses the extent to which people accept the shared cultural values which schools and universities transmit to them. It looks at attitudes to employment, and the trauma for members of a social group who defined themselves as 'working' class but who are often no longer working. It asks whether leisure time in Britain is spent productively, to promote the physical and psychic well-being of the population – or is it just wasteful hedonism?

'Gender, Sex, and the Family' traces the change in attitudes and patterns of behaviour of the sexes. Sex is biologically, but gender socially determined. So, where has a questioning of traditional gender roles led to in modern Britain? Attitudes to sex and sexuality, among young people particularly, are very different from their parents'. So how do families resolve these potential divisions? The concept of the nuclear family has undergone profound change. Male authority has been eroded. Marriage is less common and divorce is prevalent. Where is this leading in terms not just of social stability but of how people see their family roles and futures?

In 'Youth Culture and Style' we examine the way in which 'teenagers', a concept first identified in the 1950s, have their own codes of communication, fashion, behaviour, and cultural practices. We also look at the status of older people in a society becoming more youth-oriented.

'Class and Politics' deals with the question of whether people's lives and psyches are conditioned by the socio-economic rank in which they happen to have been born. The death of class has been repeatedly pronounced. We offer another view. We also look at the way in which class influences voting patterns and the extent to which people still see themselves as 'political' or of the right or left.

'Ethnicity and Language' looks at important questions around race, not just for ethnic minorities, who make up 6.8 per cent of the British population, but for speakers of Irish, Scots, Welsh, and English whose identities are partly thereby determined. It discusses the colonising nature of language and its effects on incomers and Britain.

'Religion and Heritage' assesses how far people living in Britain maintain a spiritual dimension in their lives. Religious observance appears to be in decline. But that is not the whole story. Linked to the idea of religious belief is the collective endorsement of a set of values from the past, worth handing on and preserved in the form of heritage. Heritage is more complicated than the preservation of historic monuments. It involves the idea of theme-park Britain, the Notting Hill Carnival, distinctive foods. It is very often about the incorporation of influences from the margins into the eventual mainstream.

Some of the questions we are posing are: Will British culture be annihilated by, or will it incorporate, global culture? Why does one cultural influence, one's gender for example, override another one's Scottishness, say? Is the present generation in Britain radically different from its parents? If so in what ways? If not, why not? Do the British media reflect or direct people's views and perceptions? Is Britain a melting pot of nationalities, does it allow and encourage diversity, or is it just conformist and conservative? What does it mean to be British in the twenty-first century? If 'British' is a brand, what does it signify? Quality? Style? Snobbery? Popular culture? Heritage? Social change? Stability? Perfidiousness? Good manners . . . ?

One perspective on the question of what people think it means to be British now is offered by the choices made by ten thousand people in a BBC poll at the turn of the year 2001–2. People were asked: 'Who is the greatest Briton of all time?' The top ten in the running for this accolade emerged as Captain James Cook, Charles Darwin, Sir Isaac Newton, Oliver Cromwell, Sir Ernest Shackleton, Elizabeth I, William Shakespeare, John Lennon, Winston Churchill, and Lord Horatio Nelson. Interestingly, the two people battling for the top position were Shakespeare and Lennon. Though they have some things in common (both men, both in the arts), they arguably represent contrasting attitudes towards being British.

Shakespeare represents the pinnacle of an Elizabethan cultural 'golden age' which is often contrasted to the emphasis on quantity as much as quality in the twentieth century (mass media, multinational industries, mass production). Lennon by contrast represents a different 'golden age', the 1960s, when values of freedom, liberalism, understanding, and love were promoted by a generation whose motto might have been Lennon's 'Give Peace a Chance', and its anthem Lennon's 'Imagine' (recently voted the 'greatest' number one single of all time on a Channel 4 poll of viewers). The list tells us several things about the dominant conceptions of Britishness and of 'heroes', in terms of gender, country, heritage, leadership, and fame. The fact that all those appearing in the top ten are no longer living also arguably says something about the way in which the present continues to live in the shadow of the past.

Exercises

1   How important do you think heroes are to a 'sense of identity'? From the descriptions in this chapter, and from your own knowledge, what common images of England and of Britain have you noticed, and what characteristics do you think they represent?

2   In the next chapter, you will find it suggested that the British, and the English in particular, were being presented in a certain way in Hollywood in the 1990s. Before you read this however, we'd like you to consider the following exercises.

■   Thinking of the American films you have seen, how many English actors can you remember? Have they usually played English characters? How have the English been stereotyped by Hollywood, or your own national film industry, in the past?

■   In terms of recent Hollywood films, James Bond is perhaps the most famous English character (first played by Sean Connery, a Scot). What other similar larger-than-life images of British people has Hollywood produced? How many of these originated in British novels?

■   Does Hollywood portray British women differently from British men (you might think of Deborah Kerr, Joan Collins, Glenda Jackson, Julie Andrews, Emma Thompson, or even the Americans Katherine Hepburn in *The African Queen* and Bette Davis in *The Virgin Queen*)?

3   How important do you think wider geographical perspectives, such as those offered by Europe or the Commonwealth, are to understanding British identity? How is national culture altered by these larger communities? Can you name fifteen countries that are in the Commonwealth,

and can you list them by (a) size of population? (b) year of independence?

4   British daily national newspapers are extremely varied, from the tabloid press to the broadsheets, and so are their readerships. A long-standing characterisation of newspapers categorises them in terms of the people who buy them. Listed below are the newspapers and the descriptions of their readers – can you match the one with the other

- *The Times*; The *Daily Mail*; *The Sun*; the *Financial Times*; *The Guardian*; the *Daily Telegraph*; the *Daily Mirror*; the *Morning Star*
- Read by the people who own the country.
- Read by the people who think they run the country.
- Read by the people who think they ought to run the country.
- Read by the people who do run the country.
- Read by the wives of the men who run the country.
- Read by people who don't care who runs the country.
- Read by those who think the country should be run by another country.
- Read by those who think the country is being run by another country.

5   In this chapter we have looked at some contemporary British identities. What do you know of the following people and characters who have become important or comic cultural figures to the British? Lady Godiva, Henry VIII, Queen Guinevere, Dickens's Mr Podsnap, Shakespeare's Falstaff, Biggles, Bulldog Drummond, Robert the Bruce, Lord Nelson, Lawrence of Arabia, Clive of India, and Bunyan's Christian? What are the problems with continuing to advance these characters as icons of Britishness?

6   How important do you think it is to consider language when describing other people? For example, the word 'immigrant' has not been used in this chapter but you will come across it elsewhere in this book because it is the common term used by most of the British to describe other people who have come to settle in the UK. By contrast, the British abroad are almost never regarded (by the British) as 'immigrants' in other communities or even as 'emigants' from Britain. Most often they are called 'expats' (short for expatriates). Why do you think this is?

 # Reading

Gascoigne, Bamber. *Encyclopedia of Britain*, revised edition, Macmillan, 1994. Impressive reference work, meticulously researched, which contains an A to Z guide to almost every aspect of British culture, from pre-Roman times to the present.

Porter, Roy. *Myths of the English* Blackwell, 1993. Careful analysis of aspects of Britishness from cricket to the British 'bobby'.

Room, Adrian. *An A to Z of British Life*, Oxford University Press, 1992. Handbook containing a lot of information on background detail to British culture, history, idiosyncrasies, and 'institutions' such as Ascot, Henley, and Glyndebourne.

Samuel, Raphael (ed.). *Patriotism*, 3 vols, Routledge, 1989. Detailed examination of kinds of British identity in terms of history, gender, race, politics, cultural icons, and much more.

Cultural Examples

Films

Bridget Jones's Diary (2001) dir. Sharon Maguire. Deals with the efforts of a thirty-something woman to find a man. A 'chick flick'.

Billy Eliot (2000) dir. Stephen Daldry. Funny and shrewd treatment of class and work.

Lock, Stock and Two Smoking Barrels (1998) dir. Guy Ritchie. Four London working-class men pool their money in a high-stakes card game. Things go wrong and they end up owing half a million pounds with one week to come up with the cash. Ex-footballer Vinny Jones stars in this gangster movie with 'real' background.

Harry Potter and the Philosopher's Stone (2001) dir. Chris Columbus. Orphan Harry goes to Hogwart's Academy, learns the practice of magic and has adventures. Good overcomes evil. Blockbuster film of J. K. Rowling's novel, filmed in 'heritage' Yorkshire. She insisted on British actors.

Books

Ian McEwan, *The Cement Garden* (1984). Details adolescents' response to the death of their mother in a bleak Midlands environment. A key text for unlocking UK teenagers' minds.

Joanna Trollope, *The Choir* (1992). Presents a typically British conflict between appearance and reality, change and tradition, when a venal Dean wants to close a cathedral choir school.

Nick Hornby, *About a Boy* (1998). Deals with the problems facing a laddish central character who thinks he has his life sorted out. The son of one of his girlfriends introduces him to his own emotions. Filmed with Hugh Grant.

Tony Parsons, *Man and Boy* (2000). Written with autobiographical hindsight, this novel laments the myopia of a central character who loses everything through an irresponsible fling with a colleague. Discussed in a prison as Book of the Month, on Radio 4.

Graham Swift, *Last Orders* (1997). A group of four working-class Londoners travel to the seaside when their friend dies, to scatter his ashes in the sea. A high-profile British film followed in 2002.

Penelope Lively, *A House Unlocked* (2001). Though Lively is one of Britain's best contemporary novelists, this is a non-fictional collection of memories of English country life in the twentieth century inspired by Golsoncott, the Somerset country home occupied by her family.

Television programmes

Cold Feet. Very popular British equivalent of Friends (as is the sitcom *Coupling*) but with more orientation towards drama than comedy.

EastEnders. Enduringly popular soap with fans of all ages. Set in 'Albert Square', London.

Who Wants to Be a Millionaire. Quiz programme, hosted by Chris Tarrant. It caught the imagination for its options of 'ask the audience' or 'phone a friend'.

The Weakest Link. Scathing Anne Robinson acts as a dominatrix in this quiz programme and rudely dismisses contestants who don't make the grade.

Pop Idol. An elimination contest aimed at the making of a pop star. The audience finally choose. Sequel to *Pop Stars*, whose band Hear'Say produced two hit singles in short order.

This Life. Ground-breaking, documentary-format drama series where a group of lawyers in their twenties live together in a large house.

 Websites

www.ons.gov.uk/
Office for National Statistics, UK Government Agency, produces social, health, economic, demographic, labour market and business statistics

www.statistics.gov.uk/
The official UK statistics site. Up to date and accurate

earthstation1.simplenet.com/Princess_Diana.html
A tribute in sounds and pictures from Princess Di's funeral, including Elton John's rendition of 'England's Rose' and by Blair *et al.* funeral addresses

www.private-eye.co.uk/
Online version of very influential satirical magazine. Presents alternative view of contemporary Britain

www.bbc.co.uk/history/programmes/greatbritons/
The BBC's 'Greatest Briton' site

Chapter 1

Places and peoples: nation and region

Peter Childs

■ Nation   43

■ Country   44

■ Region   48

■ County   52

■ City   55

■ Town   59

■ Village   61

■ Conclusion   64

■ *Exercises*   69

■ *Reading*   70

■ *Cultural examples*   70

■ *Websites*   71

Timeline

1536	England and Wales joined
1707	Act of Union for England and Scotland
1801	Ireland incorporated
1922	Independence of southern Ireland
1931	Commonwealth officially formed
1972	Direct rule imposed on Northern Ireland
1973	UK joins EEC
1974/5	Redrawing of county boundaries
1979	Devolution referenda
1994	Eurotunnel opened
1999	Scottish Parliament, Welsh Assembly
2000	Northern Irish Assembly

'BRITAIN' IS A SHORT form of the full name of the United Kingdom of Great Britain and Northern Ireland. Therefore, Great Britain strictly comprises the countries England, Wales, and Scotland, whereas the UK also includes Northern Ireland. On the one hand, these four countries have become part of one nation over the last five hundred years: Wales was linked with England in 1536; an Act of Union joined the crowns of England and Scotland in 1707; Ireland was incorporated in a Union lasting from 1801 to 1921, when all but Northern Ireland gained independence (taking effect in 1922). On the other hand, as European history repeatedly demonstrates, political union is not cultural union, and it has often been maintained that Scotland and Wales should have devolution, a transfer of power from the government in Westminster to a regional assembly. The pressure of this view, following referendums of the populations, resulted in the creation in 1999 of the Scottish Parliament and the Welsh Assembly, which give not independence but increased self-government. These elected bodies can be perceived as part of a transition to full national government in Wales and Scotland, though at present they are seen by some as an extra layer of government between the people and the UK government at Westminster, which retains overarching financial control and has generally centralised power rather then devolved it, especially in relation to local government below the regional level. By contrast, Northern Ireland had self-rule in most governmental areas except foreign affairs and defence prior to 1972, at which date direct rule from London was reintroduced following increased sectarian violence. However, following the Peace Agreement in 1998 and in line with Scottish and Welsh devolution the previous year, a Northern Irish Assembly and Executive was created in 2000 to end direct rule from Westminster, though continued violence and a lack of political commitment to the Agreement has threatened this, such that the reimposition of Westminster rule remained a possibility at times in late 2001 even though the IRA continued its moves towards arms decommissioning. Alongside this can be placed the fact that a *Guardian* poll in August 2001 reported that 41 per cent of Britons believed Northern Ireland should join a united Ireland, while only 26 per cent believed it should be a part of the UK.

FIGURE 1.1 Map of the British Isles showing location of counties, cities, towns, and villages discussed in the chapter

FIGURE 1.2 Big Ben in London, with the distinctive black cab in foreground

In terms of natural, as opposed to political geography, it can be argued that Britain is marked by great contrasts but few extremes. Its highest mountain is Ben Nevis (4,406 ft or 1,343 m) in Scotland, its longest river the Severn (220 miles or 354 km) which rises in central Wales but also wanders as far east as Gloucester in England. Its largest lake is Lough Neagh (153 sq miles or 396 sq km) in Northern Ireland. Officially, the mainland stretches from Dunnet Head in the north of Scotland to Lizard point in Cornwall, but most people will describe Britain as running from the famous names of Land's End, in the south, to John O'Groat's.

However, when situating British identity in terms of place in relation to culture, we should both turn to smaller geographical units, such as the ancient counties whose boundaries were contentiously redrawn in 1974, and look to the larger outside world, not least because many British people do not live in the UK. Britishness in recent years has often been defined in relation to the Continent as European political and physical links have become stronger: in 1973 the UK joined the European Community (now European Union) and in 1994 the Channel Tunnel was opened, providing a rail connection from England to France. From another perspective, their eventful history means that British people have ties throughout the world, particularly with those fifty-one countries who in 1994 were still members of the Commonwealth of Nations, a loose association of independent countries formerly of the British Empire. In between all these geographical and political groupings there has arisen not just a few but a multitude of British cultures and identities.

To give an initial outline of the UK in terms of place, we can begin by looking at three aspects: size, population, and people. The United Kingdom has a land area of just over 93,000 sq miles (242,000 sq km), a little over half of which is in England. This is one reason why England is sometimes mistaken for Britain abroad, but a stronger factor is the relatively large size of England's population – an imbalance that allows it to dominate the union, beaming its television programmes to the rest of the nation for example. In 1999, the fairly stable UK population stood at about 59½ million people.

In terms of culture, the figures in Table 1.1 can be misleading. To begin with, we should not assume that strength of cultural identity increases with size of population – indeed, many people would argue that the opposite is more likely to be the case. It is therefore not surprising that to confuse Britain with England can cause grave offence. History provides ancient reasons for this vehemence of feeling: England is named after the Angles, a tribe who invaded Britain's south-east coast from northern Europe in the fifth century and, with other conquering tribes such as the Saxons, drove the older inhabitants, the Celts, to the west. Celtic influence is still notably present in Ireland, Scotland, Wales, and Cornwall, and this ethnic difference remains one basis on which England, of the UK's four countries, is sometimes considered to have the least in common with the others. On the other hand, the breakdown into English, Welsh, Scottish, and Irish histories can also be misleading when it comes to contemporary cultural identity. The

TABLE 1.1   Resident populations of UK countries, 1981 and 1994 and 1999 (thousands)

	1981	1994	1999
England	46,821	48,707	49,752
Scotland	5,180	5,132	5,119
Wales	2,813	2,913	2,937
Northern Ireland	1,538	1,642	1,691
Total UK population	56,352	58,395	59,500

Sources: OPCS and General Register Offices; 'Mid 1999 Population Estimates', National Statistics Office

domestic histories of these four countries do not adequately represent the people of the UK today because Britain now has a richer mix of ethnicities than those associated with the ancient Anglo-Saxon or Celt. Over the last century and before, the connections created by the Empire have led to the arrival in Britain of many people from the Caribbean, the Indian subcontinent, and Africa, such that, for example, the number of British people of Asian descent is now greater than the population of Northern Ireland. Similarly, refugees from Bangladesh and Uganda, plus communities uprooted from Cyprus, Vietnam, and China, have added to the different cultural identities found in Britain. In 2000, the number of people who classified themselves as members of an ethnic minority stood at 3.8 million, a rise of nearly a million in ten years. Again, while this book deals with people within the UK, there are strong British identities to be found in, for example, Hong Kong, a British crown colony up to 1997, the Falkland Islands, over which Britain fought with Argentina in 1982, and the vast Commonwealth of Nations. So, while this chapter will focus on places within the UK, the cultural life of people in Britain is both always in flux and much wider than geographical boundaries might suggest.

Lastly, in amongst this discussion of British identities, it is also salutary to note that there are many rumours circulating about the end of Britishness. Tom Nairn's twenty-year-old book *The Break-up of Britain* is a key point of orientation in the debate, followed up by his recent *After Britain: New Labour and the Return of Scotland* (Granta, 2000). But, in the context of Europe and devolution, there are of course a range of other millennial books on the same subject, such as John Redwood's anti-Europe *The Death of Britain* (Macmillan, 1999), or Andrew Marr's book-of-the television series *The Day Britain Died* (Pimlico, 2000).

There are additionally voices from abroad, one of which I shall quote. An article by expatriate Andrew Sullivan in the *New York Times* in 1999 (21 February, 'There Will Always Be an England') uses the headline 'Farewell Britannia' on every page: 'As the century ends, it is possible . . . to talk about the abolition of Britain without the risk of hyperbole. The United Kingdom's cultural and social identity has been altered beyond any recent prediction. Its very geographical boundaries are being redrawn. Its basic Constitution is being gutted and reconceived. Its monarchy has been reinvented. Half its Parliament is under the ax. Its voting system is about to be altered. Its currency may well soon be abandoned. And its role in the world at large is in radical flux.'

Sullivan anticipates a post-imperial attempt at dismantling: 'By quietly abolishing Britain, the islanders abolish the problem of Britain. For there is no problematic "Great" hovering in front of Scotland, England or Wales. These older deeper entities come from a time before the loss of empire, before even the idea of empire. Britain . . . is a relatively recent construct,

FIGURE 1.3 The lion and the unicorn, symbolising England and Scotland, on Queen Elizabeth Gate, London

cobbled together in the seventeenth century in the Act of Union with Scotland.'

And there are of course voices from Scotland and Wales that also look forward to the end of Britishness as the route to a fuller and better national future free from England. The Welsh poet R. S. Thomas writes: 'Britishness is a mask. Beneath it there is only one nation, England', while Gwynfor Evans, the former leader of the Welsh Nationalist Party Plaid

Cymru, published in 1981 a book entitled *The End of Britishness*, arguing that 'Britishness is Englishness'. Another poet, Robert Crawford, from north of the border, maintains that 'It is hard to think today of what could be confidently called "British" culture rather than English or Scottish culture . . . Scottish culture seems to have moved into a post-British phase.'

While we can therefore still talk about 'British Cultural Identities', the emphases need to remain on the multiplicity and plurality implied by the third word, particularly given the resurgence of regionalism in recent years, suggesting that Britain as such may not exist in twenty years' time.

Nation

The British mainland, separated from the European continent by the English Channel, is the eighth largest island in the world. Its inhabitants are islanders, and their attitude towards the rest of the world has some-times been said to reflect this.

While the Commonwealth offers many indications of the cultural and ethnic influences on modern Britain, and is at the same time a sign of the UK's international links and imperial past, it is Europe's economic policies, legal dictates, and bureaucracy that is increasingly forcing the British to reconsider their identity. For some people, 'Brussels' has become a major opponent, in the face of whose recommendations and legislation they are trying to assert a national culture that they feel is coming under attack. Alongside genuine fears, such as that of a loss of local languages, there has also arisen a mythology of European Union policies: rumours maintaining that traditional British foods, such as dairy milk chocolate, crisps, fish and chips, and Cornish ice cream, are under serious threat because of EU stan-dardisation. Through appeals to such recognisable staples of national heritage, a powerful resistance to the EU has been built up, but other voices maintain that Britain's political, economic, and legislative future has to lie within a united Europe. Consequently, the split over the EU within the Conservative Party has constituted its major policy stumbling-block for many years. While the majority of British people are happy in principle to participate in an economic union, they are also defensive of their distinc-tive traditions and their cultural separation from other European countries: in other words, of their identity.

An article in the *Sunday Times* on 5 February 1995 was entitled 'Disunited We Stand'. It maintained that, while each of Britain's four different countries has a strong identity and inspires patriotic loyalties, there is no 'British' identity as such. The article noted that a 1994 survey revealed that 75 per cent of people 'north of the border' would call themselves Scottish and not British. Also, the large national and private organisations, such as British Rail, British Telecom, British Petroleum, and the British Broadcasting Corporation, all known by just their initials, are either decentralising, breaking up for privatisation, or turning into multi-nationals. The 'British' element is redundant, the article argued, and the United Kingdom is only England with other countries attached in the same way that the Soviet Union now appears to much of the outside world to have been just Russia with other communities uneasily tied to it. Such a view has made British studies courses often turn to a 'four nations' approach.

Country

To illustrate some traditional ways in which the countries of the British Isles have developed separate cultural identities, we can begin with examples of their various images and emblems. England's patron saint (and also Portugal's) is the probably fictional St George, a knight who slew a fire-breathing dragon in medieval English mythology. St George's cross is the name of the English flag, which depicts a red cross on a white background – and English national teams still play rugby and football predominantly in white. The English emblem has been the rose since the War of the Roses in the fifteenth century, when the House of Lancaster, whose symbol is a red rose, fought for the English crown against the House of York, whose symbol is a white rose. More recently, as a symbol of both tradition and socialism, the red rose has been adopted as its emblem by the Labour Party. Red is also the colour of Wales, whose mascot since 1801 has, interestingly, been the red Welsh dragon, which is the central figure on the country's flag. The patron saint of Wales is a sixth-century monk called St David, and his day, 1 March, is regarded as the country's unofficial public holiday. Wales's twin emblems are the leek and the daffodil. English and Welsh hostility is rooted in history, the relative size of populations arguably giving rise to English condescension and Welsh resentment. Welsh identities are distinctive in terms of language, literature, and culture, but Wales is also divided by language (most people speak English), politics (between those who want a republic and those who would wish for a self-governing nation within a federal UK), and geography (as in England, there is a split between south and north). The Welsh emphasise their sense of community more than the English (except those in the north of England, who are often as hostile to southern Englanders as the Scots or Welsh are), and according to surveys see themselves as more caring, genuine, and responsible than their English neighbours. Economic regeneration, the new Welsh Assembly, the resurgence of the Welsh language, and the characteristic landscape of the valleys have added to a recent growth in Welsh national feeling.

Intranational rivalry is suggested by two other adopted animals: the warring lion (England) and unicorn (Scotland). Since James VI of Scotland became James I of England in 1603, these animals have featured on the Royal Arms holding the monarch's shield. The lion has become a symbol of the strength of the crown and Britain in general, while the Scottish unicorn represents purity. In politics, the Scottish Nationalist Party is the strongest voice for the country's distinctive identity, and its most famous campaigning supporter, Sean Connery, has vowed to move back to Scotland if the country wins independence. The Scots have a stronger sense of national identity and allegiance than the English or the Welsh, perceiving themselves as tough, friendly, outdoor people who are proud of their traditions and history. Consequently, and partly because of the distinct Scottish accent, they have a higher profile abroad than the Welsh, and in some ways than the English. Scotland's patron saint is one of the twelve apostles, St Andrew, and its emblem is the thistle, a symbol of defence. St Andrew's cross forms a part of the British flag, known as the Union Jack, together with the crosses of St George and St Patrick, the patron saint of Ireland.

A fifth-century ex-slave, St Patrick made the base for his gospel preaching in Armagh, and from there led the successful resurgence of Christianity against chieftains on the British mainland. His feast day, 17 March, is an official holiday in Northern Ireland and his cross is the country's flag (it is not that of the Republic of Ireland). Northern Irish identities contain strong English, Scottish, and Irish connections, although there are people in the six counties who identify neither with traditional Irishness nor with Britons from the mainland, seeing themselves instead overwhelmingly in terms of their own local culture, with its emphasis on both hard work and an easy-going character. Ireland's emblem is the shamrock,

FIGURE 1.4 Edinburgh Festival fringe 2001

whose three-in-one leaf was supposedly used by St Patrick to demonstrate the Holy Trinity, but on the British coat of arms Ireland is represented by a harp, now most widely recognised as the logo for Guinness, the famous Irish stout. The majority of these symbols have become signs of a collective heritage and the degree to which people align themselves with such images today is negligible, but on the saints' days a few individuals do wear badges with their country's emblem in their lapels. In terms of popular culture, the Union Jack had already become simply a minor fashion design in the 1970s, appearing on watch faces and T-shirts. It was also taken up in the 1980s by football fans, who since then have visited Europe with the flag daubed on their faces (reminiscent of the Ancient Britons who would paint their faces blue with a substance called woad to frighten their enemies). Today, individuals are more likely to turn to television personalities, film and pop stars, or sports players for their country's heroes and icons.

Ireland is the second largest of the British Isles. However, unlike smaller islands which are wholly British, such as the Isle of Wight and the Shetlands, Ireland is officially partitioned. In 1921, when an agreement was signed giving the rest of the country independence, six of the nine Irish counties which constituted the ancient province of Ulster remained part of the United Kingdom – these were the north-eastern counties that were predominantly Protestant. Northern Ireland therefore has national and official links with the rest of Britain but its people share deep roots with histories and traditions south of the border, and since the Anglo-Irish agreement of 1985 the Republic of Ireland has participated in its political and legal matters. Ireland is politically divided but in several respects it is culturally united for many people, not least because the Irish have retained a national distinctiveness despite the globalising influences that are so evident in England. In the 1960s, traditional Irish music saw a resurgence which has continued; government policy has been to revive the Irish language; indigenous sports such as hurling and Gaelic football have remained popular; and Irish literature is flourishing. For example, in Seamus Heaney, the Irish have arguably produced the finest poet writing in the English language since W. B. Yeats – who was also Irish. Also, in 1993, Roddy Doyle won the most well-known literary award in Britain, the Booker Prize, with his comic novel *Paddy Clarke, Ha Ha Ha*, a popular and distinctively Irish story about a young boy growing up in Dublin.

In 1994, the Booker was won by James Kelman, a Scot, with his novel *How Late It Was, How Late*. This is a story written in Glaswegian slang, and its part-abusive, part-aggressive patter is peculiar to that city, such that its idioms are not always readily intelligible in much of Scotland outside Glasgow, let alone in the rest of Britain. In addition to a unique vocabulary, the Scots have their own legal and educational systems, a stronger Calvinist tradition than the English, and a history which has forged closer links with the French and Irish than the English. When the Scots move abroad, it is said that their national identity emigrates with them, which is significant when approximately four times as many Scots live outside of Scotland as within. It is important to remember that such feelings of belonging do not cease at the border and, in England for example, there is a strong sense of Scottish identity – as any 25 January spent at thousands of English pubs will demonstrate. This is 'Burns night', when the birth of Scotland's national poet, Robert Burns, is celebrated with drink, song, and dance in a way that Shakespeare's very seldom is. Scotland is currently also in vogue among celebrities, especially since Madonna and Guy Ritchie and the actress Ashley Judd married at Skibo Castle, where Paul McCartney may also follow suit. High-profile people who own homes in Scotland run from J. K. Rowling to Prince William, and both Jennifer Lopez and Michael Jackson have now expressed an interest in living there.

Officially, the most closely tied countries in the UK are England and Wales, which includes the large island of Anglesey across the narrow Menai Strait. Often mentioned as one unit for purposes of surveys, censuses, and polls, England and Wales are joined administratively as well as politically and economically. However, many of the arguments for devolution have rested upon the view that Wales, as well as Scotland, is readily distin-guishable from England in terms of language, culture, and history. For example, a traditional cultural event which identifies Wales separately from the rest of Britain but which is held in many forms is the Eisteddfod, a bardic competition from pre-Christian times. The name, meaning 'chairing' or 'session', derives from the ceremonial seating of the bard or poet whose work has been awarded the first prize. The Royal National Eisteddfod, conducted entirely in Welsh, is held annually in different locations throughout the country. It involves music, drama, and other arts, as well as poetry. The Eisteddfod is announced over a year in advance at a harp ceremony conducted by the Gorsedd, or Court, encircled by specially laid stones. The festival is associated with a nationalistic Welsh identity and Plaid Cymru, 'the party for Wales', was founded in a hotel room in Pwllheli during the Eisteddfod in 1925. As a cultural event the Eisteddfod remains identifiably Welsh even though there are English language spin-offs, just as Highland reels and sword dancing are Scottish. In terms of place, it is country rather than nation that remains the major cultural, though not necessarily political, grouping with which people identify.

Representations of the British are not generated only from within Britain however. In terms of culture, Hollywood remains a dominant influ-ence. In the 1940s and 1950s, English actors commonly played the roles of well-mannered, upper-class socialites. At the end of the last century, there was an identifiable trend in which male English actors took the roles of 'bad guys': killers, psychopaths, or terrorists. There was a run of such films in which the villain, though not English, was played by an Englishman: *Schindler's List* (Ralph Fiennes), *Air Force One* (Gary Oldman), *Die Hard* (Alan Rickman), and *Reversal of Fortune* (Jeremy Irons). An actor such as Anthony Hopkins, who played the part of Hannibal Lecter in *Hannibal* and *The Silence of the Lambs*, is likely to be lumped in with this group because the Welsh, unlike the Scottish and Irish, who have large populations in the USA, seem not yet to have a strong cultural identity in Hollywood. By contrast, the *Star Wars* film *The Phantom Menace* had a Scottish actor, Ewan MacGregor, and a Northern Irish actor, Liam Neeson, as its heroes. Arguably, Celtic sympathy in the USA, combined with an increased awareness of colonialism, has meant that, after the Cold War, the English have been frequently cast in the guise of oppressors, and their role in, for example, the Second World War has been ignored or downplayed by Hollywood in films such as *Saving Private Ryan* and *U-571*.

Region

It is important to remember that culture varies for Irish, Welsh, Scottish, or English people depending on which region of their country they come from. In Wales, three-quarters of the population live in the valleys and coal regions of the south, which instil a different sense of Welsh identity from the mountains and seaside towns of the more militantly anti-English north; while in England it is the heavily populated metropolitan areas that have created several of its strongest regional identities. People from these different areas are associated with specific names and local characteristics, though it is their dialect that most obviously distinguishes them. For example, those from Newcastle and Tyneside, in the north-east of England, are called 'Geordies' after a mining lamp designed by George Stephenson, while people from Liverpool are known as Scousers, after a sailor's stew of meat and potatoes called lobscouse, and anyone brought up in the vicinity of London's Cheapside is known as a Cockney, originally the name for a spoilt city child. Each of these has a strong regional identity which is reflected in television series devoted to personalities from the major cities: *Auf Wiedersehen Pet* and *The Likely Lads* about canny, tough-minded Geordies, *Brookside* and *Boys from the Blackstuff* about long-suffering but brave-faced Scousers, *Minder* and *Only Fools and Horses* about wily, enterprising east Londoners 'on the make'. The importance of regional identity can also be understood from any phone-in radio programme where presenters will almost invariably cite the area that callers are from, as though this in some significant way influenced their viewpoint, determined their record request, or mattered greatly to the show's listeners.

FIGURE 1.5 Rolling English countryside of the shires (Gloucestershire)

England is often talked about in terms of a North/South divide, which is cultural, economic, and political (the Labour Party has far more support in the north and the Conservative Party in the south). This was particularly accentuated in the 1980s by differences in unemployment levels, crime rates, and standards of living, all of which were worse in the North. The perceived divide does not occur in the middle of the country, however, and southerners sometimes refer to a cold, industrial region that is everywhere 'north of Watford', a town not particularly far north of London. In turn, some Northerners caricature many southerners as 'soft' or as 'Yuppies', an American slang word short for 'young urban professional' or 'upwardly-mobile' people. This is because people from the south-east, and particularly London, are sometimes seen as fast-living, career-minded, and unfriendly, while they are also more comfortably off and enjoy better weather than those further north. Differences between North and South have evolved over the last two centuries and are more cultural than simply industrial or economic (during parts of the nineteenth century the North was more prosperous than the South). In August 2001, *The Times* published a special issue of its Saturday Magazine, proclaiming 'It's Cool Up North'. The reasons for this assertion are several: the economy is diversifying and shifting from traditional manufacturing areas, currently in recession, into more prosperous service industries (e.g. a quarter of workers in Leeds are now in financial and business services); culturally, the north has provided the most prominent groups from the Beatles (Liverpool) to Oasis (Manchester), but now has a range of high-profile new names ranging from indie musician Badly Drawn Boy to girl band Atomic Kitten; in football, Manchester United's treble in 1999 (including the Champions' League) has been closely followed by Liverpool's cup treble in 2001 (including the Uefa

Cup), and these two teams, along with Leeds United, currently dominate the Premiership; London also no longer has a monopoly on fashion, and Manchester's Joe Bloggs label has broken several sales records since its foundation in 1995.

However, the largest number of 'enterprise zones' and development areas, assisted by government funding and incentives for industry, are in regions such as the Midlands, the north-east, east central Scotland, and south Wales – but this economic difference from the south of England is frequently exaggerated. That a southern English region such as south-west Cornwall is also a development area is often ignored because it is distant from London and the financially dominant south-east. The greatest financial distinction between London and the rest of the country is the cost of housing. In 2001, the average house price in Britain was £90,000, but it would be almost impossible to buy a home in London for anything like this price.

Other regional differences are evident in sport, food, and housing: the north has Rugby League, the south Rugby Union; the north has butties, barmcakes, and baps (all breadcakes) while the south has sandwiches and rolls; terraced housing is more common in the north, detached houses and bungalows in the south. Between these two regions lie the Midlands, a band of counties such as Staffordshire and Nottinghamshire across central England which, caught between two cultures, often seems to be regarded as the north by people in the south and vice versa. However, a strong regional identity associated with the dales, hills, and moors is felt by people in the Midlands, and the countryside of a county such as Derbyshire is often considered the most beautiful in England (by Jane Austen in *Pride and Prejudice*, for example). Also, a distinct personality attaches to Birmingham, the UK's second-largest city, and the distinctive 'Brummie' accent is as recognisable as a Scottish or Welsh one.

Language, accent, vocabulary, and idioms of speech form important regional differences. For example, Welsh, a version of which was spoken in Britain when the Romans invaded in 55 BC, is one of the oldest languages in the British Isles. Tens of thousands of people still speak Welsh, adult educational institutions run language courses, and since 1970 education in Wales, or *Cymru*, has been bilingual. About a quarter of the Welsh population speak both languages, and because Welsh and English are both officially supported it is usual to see signs written in the two languages. Also, Gaelic, another variant of the ancient Celtic languages, is still spoken by some people in Ireland, Scotland, and, to a lesser extent, the Isle of Man. Accent and idiom vary enormously throughout Britain, although since the 1990s there has been concern expressed over the spread of 'estuary English': an outer London accent and dialect characterised by features of pronunciation such as lisped 'r's and by words such as 'basically' (it is thought by some to be reducing speech variations). In England there are still great differences in regional accent but the clearest boundary is that between north and south. No English person is likely to mistake the long, soft vowels of a West Londoner who could rhyme 'garage' with 'large', for the short, hard ones of a Lancastrian, who could rhyme 'garage' with 'ridge'. As for local vocabulary and idioms, if we take Scotland as an example, some words have become national expressions and most British people will understand 'ken' (know) or 'wee bairn' (small baby). However, an English person would be unlikely to know the meaning of such words as 'wabbit' (tired and weak), 'toom' (empty), or 'reidh' (smooth).

Scottish words come from different languages that lie either side of an ancient regional divide. The majority of Scots are Lowlanders and have an ancestry that is part-Teutonic and part-Celtic. In the past, they were considered different from the traditionally more aggressive, independent, Gaelic-speaking Highlanders, who were a minority but supplied the national symbols of the tartan, bagpipes, kilt and sporran (like the Highland games, these are largely produced for tourists nowadays). However, except in the crofting (loosely, farming) communities of the west, this division is historical more than contemporary, and religious denomination, football team allegiance, and city of birth are more likely to form points of cultural identity, especially for Lowlanders. Today, Gaelic is the principal language only in the Outer Hebrides and a few other, mainly island communities.

While it is a comparatively small country, Britain still has regional television companies which, as well as making and carrying the nationally transmitted programmes, provide localised information such as Granada in the north-west of England and Central in the Midlands. Since the 1980s,

TABLE 1.2   Resident populations of largest urban districts, 1994 and 2001: thousands (percentage of UK population in parentheses)

	1994		*2001*	
Greater London	6,969	(11.9)	7,268	(14.6)
West Midlands (inc. Birmingham)	2,628	(4.5)	2,628	(5.3)
Greater Manchester	2,578	(4.4)	2,596	(5.2)
West Yorkshire (inc. Leeds and Bradford)	2,194	(3.6)	2,132	(4.3)
Central Clydeside (inc. Glasgow)	1,621	(2.8)	1,590	(3.2)
Merseyside (inc. Liverpool)	1,434	(2.5)	1,410	(2.8)
South Yorkshire (inc. Sheffield)	1,305	(2.2)	1,308	(2.6)
Tyne and Wear (inc. Newcastle and Sunderland)	1,134	(1.9)	1,124	(2.3)

Sources: OPCS and General Register Office for Scotland

regional accents have been increasingly welcomed onto the BBC airwaves, which were previously saturated by announcers with the clipped tones of Received Pronunciation, an upper-class accent used to standardise speech by public schools in the nineteenth century. Today, there are also local radio broadcasts in Welsh and since 1982 there has been a Welsh-language television channel called *Sianel Pedwar Cymru*, which means Channel 4 Wales and is abbreviated to S4C. However, national stations are more culturally influential for most people, and satellite stations for some. While there are regional weekly and even daily papers, a similar picture is true of newspapers: even locally, national media are frequently more popular than regional.

County

After region, the largest area with which the British identify themselves is their county, a geographical fusion of landscape, culture, and administration most likely to affect people in terms of its natural scenery and its historic landmarks. County boundaries partitioned ancient Britain, and three counties in the south, Sussex, Kent, and Essex, were Anglo-Saxon kingdoms. Modified in 1975, counties still form the basis of local government in England and Wales, though reorganisation in 1997 again changed the map (for example, Gwent used to be a county in south-east Wales but, since the 1997 local government reorganisation, it officially no longer exists). In terms of county types, the most famous grouping in England is the 'home counties', a nineteenth-century phrase referring to the counties around London, such as Kent, Surrey, Berkshire, Middlesex, and Essex. Some counties are known for their countryside: Cumbria's Lake District (made famous in Wordsworth's poetry) and Hampshire's New Forest (a royal hunting ground for William the Conqueror); others for their industry: Lancashire's factories and mills (described in novels by Charles Dickens and Elizabeth Gaskell) and Nottinghamshire's mines (as in D. H. Lawrence's *Sons and Lovers*).

Northern Ireland is sometimes known simply as 'the six counties'. Local government there operates now on the basis of small district and borough councils, but ancient county identities are stronger. To take one example, Antrim, which derives its name from the fifth-century monastery of Aentrebh, occupies the north-east corner of Ireland. A county of moorlands and wooded glens, it is bordered by the sea on three sides. On the north coast is the famous Giant's Causeway. This is a promontory of vertical basalt columns formed by a volcanic rift which stretches under the sea to the Hebrides, islands off the west coast of Scotland. However, Irish legend holds that a giant built this as a walkway from Ireland to a cave on

FIGURE 1.6   Typical English rural scene

the Hebridean island of Staffa, so that he could attack the legendary Scottish hero Fingal. The roof of Fingal's Cave is also formed of straight six-sided rock columns which the two giants supposedly threw at each other. Celtic mythology adds a magical dimension to local identities and has been used in Ireland in attempts to forge a national consciousness, but even English Romantic poets such as Keats, Wordsworth, and Tennyson have written about Fingal's Cave.

Most of England's thirty-nine counties have a recognisable identity and will be said to have their own particular characteristics and distinctive inhabitants. Counties have given their names to famous stretches of countryside (e.g. Surrey hills or Devon moors), to types of people (unsophisticated socialites are 'Essex girls' and those with determination have 'Yorkshire grit'), to food (Cumberland sausages and Cornish pasties) and even to breeds of animal (Staffordshire bull terrier and Berkshire pig). However, one of the strongest ways in which county loyalties are continued is through sport. For example, one of the seventeen county cricket clubs, Yorkshire, refused up until 1992 to allow anyone not born in the county to play for the team. Despite this, Yorkshire has won the County Championship more often than any other team.

Of course, geographical features are also significant. Yorkshire is separated from its historic rival Lancashire by the Pennines, a range of limestone hills popular with walkers and sometimes described as the backbone of England. Yorkshire is famous abroad for the moors on which the Brontë sisters lived, but the county is also well-known in Britain for a section of the Pennines, the Yorkshire Dales, which was designated a National Park in 1954. These Parks are areas of significant natural beauty in England and Wales protected under an act of 1949. The act prohibits building or development in such areas as Dartmoor and the New Forest in England, Snowdonia and the Pembrokeshire coast in Wales. Similar protection applies to 'listed buildings', usually those dating back before 1840. Such measures preserve the past for the heritage and tourism industries and, partly in consequence, listed buildings and National Parks are sometimes put forward as representative of an authentic Britishness that is at threat from the architecture, pollution, and city-oriented life of the present.

Yorkshire is particularly famous for having a strong identity, but this is actually true of most counties. For example, in 1995 inhabitants of Britain's smallest ex-county, Rutland, which was merged with Leicestershire in 1974, were trying to have the county officially recognised again, by raising funds through a 'Rutland' credit card. In the 1970s, this sense of local county identity was satirised in a television series called *Rutland Weekend Television*, a spin-off from *Monty Python's Flying Circus* that had nothing to do with the county – it just pretended to be run on a low budget by a small community of amateur enthusiasts.

In 1975, the Welsh counties were rearranged with others to reduce their number from thirteen to eight. Powys, in mid-Wales, covers the old counties of Montgomeryshire, Radnorshire, and most of Breconshire, but the name itself is that of an ancient province dating from about the fifth century. Like all British counties, it is steeped in history. The county contains Powis and Montgomery Castles, the Dan-y-Ogof Caves, Brecon Cathedral, and Gregynog Hall, but its most famous landmark is the Brecon Beacons, or *Bannau Brycheiniog* in Welsh. These are a collection of mainly red sandstone mountains, designated a National Park in 1957, that run for forty miles away from the English border. Along and between the mountains are standing stones from five to six thousand years ago, ancient castles, and

FIGURE 1.7   Boats waiting for the tide to come in on the north Wales coast

cairns (hill markers made from piles of stones). The forests, mountains, and reservoirs of the Beacons provide excellent grounds for outdoor activities such as angling, gliding, riding, boating, trekking, and cycling.

Since the local government reorganisations of 1974/5, Scotland has been divided into nine large administrative regions and three island areas, instead of thirty-three counties. Fife was the only county not to be renamed as a region and it now covers roughly the same area as it did before. The administrators of the Local Government Act had intended the county to be split in two but the people of Fife protested so vehemently that the plans were dropped. It is also nationally and politically significant that off the coast of Fife are the drilling ships and rigs that have been exploring for oil and gas in the North Sea since the 1970s. Some of the arguments put forward for devolution by the Scottish National Party, which had seats at Westminster and campaigned for an independent Scottish Parliament, turned on the standpoint that North Sea gas and oil are Scottish and would enable the country, free from England, to run a prosperous economy.

City

In all, the United Kingdom has over sixty cities, a title many British people wrongly think is given to a town with a cathedral. 'City' is actually a title of dignity conferred on towns of religious, commercial, or industrial importance by statute, royal charter, or tradition (for example, Coventry, Exeter, and Norwich are mentioned as cities in William the Conqueror's eleventh-century *Domesday Book* of landholdings). Occasionally new cities are created, sometimes bidding for the status, as Brighton did successfully in 2000. Britain's cities vary enormously, from the industrial giants Manchester and Newcastle in the north to the southern ports such as Southampton and Bristol. There are also the cities noted chiefly for their cathedrals, such as Hereford and Ely, and the heritage cities such as the Roman town of Chester, whose entire medieval surrounding wall has survived, or Winchester, a small city of only thirty thousand people which in Anglo-Saxon times was the capital of England.

According to the EU's 'Exploring Europe' publication in April 1996, the first five things that spring to mind when someone thinks of the UK are Shakespeare, the BBC, The Beatles, Royalty, and London, the capital of England. Within London there is a 'square mile' of offices and banks that encompasses the original walled area that is also sometimes referred to simply as 'the City' and is the financial hub of Britain's business activities. At over 7.2 million, London has the largest population of any city in Europe, although people have been steadily moving away to the outer suburbs and commuter zones since the Second World War. Britain's capital is one of the best-known cities in the world but in many ways it is different from the rest of the UK. London fashions are likely to sample different clothes and styles of the past, specialist shops sell anything from military armour to body jewellery, and musical styles are eclectic, forming such hybrids as bungle, a mixture of bhangra and jungle music, or Gujarati rock, a fusion of Western guitars with Indian sitars and tablas. Such meetings illustrate the blended histories that London now represents because its 'conglomerate nature', as Salman Rushdie records in his controversial 1988 novel *The Satanic Verses*, now echoes the cultural diversity of the old Empire. To reflect London's particular interests and identity, the position of Mayor was revived in May 2000, and its first elected incumbent was Ken Livingstone, the ex-leader of the former Greater London Council, which was itself reborn in the form of a Greater London Assembly created to run affairs in the capital.

Britain's high culture is famously represented everywhere in London from the National Gallery in Trafalgar Square and the Royal Academy of Arts in Piccadilly to the Royal Opera House in Covent Garden and the National Theatre on the South Bank. Museums in central London are around every corner from the Museum of the Moving Image (MOMI), which celebrates film and television, to the vast British Museum which was the world's first public museum and is currently Britain's second most visited tourist attraction. As much as anything in London, the British Museum serves as a reminder of Britain's imperial history, and yet it is only one of around a hundred major museums in the capital. These, from the Museum of the Jewish East End and the Museum of Eton Life to the

FIGURE 1.8   Boats and houseboats on the Thames at Richmond

Sherlock Holmes Museum and the Florence Nightingale Museum, represent the variety of Britain's lucrative cultural heritage industry.

Tradition is still celebrated all year round, from the Lord Mayor of Westminster's New Year's Parade through to the Lord Mayor's Show in November. However, in a modern consumer culture such as Britain's, the past is often used for commercial profit or for charity: 'punks' are quite likely to be arts students looking to supplement their grants by simulating a Britishness for photographers; Pearly Kings and Queens, who were originally arbitrators in arguments between traders, are now usually on show, with their coats covered in mother-of-pearl buttons, to raise money for local causes.

To many people outside the capital, 'London' conjures up a collection of buildings, landmarks, and monuments such as Buckingham Palace, St Paul's Cathedral, the Tower of London, Westminster Abbey, Big Ben, and Piccadilly Circus. However, London is best seen as not one city but a patchwork of cities stitched together: the Cockney East End, the Docklands development, the Parliament at Westminster, the administration at Whitehall, the parks and the Thameside areas, the museums, theatres, shops, and galleries of the West End, the residential areas such as Hampstead and Belgravia, the City, the exhibition area around Earls Court, and the famous suburbs from Richmond in the west to Greenwich on the east. Despite this diversity, it is the tourist attractions that survive in the popular imagination as representative of London: a fascination with Britain's past which was illustrated in the 1960s when London Bridge was bought by wealthy Americans who had it taken apart and rebuilt in Arizona.

A further, less well-publicised characteristic of London and other British cities is the rise in the number of homeless people sleeping on the streets, which exceeds two thousand, and a parallel increase in begging, which is now common in the central metropolitan areas. In London and elsewhere, 'inner-city' areas are generally less well off than the suburbs, to which the more affluent sections of society have moved (a small counter-trend has brought the middle classes into the renovated dockland areas of London and other cities). Lifestyles are different too: in the inner cities the neighbourhood and street in which people live impinge more on their sense of identity than they do in the suburbs where people's home and garden are major preoccupations and sources of pleasure. Inner-city regeneration has become a central policy for successive governments since the war, and more especially since the 'riots' that broke out in the early 1980s in the inner cities of London, Liverpool, Bristol, and Birmingham, and led to violent clashes between police and protesters against the government's race, housing, and employment policies.

The capital city of Northern Ireland is most famous throughout the world for its violence. Since 1968, Belfast has chiefly made the front pages of British newspapers for its sectarian killings, although statistically it has been a safer place to live than many American cities. Separated as they are by the fortified wall of the 'Peace Line', the Falls Road (Catholic) and the Shankhill Road (Protestant) have become notorious throughout Britain, and 'the Troubles', as they are locally called, have contributed to Belfast's population of around 300,000 having one of the highest unemployment levels in Britain. Following the peace negotiations begun in 1995, the Northern Ireland Tourist Board has been actively trying to bring visitors back to the country through a publicity campaign including newspaper and television advertisements. A largely rural country without the crowded motorways or the fast-paced life of England, Ireland's difference from the rest of Britain is illustrated by the fact that Belfast is the country's only industrial city.

The capital of Scotland is Edinburgh, cut across by the famous Royal Mile – central streets that run through the old town marking the area walked or ridden by numerous kings and queens. Though it is Scotland's first city, Edinburgh is smaller than Glasgow, whose population of three quarters of a million is about 300,000 greater. Culturally, while Glasgow is currently deemed by some to be the 'coolest' city in Britain, Edinburgh is probably most famous for its annual summer Festival and Fringe, which has grown since the war to be a series of different festivals devoted to drama, film, literature, music, and dance. The Festival, where the Fringe alone in 2001 hosted a record-breaking sixteen thousand performers in two hundred venues, sells tickets to hundreds of thousands of visitors and claims to be the largest arts festival in the world. On New Year's Eve, which is known as Hogmanay in Scotland, people gather round Tron Church in Edinburgh, just as they do in Trafalgar Square in London, to celebrate the coming year and sing 'Auld Lang Syne'.

Cardiff, or Caerdydd in Welsh, in the county of South Glamorgan, is the capital of Wales and its largest city with a population of just under 300,000. Built on a site originally developed by the Romans in the first century, the city stands alongside the river Taff (though the common nickname for the Welsh, 'Taffy', does not come from this but derives from the pronunciation of the Welsh equivalent of David, 'Dafydd'). In the nineteenth century, Cardiff became a major port when it provided an outlet for the coal mined in local valleys such as the Rhondda. In more recent decades, as the coal industry has declined so have the Cardiff docks, which used to export more coal than any other port in the world. However, in the last decade Cardiff's docklands, like London's, have been greatly renovated and the extensive redevelopment has meant that the entire waterfront has been restructured. Cardiff is also home to two strong Welsh passions: Rugby Union and singing. Cardiff is the traditional centre of Welsh rugby football and stages international matches as well as cup finals. Since 1946, Cardiff has also been the base for the Welsh National Opera, which started from amateur roots and is the oldest of Britain's regional opera companies (the others are Scottish Opera and Opera North). A new opera house was being commissioned for the inner harbour of Cardiff Bay as the centre-piece for the docklands area development, but after difficulties a Wales Millennium Centre, to house an international arts and cultural complex, is due to open in autumn 2002 instead, along the bay from the new Assembly building designed by Richard Rogers. These add to the Millennium Stadium in west Cardiff, built on the site of the old Cardiff Arms Park rugby ground in 2000. The impressive new stadium even staged the English FA Cup final in 2001, when Wembley football stadium in London was set to be replaced.

Town

On the one hand, many people regret a creeping sameness in British cities and towns – for example, in most high streets you will see more or less the same shops, such as Boots, Marks and Spencer, Next, Mothercare, Debenhams, John Menzies, Burton, Woolworth, and WH Smith. On the other hand, British towns are still enormously varied, from the seaside towns, market towns, country towns, tourist towns, and industrial towns, to the postwar 'new' towns. Some coastal towns such as Blackpool and Bournemouth are chiefly known as seaside resorts and these are extremely popular with British holidaymakers; overseas tourists are more likely to visit historic towns such as Roman Colchester or Shakespeare's Stratford-upon-Avon. Other popular spots, famous since the seventeenth century for their 'healing waters', are spa towns such as Harrogate, Cheltenham, and Buxton. Many northern towns such as Wigan and Huddersfield retain for southerners the unfair image of industrial decline they gained between the wars, while market towns in the Midlands such as Melton Mowbray in Leicestershire still suggest the traditions of the English countryside. Towns do not have the large cultural life of cities or the close-knit community feel of small villages, but they combine aspects of each, providing a balance that many people feel is preferable to the bustle of the urban areas or the relative isolation of the countryside. Each county also has a 'county town' which traditionally, but in many cases no longer, was the seat of county government. County towns can often be inferred from their names, such as Lancaster in Lancashire and Shrewsbury in Shropshire.

Traditional English towns retain many of the architectural signs of the nineteenth century. Victorian, iron-framed, glass-roofed, covered markets remain in the centres of Bolton and Halifax, for example. Many towns still have magnificent municipal buildings from their heyday over a hundred years ago and grand public houses from the turn of the 1900s.

Impressive corn exchanges, where samples were auctioned or sold, still stand in many country towns such as Bury St Edmunds and Bishop's Stortford, while imposing workplaces such as the Bliss Valley Tweed Mill at Chipping Norton in the Cotswolds and the Clocktower Mill in Burnley stand out as reminders of the industrial revolution in mill towns. Every sizeable British town has a central park such as Jephson Park in Leamington Spa or Avenham Park in Preston, and while each town is different its development of terraced housing, shops, factories, and schools around church, railway station, market, town hall and square will be familiar.

Many modern towns have arisen because of the New Towns Act of 1946. These include Harlow and Stevenage near London, East Kilbride near Glasgow, and Cwmbran in south Wales. However, of the total of thirty new towns the most well-known and recent example is Milton Keynes in north Buckinghamshire. The new towns were designed to make possible a redistribution of the metropolitan populations and they had to cope with the preferences indicated by commuter life: a traditional English liking for the countryside wedded to a practical need to be able to reach the city. The intention was always to plan towns for modern living in every aspect by blending industrial and residential areas with full leisure facilities, and by separating traffic from pedestrians through a network of underpasses and walkways. However, Milton Keynes was not built up from nothing: it was designed to unite thirteen existing villages which are now enclosed by sweeping 'bypass' roads. Britain's largest new town in terms of area and population, Milton Keynes covers 50 square miles and has about 180,000 inhabitants. Despite its image of cleanliness and hi-tech living, much of the large town is still underdeveloped and underused, and yet its diverse range of amenities and accommodation, from solar-powered to timber-framed houses, makes it a more ambitious town project than any other since the war.

Most British towns have their own distinctive characteristics or annual events that promote a local cultural identity. For example, two Welsh towns in the county of Powys are Hay and Brecon. Hay-on-Wye is a small town which has become the book trade capital of Britain. Almost every shop in the town is an antiquarian or second-hand bookseller's, and people drive great distances to spend a whole day searching the shelves; club, university, and school trips are sometimes especially arranged to come and browse at what has become the largest collection of second-hand books in the world. While Hay has developed a prestigious annual literature festival, the nearby town of Brecon is the site of a distinctly Welsh community-based jazz festival each August which attracts some thirty thousand people and takes place throughout the town in the cathedral, halls, and pubs, as well as the streets themselves. Partly because jazz is enjoyed by its fans for its musical anarchism, flair, and improvisation, its celebration at such festivals has been seen as one of the less obvious assertions of Welsh independence from English culture.

However, against this individuality we must also note that the look of larger modern British towns has been greatly influenced by the United States. British planners, in the light of a general cultural imitation of American trends, are adopting stateside practices such as the 'doughnut effect' where town centres become abandoned by shoppers for malls on the outer ring. A largely consumer culture has been imported across the Atlantic and modern buildings reflect this: shopping complexes, multiplex cinemas, theme parks, out-of-town supermarkets, Disney stores, and fast-food restaurants, some of them drive-ins. The result is a sameness that is convenient and reassuring but also, on a national scale, numbing. Most cities and towns in Britain can be expected to have a number of fast-food outlets such as Burger King, a range of clothes shops such as The Gap, a Safeway or similar shopping centre away from the town, a Super Bowl, Laserquest, or ten-screen cinema complex, leisure centres with comput-erised workout gyms, and hoardings that advertise the American Dream along with their cigarettes. Milton Keynes is a prime example of this cultural saturation. It has imitation sheep and cows, acres of Astroturf, a grid road network, huge parking lots, a Milton Keynes Bowl for rock concerts, and 'California Collection' houses. The planners' aim has been to emulate the values and facilities of the ideal American town: efficiency, convenience, easy access, cleanliness, and even air-conditioning, plus such un-British aspects as indoor gardens, straight roads, and parking for thou-sands of cars. In this, the city's designers have probably succeeded, but Milton Keynes more than any other town remains the butt of numerous contemporary jokes for the many British who unfairly caricature it as a place lacking culture, history, or interest.

Village

By stark contrast, very little international influence will be found in Britain's villages, some of which can still be described as rows of thatched cottages nestling in country fields between hedgerows and small streams. Since the war, people have moved back to rural areas, reversing the trend started by the industrial revolution. In recent decades, the number of people living in villages has increased by several million to be around 25 per cent of the total population, though only 2 per cent of the overall workforce is employed in agriculture, fishing and forestry. Agriculture accounts for about one and a half per cent of the Gross Domestic Product and there are a little under 250,000 farms in Britain. Over half of these are devoted to dairy farming or to beef cattle and sheep, while the farms primarily involved in arable crops are chiefly found in eastern and central southern England or eastern Scotland – the main crops by area are wheat and barley though the production of potatoes and sugar beet in tonnes exceeds that of barley.

Villages in Britain are traditionally associated with a close-knit society centred on a hall, which serves as a kind of community centre, a market, parish church, pub, and a 'green', which is a grass area for fairs, fetes, cricket matches and other sporting events or public gatherings. Most villages therefore promote a strong blend of social identity, because people usually have a number of roles within the community, and personal identity, associated with land ownership and family history. A village's focus is likely to be on continuity and familiarity, and it is often said that everyone will know everyone else's business. Village life, it is said, is synonymous with community, which is symbolised by churchgoing, jumble sales, charity collecting, fetes and flower shows: those who join in are welcomed and those who do not are treated with suspicion.

However, village life is changing. A modern phenomenon is the commuter village. These are hamlets or villages which have sufficiently good transport links for office workers to travel by road or rail to the major cities, such as London and Birmingham, sometimes on journeys that take several hours. Many city business people live in villages for the peace and quiet, the clean air, scenery, and wildlife – but they probably have little

FIGURE 1.9 'Save the Countryside': this protest highlights the divisions between rural and urban Britain (© Ray Bird; Frank Lane Picture Library/CORBIS)

involvement in the life of the village unless they also have children they want to bring up locally in the comparatively friendly, unpolluted, and safe environment of the country. Similarly, second homes in villages throughout, for example, the Yorkshire Dales, are not unusual. City workers come out to them at weekends or just in the summer for holidays (in 1995, the pop group Blur's number one song 'Country House' satirised this very phenomenon). Such city people are sometimes resented by the local villagers because they may force up property prices and they also pose a threat to the continuity of village life. In the 1980s, 'holiday homes' in Wales were occasionally targets for arsonists resentful of this intrusion by outsiders, particularly from southern England. The increase in village populations since the war has also occurred because more and more people, who are also living longer, are retiring to the countryside from the city. Historically, village work has been based around a farming community, but the size of the agricultural workforce decreases year by year. Britain now has nine counties that are classed as rural and, to give an indication of how they are still in some ways isolated from city life, about a quarter of the villages in these areas have no food shop, post office, or doctor's surgery. An article in *The Times* in 2001 claimed that there was still a 'village pecking-order', with landowners and farmers at the top, long-established residents, of thirty or more years, in the middle, and newcomers, of less than fifteen years, at the bottom. The article claimed that slightly below this last echelon came 'new incomers', and way down at the bottom, Londoners.

Oddly, Britain's most talked-about village is fictional. Ambridge is the setting for *The Archers*, the world's longest running radio serial. Begun by the BBC in 1950, the programme is broadcast during the week for fifteen minutes, twice a day, and by radio's standards it has a large, devoted following. In the serial, Ambridge is close to the market town of Borset in the fictional county of Borsetshire (shire is a term for the central English counties whose names have that suffix – *The Archers* was initially broadcast just in the Midlands). The on-going saga revolves around the Archer family at Brookfield farm and portrays a close-knit village community in which everyone interacts with everyone else. Episodes are full of domestic incident and minor moral dilemmas but there are fewer exaggerated, intense emotional scenes and revelations than in the television soaps. The programme has always aimed to reflect realistically and unsensationally the concerns and interests of a village community and it has a farming correspondent who ensures that the serial's treatment of agricultural issues is factual and accurate. Ambridge's counterpart in reality is Hanbury in Worcestershire, where some outside location scenes have been recorded, and the programme also has a tradition of including real people, the most noted of whom was the Queen's sister, Princess Margaret, in 1984. In 1989, the Post Office issued a set of commemorative stamps to mark the ten-thousandth episode. A similar stalwart of BBC Radio 4 has been *Gardeners' Question Time*, which has taken a panel of experts around the country from village hall to village hall since 1947. Like much of Radio 4's broadcasting, the programme thrives on consistency and from 1951 to 1980, the trio of gardening authorities remained the same, but in 1994 an entirely new panel was introduced. Such changes, seemingly trivial, are extremely contentious for the station's loyal and conservative following.

Unsurprisingly for a people who are statistically more likely to give to animal charities than to the homeless, the British have long fashioned themselves as a nation of animal lovers, and Britain has a great variety of wildlife, with an estimated thirty thousand animal species. Television reflects this with many shows such as *Animal Hospital*, supplementing the broad appetite for nature and wildlife programmes. One issue in 2001, centred on animals, tested this affection and also pointed up many differences between town and country: the foot and mouth crisis, which by September 2001 had resulted in the killing of three million sheep and over half a million cattle. The crisis arose in February 2001 and soon pointed up several areas of disagreement: some resented farmers the compensation they received for culled animals because they refused to use vaccines and also because they have long been subsidised, to the tune of a third of annual turnover (this is because, when Britain joined the EC in 1973, land prices more than doubled because the Common Agricultural Policy raised the prices paid for arables, milk, beef, and sheep); farmers felt that walkers and others, as much as the movement of livestock, spread the disease; tourist agencies resented the closing of country paths in spring while farmers disagreed with their reopening months later; farmers were dismayed that compensation (£926 million by August 2001) was paid in euros which, because of the strength of the pound, was less than it otherwise appeared; towards the end of the initial crisis, in the summer of 2001, an outrage was sparked by accusations that some farmers had deliberately contaminated their livestock to get compensation. The priorities in the toing and froing were foregrounded by the spring General Election, which farmers wanted postponing until after the crisis so that the disease was not spread by the large movement of people, while others argued that postponing the election would give out the wrong signals internationally, suggesting that Britain had been 'closed down' by the disease. The crisis added to growing concerns over food scares and the general safety of meat products.

Conclusion

In this concluding section, as well as summing up we will look at four thematic aspects of British culture that are linked to place but are shared by everyone throughout the UK: the country–city divide, travel, the weather, and the environment. As a preface to this, however, it is worth noting that there is increasing pressure for decentralisation if not devolution in the regions, and the Chancellor Gordon Brown has admitted that the 'time for regionalism' has come, as other parts of the country are increasingly angry at the disparity between London's wealth and much of the rest of the country's comparative poverty. An increasingly vocal pressure group, the Campaign for the English Regions, pointed out that London already has a public spending budget almost a quarter higher than Yorkshire and a fifth higher than the whole of the north-east. Tony Blair's response has been to set out a timetable for regional government, with referendums in 2003, when there are also elections for the Welsh Assembly and Scottish Parliament, and elections in 2004 to coincide with the next European parliamentary poll.

Apart from political borders, one of the strongest kinds of geographical division in Britain is that between those who look for the natural life of the countryside and those who prefer the amenities at hand in the city. This is a long-standing difference of taste, and in the eighteenth century the poet William Cowper, in his poem *The Task*, wrote the famous line 'God made the country and man made the town'. Today, culture in cities tends to be diverse, reflecting the highly concentrated rich mix of different peoples with varied lifestyles: life is mostly anonymous, formal, and based around groups with specialised interests. Country life by contrast is generally associated with tradition, custom, community, cultural unity, and 'the outdoor life'. The antipathy between the two is pointed up by the common expressions of pity each makes towards the other: those in the towns are stereotyped as believing that country people are deprived of life's 'basics', ranging from adequate heating to convenience stores, while those in the country are caricatured as feeling that their lives are morally superior and that urban people live in cities only because they have to (according to *The Observer*'s 2001 survey 66 per cent of people would rather live in the country).

An article in *The Times* in 2001 observed that 'although there is a part of every Anglo-Saxon soul that is pastoral . . . there is a tradition of antipathy between yokel and townie which runs through English history'. It is often maintained that rural and urban people have different attitudes to the traditions of British life and, for example, one cultural pursuit that many feel marks a division between people in cities and villages is fox-hunting, a bill to ban which was passed by the House of Commons but overwhelmingly rejected by the House of Lords in March 2001. It is a frequent generalisation that city people want what they call 'blood sports' banned; and it is just as common to hear from those in favour of what they call 'field sports' that anti-hunting campaigners do not understand, as villagers do, the need for control of the population of predatory animals in the wild. For reasons such as this, the kind of cultural division in England between north and south is also sometimes found throughout the country between 'townies' and 'yokels'. As farmers are considered by those in the towns to provide the country's food, they are blamed whenever prices are thought to be too high, as they usually are, but farmers are also resentful because they claim it is the supermarket chains who are hiking up prices while forcing producers to accept low payments or be dropped. Similarly, feeling that again they have been penalised, farmers led the fuel-duty protests that brought Britain almost to a halt in the summer of 2000. The feeling that the priorities of the countryside are being sacrificed by the government was concentrated in the formation of the Countryside Alliance, whose slogan 'Listen to Us' expresses its belief that in the face of London's policies it is powerless. The Alliance has arguably had little success even though its rallies in the capital have brought out more protesters on London's streets than any other recent cause. The Alliance fashions itself as the countryside fighting for its liberty, and it defends hunting, fishing, shooting, and the interests of farming communities as well as campaigning on conservation and the environment. Lastly we must note that in addition to the country and the city, there is a third place of escape for people from either of these communities: the coast. Because all Britons live on an 'island' there is a strong coastal culture incorporating trawler fishing, watersports, ports and docks, shipping, yachting, and, for visitors, the British tradition of seaside holidays, with its staple ingredients of piers, buckets and spades, postcards, amusement arcades, deckchairs, donkey rides, and promenading. Again, there are also dozens of smaller islands off the British mainland, and the largest of these, the Isle of Wight off the south coast of England, is a county in its own right.

These areas are of course linked by travel on road, rail, air, river, or sea. Three in four British households today own at least one car. In the 1930s, more miles of road in Britain were covered by bicycle than by car, but now it is mainly those conscious of their health and the environment who choose two wheels over four. Commuting by train, on the main network or the London Underground, is a daily activity for millions of Britons – many of whom will complain that the rail services are far worse than on the Continent. In response to this constant criticism, a charter was introduced in the early 1990s to compensate people for delays, cancellations, and poor reliability. London's main airport, Heathrow, is the busiest in the world, although only 20 per cent of its forty million annual customers take domestic flights. Additionally, though they were superseded as a mode of transport in the nineteenth century by the railways, Britain is carved across by hundreds of streams and rivers, some with houseboats, and over four thousand miles of canals and waterways. Also, recently trams have been reintroduced in cities such as Manchester, a light railway links the city area in London with the docklands, and a monorail has been built above the streets in the centre of Sheffield.

An influence that on another level links city, country, and coast is a shared climate. In the eighteenth century, Samuel Johnson said that 'When two Englishmen meet, their first talk is of the weather.' Throughout Britain today the weather is still the most frequent topic of conversation, and not usually for agricultural reasons but simply because it is so changeable. Many British people will be only too willing to offer a forecast of likely shifts in the weather. On top of experience and barometers, several other, often proverbial methods of prediction are sworn by. For example, a herd of cows sitting in a field is thought to indicate rain, as do twitching bunions and rheumatic attacks. Similarly, the old saying, 'Red sky at night, shepherds' delight; red sky in the morning, shepherds' warning' is passed down from generation to generation as a sure method of anticipating fair or foul weather throughout the country. The national hobby of predicting rain, sunshine, hail, thunder, snow, or sleet is nicely summed up by the annual bets on whether there will be a white Christmas. Perhaps because of their obsessive interest in the weather, the British are generally sceptical of official forecasts. Although this scepticism is distinctly unfair, it was bolstered in October 1987 by a freak hurricane which a BBC television weather forecaster famously asserted would pass Britain by. The storm blew over fences and light buildings, brought down telegraph wires and poles, put television stations out of action, resulted in eighteen deaths, and left many cars crushed by fallen trees. Memories of 1987 were frequently invoked in the winter of 2000, when 'freak' floods left many villages under water and thousands of people homeless.

Britain in fact has a moderate climate in terms of its temperature, which has never been recorded as high as 100° Fahrenheit or as low as −18°F. Generally, it is between 35 and 65°F, and the climate is milder in England and Wales than in Scotland. The weather remains a constant talking point in Britain because of its local variations and its seasonal oddities: for example, though winter runs from December to February, a cricket match has been 'snowed off' in Buxton, Derbyshire, in June. August, in high summer, is one of the wettest months of the year and many Britons will swear that May and September are usually sunnier months. Rainfall differs greatly between regions and average annual levels vary from 500 mm in East Anglia in southern England to 5,000 mm in the Scottish Highlands.

Lastly, a country is frequently discussed in terms of its environment. For different reasons, the human maintenance and manipulation of the environment is of particular interest to two groups of people: environmentalists and the disabled. While they lagged behind other Europeans, the British became increasingly sensitive to ecological concerns, as the following examples indicate. The British Green Party, founded in 1973 as the Ecology Party, polled 15 per cent of the European Parliament votes in 1989. Most large cities are now circled by a 'green belt' on which little building is allowed. The Forestry Commission, which has its headquarters in Edinburgh, was set up in 1919 because of the timber shortage that became apparent in the First World War. By the 1980s, through grants and government administration, it had already reached its 2000 target of nearly 5 million acres of forest land. Recycling centres have also been stationed at shopping centres and other public places, for people to bring along their old newspapers, glass, clothes, and aluminium. The campaigning environmental group Friends of the Earth has been prominent in Britain since 1970, lobbying on world issues such as rain forests and global warming as well as on local British concerns including beach pollution and the privatisation of the water authorities in 1989. Greenpeace, the Campaign for Nuclear Disarmament, Earth First!, and various 'New Protest' groups, sometimes associated with New Age travellers, discussed in Chapter 7, have all also been active in Britain over the last twenty years.

A further issue of the (particularly built) environment is disability. Though many people in Britain have been slow to recognise the special needs of the disabled, supermarkets nearly always now have designated parking spaces close to the entrance, theatres often have signed performances, public buildings may be denied planning permission if they do not include wheelchair access, and most employers now claim that their equal opportunity policies mean that jobs are open to all people regardless of age, ethnicity, gender, or disability. Despite this, legislation has been difficult to pass, and disabled people are not well represented in films or on television, although a regular Radio 4 programme entitled *Does He Take Sugar?* attempts to provide a platform for issues of disability and the representation of the 'differently abled'. However, with respect to people's misconceptions, a high-profile media figure such as the scientist Stephen Hawking (who has motor neuron disease) or the pop star Ian Dury (who had polio) can do more than such a minority programme to raise general awareness of the difference between a physical 'disability', which usually relates to a specific aspect of life, and general, particularly mental, abilities. The general appreciation of disabled people has probably been raised greatly by the profile of the current Home Secretary, David Blunkett, who is blind, as well as the increasing willingness of television companies to give disabled sport more exposure. Overall, the campaign for responsible and fair adaptation of the natural and built environment has been seen as one of slow progress as organised groups lobby and protest on specific issues of personal or social importance against businesses whose interests are by contrast shortsightedly commercial.

As a final word, it can be said that, while the Union Jack can be seen flying at international conferences and decorating lapel badges, it is as often used today as a design for underpants, a pattern for dyed hair or face-painting, and a favourite symbol of the far-right British National Party. In other words, it is chiefly an emblem now of Britain's past and will be used nostalgically, ironically, and even callously as a sign of solidarity against others. Britons have always defined themselves as an island people, whose singularity and separateness is illustrated by the channel of water dividing them from the Continent. However, the British now have an undersea tunnel that connects them with France, they are hostile to federalism but committed to joining Europe, they are soaked in influences from the USA, and are succumbing to a global culture that may leave them disunited but curiously alike. This chapter has illustrated how, in terms of place, 'Britishness' is a problematic tag for people living in the UK, and that it perhaps best serves simply as a national label for traditional values and issues that lie between the local or global concerns with which individuals are increasingly more likely to identify themselves.

Exercises

1   What different kinds of regional identity do you think there could be said to be in Britain? How many regional variations in accent can you think of?

2   Can you name any personalities or politicians who seem to you representative of a distinctive kind of Britishness? Can you say which country or region they grew up in?

3   Do you think there is any correlation between climate and culture or character, and do you think there are any dangers in promoting such beliefs?

4   Try to locate six other British cities on Fig. 1.1. What do you know of each city and how do you think cultural identities might be different in each?

5   *The Times* published a special issue of its Saturday magazine, proclaiming 'It's Cool Up North' in August 2001, which listed the following as representaive of the old and new north. Looking at each pair, how would you describe the differences between the old and new representatives?

Old North	*New North*	
Bill Shankly	Gérard Houllier	(Liverpool football managers)
The Tower Ballroom	Manumission in Ibiza	(Dance venues)

The Animals	Atomic Kitten	(Bands)
Blackpool Tower	The Angel of the North	(Major sights)
L. S. Lowry	Damien Hirst	(Artists)
Cloth caps	Designer shades	(Headgear)
William Wordsworth	Simon Armitage	(Poets)
The Likely Lads	*The Royle Family*	(Television shows)
Saturday Night and Sunday Morning	*East Is East*	(Films)

 # Reading

Champion, A. G. and Townsend, A. R. *Contemporary Britain: A Geographical Perspective*, Edward Arnold, 1990. Looks at Britain in the 1980s and at the relationship of policies and practices with the land (considers the north/south divide and the rural/urban debate).

Daudy, Phillipe. *Les Anglais: Portrait of a People*, translated by Isabelle Daudy, Barrie and Jenkins, 1991. A French overview of the British.

Jacobs, Eric and Worcester, Robert. *We British: Britain Under the Moriscope*, Weidenfeld and Nicolson, 1990. Analyses the results of surveys about subjects ranging from politics to drugs.

Kearney, Hugh. *The British Isles: A History of Four Nations*, Cambridge University Press, 1989. Suggests that while English, Irish, Scottish, and Welsh identities are strong, a British identity is lacking.

Simpson, J. (ed), *Dictionary of English Folklore*, Oxford: Oxford University Press, 2000. Up-to-date guide to the arcane aspects of English heritage.

 # Cultural Examples

Films

Solomon a Gaenor (2000) dir. Paul Morrisson. Best Foreign Language Oscar-nominated movie set in the Welsh valleys in 1911. A Welsh girl falls in love with a Jewish boy, but the local community threatens their happiness.

Snatch (2000) dir. Guy Ritchie. Modern London gangster comedy, starring Brad Pitt as an Irish gypsy and directed by Madonna's husband; a follow-up to *Lock, Stock and Two Smoking Barrels*.

The Full Monty (1997) dir. Peter Cattaneo. Comical film about unemployed workers in Sheffield who become male strippers. The biggest box office attraction of the year in the UK.

Into the West (1992) dir. Mike Newell. Irish mythology, travellers, and inner-city life.

Local Hero (1983) dir. Bill Forsyth. Poignant film about a Scottish coastal community threatened by a multinational oil corporation.

Riff-Raff (1990) dir. Ken Loach. Social comment, set on a building site: strong regional characters.

24-Hour Party People (2002) dir. Michael Winterbottom. Fact-based film about the 'Madchester' years, concentrating on the rise of Factory records and the Haçienda club, putting Manchester at the heart of the British music scene.

Books

Sue Townsend, *The Queen and I* (1992). Fantasy about the Queen living on a Midlands housing estate.

R. S. Thomas, *Neb* (1985). Autobiography, written in Welsh, of Wales's most celebrated late twentieth-century poet.

James Kelman, *How Late It Was, How Late* (1994). Novel of Glaswegian street life.

Seamus Heaney, *North* (1975). An attempt by the Nobel-winning poet to place contemporary Northern Irish history in the context of European history and prehistory.

Nick Hornby, *How to Be Good* (2001). Comic novel about the priorities and anxieties of London life in the new century.

Laurie Lee, *Cider with Rosie* (1959). Most famous and still much-loved celebration of English village life.

Television programmes

Last of the Summer Wine. Comedy about three retired men in a Yorkshire village.

Monarch of the Glen. Spoof drama series about life on a Highlands country estate.

Brookside, EastEnders, Coronation Street.

Urban living in Liverpool, London, and Salford respectively.

Emmerdale. Previously called *Emmerdale Farm*, this is a serial about (now somewhat loosely) agricultural and village communities in England.

The Old Devils. Serial adapted from a Kingsley Amis novel, about a reunion of friends in Wales (S4C provides many of the best programmes about Wales).

World of Pub. Comedy set in a London pub, heavily reliant on rhyming slang and Cockney caricatures.

The League of Gentlemen. A satire of rural life set in the fictional village of 'Royston Vasey', where outsiders are treated with deep suspicion and the standard question asked of any unfamiliar person is 'are you local?'

Velvet Soup. Acclaimed and occasionally surreal new Scottish comedy sketch show.

Websites

www.statistics.gov.uk
    The latest official UK statistics, grouped in thirteen themes

www.ukvillages.co.uk
    Over 27,000 websites and online community centres for villages across Britain

www.thisislondon.co.uk
  News and information site for the capital

www.edinburghfestivals.co.uk
  Guide to the annual Edinburgh festival

news.bbc.co.uk
  Excellent online BBC news coverage

www.whatthepaperssay.co.uk
  Digest of regional and national British press

www.londonnet.co.uk//ln/index.html
  Claims to be the best guide to London on the Web

www.countryside-alliance.org/
  Website of the Countryside Alliance

www.24hourmuseum.org.uk
  Vast access point to Britain's museum collections

www.ordnancesurvey.co.uk
  Free map service with historical mapping of Britain

Chapter 2

Education, work, and leisure

Mike Storry

- Schools   75
- Colleges and universities   78
- Educational changes and trends   79
- Employment   83
- Unemployment and economic change   87
- Leisure around the home   90
- Public entertainment   92
- New patterns in leisure   100
- Trends in entertainment   103
- Conclusion   107
- *Exercises*   108
- *Reading*   109
- *Cultural examples*   109
- *Websites*   110

Timeline

600	Foundation of King's School Canterbury
1249	Foundation of Oxford University
1902	Education Act establishes state secondary education
1936	Television starts in England
1944	Education Act: grammar schools
1954	Independent Television Act licenses alternative broadcasters to BBC
1967	Plowden Committee recommends child-centred learning
1969	Foundation of Open University
1970	Equal Pay Act
1971	Industrial Relations Act (judiciary to arbitrate industrial disputes)
1975	Employment Protection Act
	Sex Discrimination Act
1976	Foundation of (private) University of Buckingham
1983	Unemployed: 10 per cent of workforce
1988	Education Reform Act
1990	Education (Student Loans) Act
1992	Polytechnics become universities
1993	Trade Union Reform and Employment Rights Act
1994	Criminal Justice Act opposed by Ramblers' Association

W E HAVE LINKED WORK, education, and leisure in the title of this chapter in the belief that very often people's work is determined by the education they receive and that their leisure activities complement their work.

The timeline above picks out a number of significant historical points. From it you will see that schooling for the top echelon of British people started in AD 600, through royal patronage. Concern with people's conditions of work came only gradually and change was achieved slowly through the Factory Acts of the nineteenth century. These aimed to prevent child labour and to restrict work to ten hours a day. Today, the 'working week' generally covers 9 am to 5 pm, Monday to Friday, although few people still work those exact hours and many are now employed on 'flexitime,' with unfixed times for arriving at and leaving work. Britons work the longest hours in Western Europe and attempt to express their real selves through leisure activities, both in the private space of the home and outside it. This chapter will look at the part played by education, work, and leisure in forming British people's identities, and will deal with those topics in sequence.

Schools

There are about 33,000 schools in Britain with 10,082,000 pupils and 597,000 teachers. There are separate state and private systems. The latter has 2,421 schools; 164 state grammar schools survive. The school year runs from September to July and children normally start school in the September following their fifth birthday. The school day is usually from 9 am to 3.30 or 4.00 pm and children are allocated places by the Local Education Authority (LEA) in the schools nearest to them, though these allocations are subject to appeal. The government has encouraged the exercise of parental choice by promoting competition among schools and adopting a policy of incentives for 'good' schools and a laissez-faire attitude to the closure of those which are becoming less popular. League tables of school exam results have been published since the early 1990s.

The state offers 'primary' (for ages five to eleven) and 'secondary' (for ages eleven to eighteen) schooling. There are a very few 'middle' schools for children aged ten to thirteen and some 'special' schools for children with learning difficulties. These are the main state schools, although there are others in for example hospitals and youth custody centres. Pupils are permitted to leave school at sixteen but a majority (2000: 73 per cent) stay on or move to Local-Authority-controlled Further Education (FE) or sixth form colleges.

The present state system evolved from a gradual move towards universal educational provision which started in the nineteenth century. Poorly funded 'board' and 'hedge' schools (the former managed by a local school board, the latter outdoors) taught pupils up to the standard leaving age of fourteen years (most recently raised from fifteen to sixteen in 1976).

In 1944, R. A. Butler's Education Act introduced the '11 plus' examination. All children took this test at the end of primary school, and those who passed had their fees paid at the local grammar school. This change had significant social and cultural effects in Britain. It made possible a degree of social mobility hitherto unknown and eroded notions of those with ability coming only from higher social strata. It introduced to postwar Britain a 'meritocracy,' and made a significant contribution to the affluence of the 1950s and 1960s.

On the negative side, it distanced children from their less well-educated parents. But perhaps the worst effect of the 1944 Education Act was that some people saw it as 'discarding' the 80 per cent of children who were assigned by the test to secondary-modern schools. Children were labelled as 'failures' at the age of eleven and this led to a cumulative loss of ambition, achievement, and self-esteem. Many became alienated and reluctant to integrate into society. In due course, this offered fertile ground for the growth of such youth-cultural subgroups as mods, rockers, and punks. Secondary-modern school pupils and teachers were demoralised by the knowledge that the most favoured students had been 'creamed off' to the grammar schools and by the fact that, despite the rhetoric of 'appropriate provision', they were part of second-class educational establishments in a system of 'separate development,' a sort of cultural 'apartheid'.

Partly because of the above malaise, the Labour government, in the 1960s, endorsed a system of 'comprehensive' schools. These were co-educational (most grammar schools were single-sex) and for all abilities. Some 'comps' exchanged grammar-school-type streaming (grouping pupils according to performance) for mixed-ability teaching. Here pupils of differing capabilities shared the same classrooms in the belief that the bright would help the weak and that improved social development would compensate for any lack of intellectual achievement. It was hoped that this would eventually lead to cohesiveness rather than competitiveness in society at large. Other comprehensive schools adopted what they saw as the best of existing educational practices, including intellectual rigour, while reducing emphasis in their curriculum on classics and sport.

In the private system, 'preparatory' schools educate children from the age of five, prior to their entering the 'public schools' at thirteen. Confusingly, famous private schools such as Eton and Harrow, Winchester, or Stonyhurst are known as 'public schools'. (The expression 'public school' originally referred to a grammar school endowed for the public.) That system of education is now, as *Chambers Dictionary* puts it, 'for such as can afford it'. There are also schools which have some state and some private support. By 1995 the parents of children in approximately a thousand schools had voted to opt out of the control of local authorities and be funded directly from central government, that is become 'Grant Maintained'.

State schools in Britain are non-denominational. Of the state-supported ones which have a religious affiliation, (known as 'faith schools') the majority are Anglican, but other denominations of schools exist: principally Roman Catholic and Jewish. Their capital expenditure is covered by the state and their running expenses are paid by the members of their congregations. A contentious issue has been that the same financial support was not made available to Hindu or Islamic schools. This became a major issue in Bradford and other places with large Muslim populations where poor educational provision was partly blamed for riots there in June 2001.

To monitor pupils' performance, the government introduced a series of 'Standardised Assessment Tests' (SATs) – taken at age seven, eleven, and fourteen. However, the major public exams which pupils face are those taken in individual subjects at sixteen and eighteen respectively: the General Certificate in Secondary Education (GCSE) and Advanced ('AS') levels. In Scotland students gain Lower and Higher Certificates. University entrance is typically based on good grades in approximately six GCSEs and three 'AS' levels. Other qualifications open to those school leavers who want to attend college are AVCEs, BTECs, HNCs, City & Guilds, RSA, and GNVQs.

The school system has a reputation for quality. However a number of factors – continual reforms; the over-prescriptive National Curriculum; inspections without feedback – have produced low morale among teachers, many of whom leave the profession.

In 1998 Britain was just ahead of Portugal, at second-to-bottom in adult literacy in the OECD (Organization for European Co-operation and Development). A 2000 report by the National Skills Task Force found that seven million adults in Britain were functionally illiterate. This was described by Estelle Morris, the Education and Skills Minister, as 'quite frightening'.

The government is trying to address these problems but, despite the rhetoric, spending on schools in 1999, of £2,433 per pupil in primaries, and £3,823 in secondaries, was 1 per cent below the OECD average of 12.9 per cent of all public expenditure.

Colleges and universities

On leaving school at eighteen, 41 per cent (1996/7) of pupils become students at universities and colleges. Including the Open University, which is mainly part-time, there are 110 universities in Britain: 93 in England, 13 in Scotland, 2 in Wales and 2 in Northern Ireland. They have 1,802,000 students and 78,900 lecturers (2000). The standard length of undergraduate study in Britain is three years for a Bachelor of Arts or Science degree (BA/BSc), and up to seven years for 'vocational' degrees (that is ones linked to a specific job), such as medicine, dentistry, veterinary courses or architecture. Students of subjects such as civil engineering spend an intermediate year in industry (a 'sandwich' course). Many universities offer the Bachelor of Education (B.Ed) degree which is a four-year course geared towards classroom experience. The majority of primary-school teachers qualify by this route. The standard way to train to be a secondary-school teacher is to do a three-year university course in a specialist subject such as biology, history or mathematics followed by a one-year Post Graduate Certificate in Education (PGCE) which includes teaching practice.

Students on Master's courses (MA/MSc) study for at least one year, and those doing Doctorates (PhDs) for upwards of three years. Students finance their studies with great difficulty. Grants were pegged at 1982 levels and abolished altogether in 1994. A system of loans was introduced in 1990/1, and in 1997 for the first time students had to pay £1,000 towards fees. Hence today they experience real financial hardship. Only those with parents who can afford to subsidise them are without money worries. The percentage of working-class young people attending university is declining.

Oxford and Cambridge (known collectively as 'Oxbridge') are the oldest universities in Britain. Though much expanded, their student numbers are still small, compared with London's 102,000. In 1998/9 Oxford had 16,185 students in residence; Cambridge 17,350. Other old universities are Durham and St Andrews, and they are distinguished from the so-called 'redbrick' universities founded around the beginning of the twentieth century (for example Birmingham, Liverpool, Manchester) through their emphasis on traditional subjects. 'New' universities created in the 1960s include Lancaster, York, Keele, and Sussex. In 1992 all the former polytechnics (originally colleges with a technical bias) changed their names and joined the existing forty-four universities.

Britain has two other main universities (apart from the European campuses of several American ones): the University of Buckingham (1991: 8,627 students, 1997: 798 students) and the Open University (1997: 200,000 students). The former was Britain's first private university the latter offers a wide range of degree programmes delivered partly by television and radio, appealing to those who are already engaged in full-time work, and whose only all-day attendance commitment is to a week-long annual summer school. Students have to fund themselves.

Access to higher education is still determined by the class one happens to be born into. For example in Britain as a whole, currently 80 per cent of children from professional middle-class families study at university, compared with 17 per cent from the poorest homes. Moreover at the extremes of opportunity, in 1999 in the Solihull suburb of Knowle, a population of 11,700 had 150 pupils starting degree courses, while Clifton East in Nottingham, with a population of 8,400, failed to send a single pupil to university.

The educational sector which has been most influential in raising Britain's profile abroad, the public (that is private) schools one, has benefited from the difficulties experienced by the state sector. Some public schools have chosen to pick the best elements out of the National Curriculum. The proportion of pupils attending public or independent secondary schools has risen, as the public sector has atrophied. Independent school pupil numbers have remained fairly constant at around 560,000 at a time of declining total school rolls. Parents are eager to benefit from the fact that the private sector has always had a disproportionately high influence on British culture and society, dominating very many aspects of British public life, from Whitehall to Shire Hall, from Parliament to local constituency parties, from the Institute of Directors to local Chambers of Commerce.

Educational changes and trends

Major recent educational changes have been: the imposition of a National Curriculum (as opposed to one agreed with local authorities and Her Majesty's Inspectors (HMIs)); the introduction of pre-GCSE examinations; and the publication of league tables of schools' performances (since abandoned in Wales and Northern Ireland). Opponents of a national curriculum felt it was closing down room for individual initiative and saw it as sinister in its regimenting of pupils. They referred to a French Minister of Education who boasted that he knew at any hour of the day which page of which book pupils would be turning. Supporters of a national curriculum promoted it as a necessary educational reform which would ensure uniform standards in schools.

Reform was necessary if only because of the underachievement and disaffection of many children in school. People can still relate to George Orwell's statement in the 1930s: 'There is not one working-class boy in a thousand who does not pine for the day when he will leave school. He wants to be doing real work not wasting his time on ridiculous rubbish like history and geography' (*The Road to Wigan Pier*, 1937).

To the consternation of those working and studying in them, Tony Blair (educated at the Edinburgh public school, Fettes College) in 2001 referred to comprehensive schools as 'bog-standard'. The School Standards Minister, Stephen Timms, echoed this view in 2001, complaining of 'one-size-fits-all' educational provision. Because many children are bored by the GCSEs they are doing, the government is proposing to enable them to embark on apprenticeships two days a week at fourteen years of age, once forty thousand industrial placements have been found.

Previous such initiatives have failed amid complaints that firms have exploited students on work experience as unpaid labour. Ken Spours, of London University's Institute of Education, said: 'In the era of league tables, it could mean schools just getting rid of their disruptive pupils – and I don't see industry falling over themselves to take them.' Some see this leading to a divisive two-tier education system where some children are denied good-quality education and others, with a privileged background, are enabled to flower.

Some schools are considering offering the International Baccalaureate as an alternative to AS levels, particularly after the new sixth form curriculum's chaotic first year. Traditionally the lower sixth year is one without examination, where pupils are given space to find their feet in independent study and develop a love of a subject. Instead the AS system placed them under great pressure to perform, and they had to endure public examinations three years in succession. However the Education & Skills Minister, Estelle Morris, is now promising schools more flexibility.

Debate on educational change has featured in much popular culture, including *Grange Hill*, a children's soap opera set in a comprehensive school and in the soap *Brookside*. Contrasting the worlds portrayed there, or in a film such as *Kes* (1969, re-released 2001), with those of films such as *Good-bye Mr Chips* (1939) or *The Belles of St Trinians* (1954) shows the extent of the changes in both education and representation that have taken place. The former relate to the everyday lives of their viewers. The latter invite audiences to peep into a privileged world to which few of them will ever have access.

Schools matter to people because education is not just about the delivery of syllabuses. Primary schools in particular are the sites for the transmission from one generation to the next of shared culture. The culture is of the classroom, but also of the playground. Children socialise there.

The playground is a concrete jungle where children practise their games and learn, where society's folk memories and myths are recycled through chants. The song 'A Ring a Ring a roses / A pocketful of posies / Atishoo! Atishoo! / We all fall down' contains memories of the Black Death which swept Europe in the Middle Ages. Another reminder comes when, on the passing of an ambulance, children say: 'Touch your collar / Never swallow / Never catch the fever.'

In choosing a school for their children, parents worry about potential academic progress, but also about the prevalence of bullying, the development of life skills, and the kind of social, cultural, and spiritual experience offered by the school. Furthermore, because schools are so important in the formation of shared cultural identity, people are interested in the way in which prominent public figures choose to educate their children, and comment on their decisions. For example, Prince Charles was the first member of the royal family not to be educated by palace tutors. He was sent to Gordonstoun in Scotland. His own sons William and Harry were sent to Eton. For ordinary parents this humanised the Royal Family, who became subject to the same anxieties and uncertainties of sending children to school as they did. Conversely, people sensed hypocrisy when Prime Minister Tony Blair bypassed the state system and sent his sons to the exclusive Catholic public school, Brompton Oratory.

In choosing a school, some parents also consider the availability of an 'old school tie' network, which may help their child to get a job and develop socially useful lifelong friendships. In Britain as elsewhere, those who have shared experiences during their formative years forge a common cultural bond which enables them to operate along co-operative and self-help lines. The most famous of such networks may be the grouping of old Etonians, Harrovians, and other public schoolboys, known as 'the Establishment'. Girls' schools offering access to this network would be Roedean, Benenden or Cheltenham Ladies College. Britain works on a system of contacts among people whose business, professional, sporting, and social lives produce a shared cultural milieu. This is evident in the number and social status of clubs nominally representing various interests but in practice simply enabling members to socialise, for example: Rotary or Round Table, golf, and sailing clubs. Cubs and Brownies, Scouts and Guides induct British children into this club mentality.

It has always been the case that pupils from single-sex schools have performed better than those at mixed ones – without the distractions of the opposite sex, so the argument goes. This has applied more to girls than to boys. Thus, in the 2001 GCSE tables the top nine schools nationally were girls' schools. Recently moreover the trend in school and university education is that girls seem to be performing much better than boys. Various factors have contributed to their increased pre-eminence. Today more women in prominent jobs offer role models. Feminism has changed girls' expectations and encouraged their ambition. A profound shift appears to be taking place where boys are 'the weaker sex', the ones who need encouragement and the raising of their self-esteem. This is one of the problems being addressed by educators. The Labour government appears less doctrinaire than previous administrations. They are prepared to support grammar schools where appropriate rather than the comprehensives which Labour introduced in the 1960s. They are also prepared to borrow ideas from private schools and in extreme cases to allow failing inner city schools to be managed by private companies. However, they are also putting less money into education than the OECD average, by a full percentage point.

Spending per pupil in 1999, at £2,433 for those at primary schools and £3,823 for those at secondary schools, was lower than the OECD average of £2,880 and £3,869 respectively. A report by the National Skills Task Force in 2001 indicated that seven million adults in Britain are functionally illiterate, and this perhaps explains Labour's emphasis on 'education, education, education', where attention will be directed mainly to schools.

An educational trend that some people see as disturbing is that recent governments have encouraged a shift at third level, from education to training. The word 'education' comes from the Latin *educo* meaning to lead out or develop qualities which are within. This is meant to produce the fully rounded individual with a healthy mind in a healthy body (*mens sana in corpore sano*). Critics suggest that because the majority of students are in the formative eighteen to twenty-two phase of their lives it is a mistake to concentrate solely on *instruction*, which implies pouring knowledge into them and ignores the stage of personal development that they have reached. Training is to do with the supply of workers and is not concerned with the individual. Education, on the other hand, develops qualities and offers personal cultural fulfilment. Opponents, on the other hand, say that publicly funded education should be pragmatic and does have a duty to supply society's need for skills – the piper *is* entitled to call the tune.

The university scene is more successful. According to figures from the OECD, in Britain in 1999 35.6 per cent of twenty-one-year-olds graduated from university. This is the highest percentage in Europe. Moreover in 2001 a report on graduate employment commissioned by the Higher Education Funding Council found that more new UK graduates expressed satisfaction with their college courses than did their counterparts in Europe and Japan. Government figures in 2000 showed that only 17 per cent of students in the UK leave universities without a qualification, the second lowest drop-out rate in the world (after Japan).

As regards the place held in British society and culture by universities – they have always taken criticism from both the political left and right.

The left sees them as elitist nurseries for the children of the bourgeoisie. Conversely, the political right sees them as populist hotbeds of left-wing radicalism where the next generation is encouraged into the ways of socialism and opposition to authority. However, even when the lines of political division are being redrawn, university graduates (especially from Oxbridge) still dominate the political leadership of Britain. For example, Tony Blair and Margaret Thatcher both went to Oxford, and almost two-thirds of the people appointed by Tony Blair to the Labour Cabinet since 1997 were educated at Oxford or Cambridge. (His initial 1997 'redbrick' Cabinet was partly imposed on him by Labour MPs, who in opposition have the right to elect the top team.)

Despite sometimes rancorous debate, individuals still feel positive about education. A wide range of them, having had the experience of being in the school play, practising team sports such as hockey or soccer, or such extra curricular activities as chess or judo, develop and retain a shared sense of pride in their schools. Rivalry between schools is felt by children who are publicly labelled by the uniforms that most British schools make them wear. When they leave school, reports of their achievements will often indicate their schools – so, for example, members of the Oxford and Cambridge rugby teams have their colleges *and* schools listed thus: Carr, Kenneth: Merton; St Anthony's Comprehensive, Luton. Smith, John: Churchill; Shrewsbury School. Students will often visit their old schools and join Old Girls or Boys Associations, which meet to arrange social functions. Throughout their lives people who went to Eton, Harrow, or Winchester schools are referred to by others as Old Etonians, Old Harrovians, or Wykehamists (Winchester School was founded in the fourteenth century by Bishop William Wykeham). And they see themselves in this way also. Well into middle age someone will pride himself on being a *public* school boy. Professor Richard Hoggart saw himself all his life as 'a *grammar* school boy'. For Hoggart this implied someone who forever has to jump hurdles, which he places for himself, in order to retain a sense of self-worth.

Even primary schools have reunions, as people feel a need to re-experience the comradeship and spirit of community of their youth. No matter how old people are, school is where they acquired their first long-term friends, developed their social personalities, and gained a deep and lasting sense of communal identity.

Employment

Education and work are linked in that an individual's success at school often determines the kind of job he or she goes on to do. The relationship is not always this straightforward, but often there is a connection between upward and downward trajectories at school and in the workplace. An important effect of the many divisions in British education – between state and private, Oxbridge and redbrick; vocational and academic – is that the workforce experiences ideas of stratification which have been superseded in many other countries. Thus the British workforce is distinguished by its divisions rather than its cohesiveness. Remuneration replicates social division. Process or factory workers have always received (weekly) wages, while predominantly middle-class managers have received (monthly) salaries. There are still quite separate ladders of achievement in numerous workplaces and it is almost impossible for people to cross from one to another despite the fact of John Major, somebody who did not attend university, let alone Oxbridge, exceptionally rising to become prime minister.

Further examples of the continuing stratified nature of Britain unfortunately abound. British company reports still append names to photos of directors while referring to technical processes beneath photos of workers. The civil service is divided into administrative, executive, and clerical grades; industry into management and shop floor; banks into directors, managers, clerks, and cashiers. These divisions may not be in all cases watertight, but very few people at the top of British industry have risen from the bottom, and this both reflects and determines a British cultural identity based on the social and economic divisions which separate groups of people from one another.

Tables 2.1 and 2.2 show the distribution of workers between different industries and the national unemployment rate in recent years. From these figures it is tempting to suggest that the recent success of the Labour government is entirely due to their control of this single problem. Conversely, should this trend reverse, Labour might be less likely to retain office.

Attitudes to work are determined culturally, and work in general has always had a low cultural profile. If we 'read' British society through literature, we can see that most works of fiction for example either don't refer to work or, if they do, denigrate it. In Jane Austen's novels, people who are in trade are not quite respectable; the correct thing to do is to own land and to live off one's rents. Neither Elizabeth Bennet's Mr Darcy nor Emma Woodhouse's Mr Knightley works for a living. Bulstrode in George Eliot's *Middlemarch* (1871–2) is a banker and thus in a profession which is not yet entirely respectable. In Dickens's novels people try to separate their public (working) selves from their private (domestic) lives in the belief that everybody wants to escape from work. Wemmick, the law clerk in *Great Expectations* (1860–1) pulls up a drawbridge when he goes back to his home where his 'aged parent' lives. Home is sacrosanct. Work is a necessary evil.

Work is rarely portrayed seriously or in detail in British films. Karel Reisz, Tony Richardson, and others of the 1950s New Wave cinema were seen as daring for approaching the subject of work at all in *Saturday Night*

TABLE 2.1   The workforce in Britain, 2001: %

Agriculture, forestry, & fishing	1.3
Manufacturing industries	16.1
Construction	4.8
Wholesale & retail	17.0
Hotels & catering	5.8
Transport & communications	6.1
Banking, finance, & insurance	4.1
Real estate/business	14.7
Education	7.9
Health & social work	10.5
Total no. of men in employment	12,356,000
Total no. of women in employment	11,985,00

Source: 'Labour Market Trends', National Statistics, Crown Copyright 2001

TABLE 2.2   Unemployment in Britain, % of workforce

1980	5.1	1991	8.0
1981	8.1	1992	9.7
1982	9.5	1993	10.3
1983	10.4	1994	9.4
1984	10.6	1995	8.0
1985	10.9	1996	7.2
1986	11.1	1997	5.5
1987	10.0	1998	4.7
1988	8.0	1999	4.3
1989	6.2	2000	3.8
1990	5.8		

Source: 'Labour Market Trends', National Statistics, Crown Copyright 2001

and Sunday Morning (1960) and *Room at the Top* (1959). In fact, although there are some 'documentary' scenes from the factory floor in the former, the film concentrates on a love story. The same is true of David Lodge's novel *Nice Work* (1988). Even 'revolutionary' drama such as Alan Bleasdale's lauded television series *Boys from the Blackstuff* (1991), which shows how work is integral to a sense of both identity and culture, feels a need to portray workers as 'cheeky chappies' who avoid 'hard graft'. On the other hand, Willy Russell's popular escapist films *Letter to Brezhnev* (1985) and *Shirley Valentine* (1989) deal directly with work in and outside the home, and yet they offer their audiences a fantasy of escape from the tedium of work into romances with 'exotic' foreigners.

Unlike novels and films, television curiously, has produced a spate of series about work. They have accelerated beyond such hospital dramas as *Casualty* or rural veterinary practices such as *All Creatures Great and Small* to include the military (*Soldiers*), fire-fighting (*London's Burning*), and many others. Television comedy series set in workplaces include *The Brittas Empire*, *Drop the Dead Donkey*, and *Dinner Ladies*, set in a leisure centre, an office, and a canteen respectively.

A film which offers a useful case-study because it did very well at the box office, and therefore may be seen to reflect popular British aspirations and values, is *Four Weddings and a Funeral* (1994). The story pursues some friends around Britain and examines their social lives in the context of the ceremonial rituals of the title. The whole is placed in the context of an Anglo-American 'special relationship,' which is part shared cultural history and part wish-fulfilment designed to appeal to different agendas on both sides of the Atlantic. As in other films such as *Remains of the Day* (1994), *A Handful of Dust* (1988), or *The Shooting Party* (1984), it adds social comment to a familiar recipe of stately homes in a timeless, upstairs/downstairs England peopled with fascinating eccentrics and nameless servants. This has been called a 'Merchant/Ivory' version of Britain (from the names of the director and producer who made *Room With a View* (1985) and *Howards End* (1992)). *Four Weddings and a Funeral* offers a version of Britain which contains a mixture of traditional and new clichés. Bohemianism, the gay community and monarchy are all contained in the non-threatening framework of British compromise. Meanwhile there is absolutely no mention of work. The film comes from the same mould as *Chariots of Fire* (1981) and *Another Country* (1984), which ultimately praise the leisured Britain that they depict and steadfastly ignore the means of getting a living. In such pointedly socially divided worlds, work persists in its cultural representations as something the upper classes do not do and the working classes wish not to do.

To illustrate further British culture's negative representation of work, we can look at one or two examples from Britpop. The 1995 Blur album is called *The Great Escape*. Its front cover has a picture of someone diving from a motorboat into a beautiful Mediterranean sea. Its back cover has the four members of the group dressed as urban professionals huddled around a computer. Here, as with most popular culture aimed at the country's mass population, the dominant British view is that work is a treadmill from which people dream of escaping (Blur's other album titles also suggest this: *Leisure*, *Modern Life Is Rubbish*, *Parklife*).

The possibility of a life of leisure is also a fantasy indulged in every week as the National Lottery winning numbers are announced on television and millionaires are literally 'made' overnight. It is assumed that winners will give up work without regret, but many have to be counselled by therapists to cope with (partly their wealth but largely) their position away from the community and working life they have known.

People establish and share identity at work through participation in such incidental 'social' aspects as car pools, coffee clubs, office sweepstakes (betting on horses), company sports clubs, and celebrations for engagements and birthdays. More people meet their future spouse through work than in any other way.

On leaving the office or the factory, there is often a shared drink with work mates and nights out to celebrate new jobs, retirements, and weddings. (The latter are known as 'hen' and 'stag' nights for women and men respectively.) They take place in night clubs, pubs, or working men's social clubs. Many relationships carry on outside work, and workers do jobs ('foreigners') for one another. This kind of social side to work obviously all comes to an end when jobs are lost.

Despite the taboo against cultural representation of work, in practice British society is constructed so much around employment that those who are cut off from it are also isolated socially. Britain was the first country to industrialise and is one of the first to have to devise programmes for coping with the problems of post-industrial and even post-agricultural society (in 1950 25 per cent of the workers in Britain still worked on the land – the figure today is under 2 per cent). It has to supply redundant workforces with wide-ranging help, from counselling to setting up small businesses, from make-work schemes to volunteering.

Unemployment and economic change

The work ethic is very strong in the UK, and for a majority of the British population their identity is shaped by the notion that they *work*. However, one of the main features of the working classes in the post-Thatcher period in Britain is that a greater proportion of them than of either the middle or upper classes is *not* working. Loss of work to a class which defines itself as *working* is traumatic and will be dealt with further in Chapter 5. It is hard for outsiders to appreciate the trauma of growing up within such a situation. Yozzer Hughes, a chief character in Alan Bleasdale's *Boys from the Blackstuff*, became a cult figure with his catchphrase of 'Gizza job', partly because so many people could empathise with him. This has also been a major theme in soap operas such as *Brookside* and *EastEnders*.

Women in employment have fared less well than men. There is a much higher percentage of women in work than there was in the postwar period, and there are now more women in the workforce than men. However, for a number of reasons, including prejudice and part-time working, women have often failed to gain promotion to posts of greater responsibility. The term 'glass ceiling' is applied to this consequent upper limit of women's progress in company careers. Their rate of unemployment (among those seeking work) is less than half that of men but their average pay is only 75 per cent of men's in similar occupations. However unemployed ethnic-minority women and men are even more disadvantaged than mainstream workers, with rates of 17 per cent and 24 per cent respectively. The rate of unemployment for Muslims is estimated to be 27 per cent whereas for Christians it is under 10 per cent.

Unsurprisingly the above climate has led to a decline in a sense of job security. According to government reports, unlike previous generations middle-aged people now do not feel secure about their financial prospects. When the chairman of a major bank predicts job losses in his industry of 20,000, others see *their* jobs as precarious, and people are cautious about spending. For example at 12.2 per cent the percentage of disposable income that people now save is 50 per cent more than it was in the 1960s. John Major's prediction of 'wealth cascading down through the generations' has a hollow ring for this generation. Karl Marx's predictions about the 'casualisation of labour' appear to be coming to pass, and certainly many more people are being employed on temporary or part-time contracts. Instead of seeing this as the apocalyptic end to capitalism however, some business analysts prefer to see it as following the pattern of the United States and supplying a more flexible productive base which ultimately regulates more efficiently the balance between supply and demand in the labour market.

For the last hundred years the south-east of England has been the most prosperous part of Britain and for a time in the 1980s, people there enthusiastically endorsed the concept of corporate Britain. They were enabled to participate in company share-purchase schemes, and they supported the under-priced privatisation sales of utilities such as electricity, water, and telephone companies. The majority of small shareholders (they were known as 'Sids', because of a British Gas privatisation advertising campaign with a character of that name) took their profits and sold out, in the spirit of the entrepreneurialism which was being recommended to them by government. Some did sense themselves for a time as empowered and as part of corporate Britain. Other people felt that, because the industries were owned by the country, *their* national assets were being sold to those sufficiently well off to have money to invest in them. So this was seen as yet another way of shifting money from the regions to the well-to-do south.

People on the political right argued that Britain had become a poor country because it has created a climate of dependency: its citizens lacked initiative, relied on the 'nanny' state to look after their every need and thus avoided their personal responsibilities. This hard-edged Thatcherite view led to a situation where, in the interest of industrial efficiency, jobs were being axed at precisely the time when council tenants were being encouraged by the government to buy their state-owned homes ('council houses') on very good terms. Some individuals simply couldn't cope and returned their house keys to their mortgage providers. At one point in the early 1990s, homes were being repossessed at the rate of a thousand per week, and even among the more affluent there were up to one and a quarter million people in Britain with 'negative equity'. That is, the loan they had taken out from the bank was greater than the value of the house they borrowed it for. No wonder the Labour government, with its pledge to increase employment rather than just to bolster capital, was welcomed into office in 1997.

Attitudes to work in Britain have also undoubtedly been affected by the decline in religious observance. Protestantism has had a particularly close relation to work. A belief in the moral importance of work (*laborare est orare* – to work is to pray) was especially notable in the late eighteenth century, with the growth of commerce in London, and in the early nineteenth century, with the start of the industrial revolution. The popularity of Daniel Defoe's *Robinson Crusoe* (1741) shows how ingrained in the culture was the idea of the 'self-employed' individual who, out of a sense of religious duty, struggled against odds to succeed. He 'justified his existence' through work. This ideology appealed to people who until recently had been largely rural and self-employed, but who, because of the 'division of labour', were now forced to do single unsatisfying city-based jobs.

In *Religion and the Rise of Capitalism* (1926), R. H. Tawney drew attention to the link between people's religious beliefs and their relative wealth. He attributed Britain's economic well-being to the Protestant work ethic – the idea that we are put on earth not just to live and to eat, but to work hard (partly as descendants of and inheritors of the sin of Adam and Eve (work as 'punishment')). People who believe in the sanctity of work become rich. Conversely the more unworldly the religion the less likely the religious congregation is to become rich. The situation is undoubtedly circular – economic decline may test religious commitment, which in turn limits adherence to the work ethic. The latter is based on a religious belief, but, in practice, people of all persuasions have come to believe in work as a good thing and as a defining characteristic of being British. Again this has increased psychological and social trauma for those unable to find jobs.

If, for one reason or another, both culturally ingrained commitment to work is eroded and opportunities are taken away and replaced with the mentality induced by enforced dependency upon the state, people have to find outlets elsewhere. Their energies have been channelled into leisure, and this displacement has taken place in Britain progressively throughout the years of unemployment and the move to casual work. Shopping as a leisure pursuit has been encouraged because it fills people's time and is good for the economy. The graph of the decline in the number of permanent jobs, is crossed by the ascendant one of ownership of video recorders, the practice of sports, and other indoor and outdoor leisure pursuits.

Leisure around the home

In dealing with leisure we are concerned not just with how people occupy themselves but with the cultural significance of their hobbies and practices. This applies to group and individual activities. We may divide the leisure pursuits which British people engage in into private and public. These are crude designations, but they do offer a way in to understanding how leisure affects cultural consciousness and identity.

As mentioned in the Introduction, the dominant medium for cultural exchange in Britain is television. It is difficult to pinpoint the moment at which television became a significant part of the national cultural consciousness, but many oral histories of older people refer to the novelty of watching the June 1953 Coronation of Queen Elizabeth II on television. This they did in company with friends, relations, and neighbours. The move from listening to the Football Association Cup Final on 'the wireless' (radio) to watching it on television, marked a further important change. Particularly since the 1960s, daily consumption of television has risen as broadcasting expanded from evenings only, to daytime, to the mornings – so-called 'breakfast television'. Television watching is now effectively available twenty-four hours a day, especially with video and numerous cable and satellite stations. The average time spent watching television is nearly three hours a day. The young and the old watch more, the middle-aged a lot less. Television is a powerful social adhesive in Britain. Following stories on television provides people with topics of conversation, allows them to get to know one another's tastes and preferences, and enables them to explore the current social and cultural preoccupations that television directs them towards. Workmates and friends are bonded together by their responses to the news, sitcoms, dramas, or soaps that they have seen on television.

It is clear that the change in the importance to their lives that people attach to television had come about by 1974. At that time Edward Heath, Britain's prime minister, made two mistakes in devising strategic responses to the emergency of the oil crisis. In order to save electricity, he brought in a three-day working week, and he made the television companies finish broadcasting each evening at 10.30 pm. In other words, he prevented people from working and he interfered with their watching of television. They were not prepared to put up with either of those changes. There was widespread opposition to the government and undoubtedly the above measures were factors in Heath's loss of the General Election in 1974.

Television's place is very much in the home. So, for example, when pubs introduced large-screen televisions for specific sports events and promotions in order to increase custom, their success was limited, because pubs are places more for social interaction than for 'watching the box'. Many people prefer to attend football matches and get much more of a sense of shared identity from their support for the same team. There is a 'family' atmosphere at some of the big clubs, despite the fact that there are forty thousand people present. Such large attendances indicate a wish for a shared sense of community which television alone can't provide. In 2001, attendance at football matches is increasing and numbers watching it on television are declining.

However in a country with all sorts of signs of social breakdown, from child murder and random knife attacks in the cities to rural suicides and abduction, people cling to electronic expressions of community. They watch their own society through television dramas such as *Casualty* or *The Bill*, which offer excitement set in an everyday context, or soap operas such as *Emmerdale* or *Heartbeat* which invoke an idealised rural past. Young people especially relate to soap operas. Reference was made above to *Grange Hill*, but by far the most popular soaps followed by people in the age group fourteen to twenty-five are the Australian serials *Neighbours* and *Home & Away*. A slightly older age group watches *EastEnders*, *Brookside*, and *Coronation Street*. Given the success of US culture in numerous areas of British life, there is a surprising lack of interest in American soaps. Exceptions are ones set in ostensibly coherent communities such as *Cheers* or *Northern Exposure*, and are usually comedies. Characters in these programmes supply viewers with topics of conversation which provide the potential glue for their own social community. Table 2.3 shows the relative popularity of television programmes.

Besides television, the major leisure activity of many British people is their hobby. The hobbies or minority interests pursued by Britons are numerous, wide-ranging and passionately indulged in. They are part of the people's identities. Such minority activities include philately, train-spotting, ferret-keeping, fishing, pigeon-fancying, bird-watching, scouting, swimming, cycling, fell-running – just counting along a scale of physical activity. Most of these hobbies will have magazines to accompany them, or at the very least a newsletter. The number of browsers in high-street newsagent evidences the range and diversity of Britain's leisure interests

TABLE 2.3   Most popular television soap operas, series and quizzes, 2001: millions of viewers

EastEnders	51.8
Emmerdale	49.7
Coronation St	43.5
Neighbours	23.1
Who Wants To Be A Millionaire	21.5
The Weakest Link	17.7
London's Burning	8.5

Source: BARB, 2001 (aggregated figures for a week's viewing, which may cover more than one transmission)

and perspectives, as do Tables 2.4–6. Table 2.5 shows how, over the past twenty years, there has been a significant shift particularly in men's magazine reading habits. *FHM* (a lifestyle magazine), *Loaded* (a 'lads' mag'), and three television guides may constitute men's sole current reading, and accurately record a move from interest in active leisure and general topics towards television watching. The magazines which sell best to women are almost exclusively gender-specific: *Take a Break* (3,383,000), *Woman* (1,858,000), *Bella* (1,943,000), *Woman's Own* (2,191,000), and *Chat* (1,480,000) NTC Publications 2001.

Reading of books, the other major domestic leisure-time activity, has held up well. Book buying ironically is stimulated by television. *Brideshead Revisited* (1945) and *Pride and Prejudice* (1813) sold many more copies after their television series than they ever did previously. Table 2.5, which covers books which people buy for themselves, is divided along gender lines and concludes this section on 'indoor' entertainments.

Public entertainment

We will now look at some entertainments outside of the home which British people use to occupy their free time. The principal place of entertainment outside the home that people automatically think of in relation to Britain is the public house or 'pub'.

Pubs and cinema

In the past, pubs have performed different social functions. Traditionally they were a male preserve. Various sociological studies have suggested that until the 1950s the British pub was a more welcoming place for a man than

TABLE 2.4 Readership of selected newspapers and magazines, 2000:
thousands (percentage of potential readership in parentheses)

The Sun	9,522	(21.0)
Daily Mirror	5,843	(13.0)
What's on TV	4,513	(9.7)
Radio Times	3,649	(7.8)
Readers' Digest	3,391	(7.3)
Take a Break	3,383	(7.5)
Daily Telegraph	2,390	(5.0)
Auto Trader	1,923	(3.0)
BBC Gardeners' World	1,736	(4.1)
The Times	1,718	(4.0)
Cosmopolitan	1,537	(3.0)
The Guardian	1,093	(2.0)
The Big Issue	1,152	(2.5)
Private Eye	566	(1.2)
J17	556	(2.1)
Motorcycle News	529	(0.9)
What Hi-Fi?	506	(1.7)
The Economist	383	(0.7)
Practical Photography	305	(0.7)
The Face	217	(0.5)

Source: National Readership Survey, 2000

TABLE 2.5 Most popular magazines read by men, % of potential readers

1980	1990	2000
Reader's Digest 20	Reader's Digest 14	FHM 20
Custom Car 9	What Car 7	Sky Customer 9
Do-It-Yourself 6	Classic Cars 5	Cable Guide 6
Mayfair 6	National Geographic 5	Loaded 6
Hot Car 6	Golf Monthly 4	Skyview TV Guide 6

Source: Social Focus on Men, ONS

his home. It was familiar and cosy (small bar-rooms were called 'snugs'), with a fire and games such as darts and dominoes. This changed when houses in the 1950s, a period of increasing affluence, were brought up to

TABLE 2.6   Most popular types of books bought, rank and type, 1999 (1994 rankings five years ago in parentheses)

Women		Men	
1	General fiction (Cookery)	1	General fiction (Crime/thriller/detective)
2	Romance (Romance)	2	History/archaeology (English dictionaries)
3	Crime/mystery (Crime/thriller/detective)	3	Adventure/thriller (Car repair manuals)
4	Historical novels (English dictionaries)	4	Autobiography (Cookery)
5	Cookery/food/drink (Puzzle/quiz books)	5	Sports/games games (Computer manuals)
6	History/archaeology (Gardening/indoor plants books)	6	Science fiction/fantasy (Sports/games books)
7	Autobiography (Food/drink)	7	Sheet maps (Gardening/indoor plants)
8	Adventure/thriller (Historical novels)	8	Crime/mystery (Sports/games instruction books)
9	Science/medicine (Classics/literature)	9	Business/economics (Road atlases of Great Britain)
10	Psychology/social sciences (Baby and childcare books)	10	Bible/religion (War/adventure stories)

Source: *Books and the Consumer* 1999, Book Marketing Limited

date and made more attractive with higher standards of draught-proofing, labour-saving appliances, new furnishings, and even central heating in some cases. Britain in the 1950s was a 'home-centred society'. It was then less acceptable for a woman to go into a pub alone, than it was for a man. Some city-centre pubs specified 'men only' and many covertly discouraged single women. Today they are much more welcoming to people of both sexes but few older women will say they feel comfortable going into a pub on their own.

Among 'outside' entertainments, 'going to the pub' has been through periods of popularity and decline in British social life. In numerous novels, including those of Henry Fielding, Charles Dickens, and Thomas Hardy, it is seen as a traditional feature of British life. Nowadays though, with the percentages of men and women who never drink alcohol at 15 per cent and 20 per cent respectively and rising, pubs are struggling. However, with the churches in Britain in decline, as congregations age and Sunday attendances fall, pubs are finding a new role. They fill the social vacuum created by religious decline, and perform the function of community meeting place and so are still, in the new century, very much central to British life. That this is the case is shown by the many pubs in soap operas, including 'The Vic' in *EastEnders* and 'The Rover's Return' in *Coronation Street*.

Pantomime, performing arts, and cinema

At Christmas time, pantomimes form an important aspect of British cultural experience. Unknown on the Continent, they are staged in theatres, village halls and community centres of all sorts, amateur and professional. Well-known television personalities, soap stars, or even politicians appear in them. Parents attend with children, and in a controlled dramatic environment 'pantos' offer a 'safe' form of initiation into the adult world. They contain a number of standard ingredients: cross-dressing (the 'Principal Boy' is always a woman; the 'Dame' is a man); double entendre (parents can understand lewd meanings which pass over the heads of their children); contemporary reference (current politicians, or aspects of daily life such as the National Lottery are guyed); ritualised audience participation, where children get to shout: 'He's behind you', or 'Oh yes it is' / 'Oh no it isn't'. They very often involve reworking of myths, as in *Babes in the Wood*, or *Cinderella*, where the badly treated individual gets justice and their rightful place in the world and there is a sentimentally happy ending for the grannies.

When London theatre was suffering during the post 11 September tourist absence in 2001, pantomime there and elsewhere in Britain was booming. Thousands of people flocked to pantos which earned millions of pounds of profit. At a time of military intervention in Afghanistan and global uncertainty, people sought out traditional family entertainment. To assuage their fears of the bogey man Osama bin Laden, a character with his name was incorporated into the year's most popular panto, *Aladdin*. Others doing well included *Cinderella*, *Beauty and the Beast*, *Puss in Boots*, *Snow White and the Seven Dwarfs*, *Peter Pan* and *Dick Whittington*.

Theatre, ballet, and opera give Britain a high cultural profile particularly with overseas tourists, even though they remain minority pursuits in Britain. They are patronised by older, well-to-do people in London and the major cities. Perhaps because the largest concentration of these cultural resources is in London with its National Theatre, Royal Shakespeare Company, English National Opera, and Royal Ballet, they tend to be seen as 'elitist'. However, theatres are in fact dispersed around the regions. Liverpool has a Royal Philharmonic Society. Manchester's Royal Exchange Theatre offers high quality drama. Leeds-based Opera North is thriving and Scottish and Welsh Opera companies are well received on their countrywide tours. Despite a difficult financial climate, several concert halls were either built or refurbished in the early 1990s including

Manchester's £42 million Bridgewater Hall, Birmingham's Symphony Hall and Liverpool's Philharmonic Hall.

Some of these art forms are supported mainly by overseas tourists (London West End theatre productions such as Andrew Lloyd Webber's *Cats*, Willy Russell's *Blood Brothers*, or Agatha Christie's *The Mousetrap*), but some have a devoted local clientele. It is necessary to bear this in mind when looking at the respective 2000 attendance figures for theatre (36.7), classical concerts (11.6) and opera (6.64) (as percentage of all adults: Target Group index BMRB 2000). And one should be aware that, in addition to these, there are an estimated seven hundred youth theatres catering for 53,000 participants.

Going out to the cinema is still a staple part of British life and appears to be on a rising trend. (after a long period of declining attendances). There were more than 140 million attendances in 2002 (largely thanks to *Harry Potter* and *The Lord of the Rings*), despite the competition of television. (This compares with the peak 1965 of 327 million). However, the majority of all cinema going is still done by under 5 per cent of the total population, and the range of films on offer has not widened, despite the increase in the number of multiplex screens, which are owned by large multinationals and which show mainly Hollywood films. So cinema attendance, as a cultural practice, has yet to regain its 1960s popularity, but can still be a cohesive social force, particularly for young people.

Sport

The major outdoor leisure outlet in Britain is sport. People in Britain spend a great deal of their leisure time either participating in or watching it. The main sports practised in Britain during the winter are rugby and soccer. Rugby is controlled by the Rugby Union, soccer by the Football Association. The traditional division between lower-social-status professional soccer players (who need to be paid) and higher-social-status rugby players ('gifted amateurs') has been eroded by the Union's decision in 1995 to relax its rules to allow professional rugby clubs. Soccer is known as 'a gentlemen's game for roughs' and rugby as 'a roughs' game for gentlemen'. One of the many paradoxes of British society is that, although most of the public (that is private) schools in Britain play the middle-class game of rugby as their main winter sport, both Eton and Harrow, Britain's most exclusive schools, have always played soccer. Nationwide attendances at soccer matches in the 1999/00 season totalled 25 million. This compares with the peak figure in 1954/5 of 34 million.

There are two major groups of professional clubs, who play in either the Premier or the Football league. There are also two main competitions: the League Cup, which is based on points, and the FA Cup, which is a knockout competition. Going to a football match between major clubs such as Arsenal, Liverpool, or Manchester United can be a powerful experience. Supporters of rival teams are segregated at football matches and often ritually taunt one another. For example, supporters in the Kop (a terrace at Liverpool named after a lookout hill from the Boer War: Spion Kop) used to sing: 'See them lying on the runway . . . ' to Manchester United supporters – to remind them of their team's plane crash in Munich in the late 1950s. Most of the chanting is not so vicious; a milder taunt nowadays is to sing 'Always look on the bright side of life . . . ' to your rivals, when your team has just scored a goal. Much debate centres on whether football supplies a safety valve for, rather than an encouragement to violence, and it is argued that aggression is harmlessly released in the above ritualised exchanges between supporters. Supporters are thought to feel a necessary sense of shared community through loyalty to their team and local pride when it wins. A measure of the seriousness with which supporters take their soccer is contained in the Liverpool manager Bill Shankly's remark: 'Football isn't just a matter of life and death. It's far more important than that.'

In summer, the game of cricket is played widely on village greens, as well as at the professional level, and is a genuinely popular 'grassroots' game about observance of rules, fairness, and a pitting of wits and talent between equally matched teams. However, there are class associations to all British sports and in the case of cricket there is a history of contention for 'ownership' of the game. For example many British stately homes have an adjacent cricket pitch and pavilion and over the years encounters have taken place there between 'gentlemen & players'. This again underlines the British distinction between the upper classes (gentlemen), who are leisured and admirable, and the lower (players) who work and are disparaged.

This may also be seen in rugby. Rugby League was founded as a breakaway from Rugby Union famously at the George Hotel in Huddersfield in 1895. Basically the players were impoverished northern working men who wanted to be paid for giving up their precious Saturday afternoon to play a game of rugby.

Significantly, professional soccer is associated with Britain's cities whilst cricket, which may well be played in urban centres such as Old Trafford (Manchester), Headingley (Leeds), or Lords (London), is associated with rural Britain. So while football clubs are named 'Leeds United' or 'Manchester City', professional cricketers play for counties, such as Kent, Somerset, and Gloucestershire.

Variations occur in the terminology used to describe people watching leisure entertainments. Those who watch soccer, rugby, cinema, television, theatre, or opera are known respectively as 'crowds', 'spectators', 'audiences', 'viewers', 'theatre goers', or 'opera buffs'. These terms form part of a spectrum of cultural snobbery. Soccer fans are traditionally working-class and are called 'crowds', suggesting they are amorphous. Middle-class people who watch rugby are 'spectators' – they are dispassionate onlookers. 'Audiences' are more sophisticated again because they listen. 'Viewers' is a euphemism which denies the passivity of the television 'couch potato'. 'Theatre goer' implies some form of dynamism and the word 'buff' comes from the uniform (made of buffalo hide) worn by smart regiments.

There are many other outdoor sporting events in Britain, particularly in the summer, which attract national and international interest. However there are many more, less publicised ones, which supply the high point in individual enthusiasts' years. Surprisingly, local events can sometimes be better patronised than national ones. For example thirty thousand runners take part in Gateshead's annual Great North Run, compared with the twenty-six thousand who take part in the London Marathon. The former is hardly alluded to in the national news media with their metropolitan emphasis, but the latter is hyped and televised. Impressionistically, the degree of health consciousness, fitness, and dietary awareness is higher among the British young than the Americans. But young Swiss, Germans, or Canadians are much more likely to swim or ride bikes than the British. There is no British equivalent to the Continental 'parcours' (outdoor fitness areas in national parks), and facilities such as the National Rowing Centre at Nottingham or the Manchester Velodrome (for cycling) are over-stretched and of no help in keeping the generality of people fit. Most exercise takes place indoors for women, and increasingly for men. Health and fitness clubs or gyms became very popular throughout the country in the 1990s (cynics say because they are dating agencies), and large numbers of people regularly attend aerobics or 'step' classes.

In a study published by the Office for National Statistics in 2001, the following sports were most popular among the four-fifths of men, randomly interviewed, who took part in at least moderate physical activity: walking (48 per cent), snooker (18 per cent), cycling (15 per cent) and swimming (13 per cent) were more popular than football (10 per cent). Despite this focus on fitness, cigarette smoking among the young is again on the increase – particularly among young women.

Festivals

Arts festivals take place annually in most large cities, and smaller places such as Glyndebourne and Buxton have their own opera festivals. Pop and rock festivals in particular have become a feature of youth culture. The best known are at Glastonbury and Reading. Entrance fees are relatively high at £103 for two or three days but they are extremely well attended by upwards of twenty thousand people. Glastonbury was cancelled in 2001, but is scheduled for 2002.

Museums

In this survey of communal leisure activities, we can also say that a traditional version of British culture is nurtured in a range of public institutions: mainly museums and art galleries. In the past it has tended to be high culture which is conserved here, and they were places of obligatory pilgrimage for schoolchildren, who in the course of their subsequent lives never returned. In recent years, this has changed. The institutions have become much more imaginative, and their collections have been partially devolved to the regions. The Tate Gallery of modern art now has branches in Liverpool and St Ives as well as two in London and there is a branch of London's National Portrait Gallery at Bodelwyddan Castle in north Wales. Instead of a single unchanging stock, museums now tend to stage more 'thematic' exhibitions, such as Liverpool Maritime Museum with its slavery exhibition, or its Labour Museum which deals with the material conditions of people's lives rather than high culture. Responding to public interest, in 2001 London's Victoria and Albert Museum rearranged its collection to offer 'British Galleries'.

Holidays

Leisure was originally the preserve of the upper classes. Only they had the time and money to tramp their own grouse moors in Scotland, or sail their yachts with professional crews at Cowes. For example the industrialist Sir Thomas Lipton was able to finance his own Americas Cup yachting challenges and pay his crews in the 1930s. So when leisure became available to ordinary people through decreased working hours and paid annual leave, by and large in the 1950s, it gave social status to those benefiting from it. This soon changed, as catering for larger numbers of leisured people on a year-round basis turned into an industry. Treatment of holiday-makers became more systematic, more professional, less deferential and less status-aware.

Since the 1960s the two-week annual holiday is more likely to be spent abroad. Package holidays were introduced to Britain in the 1950s by the Russian entrepreneur Vladimir Raitz, founder of Horizon holidays. The beneficiaries were the hoteliers of France, Spain, and Florida, and those losing out were British seaside landladies at traditional resorts. The most popular overseas holiday destinations for Britons in 2000 and the numbers going to them were France (11,887,087), Spain (11,130,005), and the USA (4,327,211). British people have become obsessed with holidaying abroad. David Lodge suggests in his novel *Paradise News* (1992) that tourism is the new world religion. The Hoover company so underestimated the demand for a holiday scheme it was promoting in 1993 that it lost £200 million.

FIGURE 2.1 The traditional British holiday is a trip to the seaside, and to such sites as the pier at Brighton

New patterns in leisure

Gambling

Betting on the sport of the rich – horse racing – has always been practised by the working rather than the middle class, whose puritanism in regard to gambling has been tempered only by government-sponsored Premium Bonds and the National Lottery.

The latter has become a major national talking point in Britain, which was the last country in Europe to introduce one, in November 1994. As a social and cultural phenomenon it is especially interesting. It generates comment in the media, between politicians and among people in general. It has brought a whole new clientele into gambling. Tickets are sold through newsagents and Post Offices – where everybody goes – whereas other forms of gambling such as on horse racing are contained within betting shops where passers-by may not even see in through the windows and where the family is virtually excluded. Many people, once a year, will place a bet on the Grand National or the Derby, but with the Lottery, and its sequel 'Instants' scratchcards, everyone has a 'flutter' (a bet) week by week.

The National Lottery has become an important social and cultural phenomenon. Its revenues, at £65 million per week, are well above initial estimates of £14–35 million, and nine out of ten adults are claimed to buy tickets on occasions. It is clearly a financial success. This is especially striking since the bookmakers Ladbrokes have likened the chance of winning the jackpot to that of Elvis landing a UFO (Unidentified Flying Object) on the Loch Ness Monster. The odds are about fourteen million to one.

George Orwell, writing in 1948, imagined it with quite uncanny accuracy:

> The Lottery, with its weekly pay-out of enormous prizes, was the one public event to which the proles [workers] paid serious attention. It was probable that there were some millions of proles for whom the Lottery was the principal if not the only reason for remaining alive. It was their delight, their folly, their anodyne, their intellectual stimulant. Where the Lottery was concerned even people who could barely read and write seemed capable of intricate calculations and staggering feats of memory.
>
> (Orwell: *1984*, p. 71)

It is tempting to say that the Lottery is really about the possibility of social change. It has caused social upheaval and division. Predictably some people have not been able to cope with huge winnings. Many legal cases have centred on breaches of trust among workmates, within families and between friends.

The weekly television programme on Saturday nights where the draw is made has twelve million viewers for its mixture of orchestrated hype and celebration of greed. The proceeds are devoted to 'good causes', many of

FIGURE 2.2   English samba band (sponsored by a National Lottery grant)

which are associated with heritage or 'high' culture such as Sadlers Wells ballet, or the Royal Opera Company. It has introduced the word 'rollover' (un-won prizes carried forward) into the dictionary. It has increased the number of what were previously (football) 'pools winners' (in its first year it produced more than 100 millionaires) and so raised their profiles as social and cultural phenomena.

A number of lobbies have predictably come out against the Lottery: church leaders, directors of charities helping the poor, other charities whose revenues have fallen, and the companies who previously received the money gambled on football, via their weekly 'pools coupons'. They raise the following main objections: people are spending money they can't afford; revenues are being diverted from the poor to the rich; the state is encouraging gambling; less money is going to charity overall.

Public acceptance of the Lottery and people's enthusiastic identification of themselves as prepared to take a risk may, however, represent a sea change in Britain's attitudes to gambling, entrepreneurialism, and the new rich. In much British middle-class culture and entertainment – from the novel to plays to television sitcoms – the most reviled characters have been the *nouveaux riches*, whether as individuals or as a class. Mrs Malaprop, Josiah Bounderby, and Hyacinth Bucket are examples of people whose wealth and pretension exceed their level of cultural attainment, sensitivity and good manners. A television series such as *Fawlty Towers* probes the interrelationships between class, snobbery, deference, respectability, good manners, money, and service, in the crucible of a home-*cum*-'guest-house'.

A lot of the criticism of the Lottery is based on the fear that one class will be subsidising another's pleasures. A major complaint about the disbursement of funds is that places of entertainment for the rich have benefited. What irks many people is that winning the Lottery goes against their idea of 'natural justice', as defined by the middle classes, in terms of the work ethic we discussed earlier: 'unearned' money is frowned upon. Also, when someone with a criminal record won several million pounds, the *Daily Telegraph* expressed its readers' sense of outrage that such 'undeserved' luck should happen. But the paper itself is caught in the bind of accepting and promoting such aspects of capitalism as free enterprise and entrepreneurialism yet not liking one of the inevitable consequences.

Trends in entertainment

In the last hundred years there have been major shifts in the cultural influences that British people cite as reflecting their tastes. In the past, common reference points would be individual musical hall performers such as Marie Lloyd, or singers such as Vera Lynn or Gracie Fields – people giving live performances in theatres around the country. With technology and the growth of radio and television, *groups* of entertainers came to predominate. The Beatles or Rolling Stones, Blur or Oasis are obvious examples. The same is true of radio and television comedy shows where a team (the Goons, Monty Python, the Goodies) was involved in making the show. Now, on the other hand, possibly because of a new cult of individualism, the emphasis has moved away from the group to the individual in entertainment. Young people in Britain today name as their formative cultural influences such lone stars as Vic Reeves, Jo Brand, Ruby Wax, Steve Coogan or Victoria Wood.

FIGURE 2.3 Shopping is now the number one leisure activity in Britain

A current television trend that the Salvation Army, among others, finds disturbing is the increase in confrontational shows. They claim that they encourage 'greed and deception'. Anne Robinson's *The Weakest Link* is deliberately rude to its contestants. In ITV1's show *Shafted*, which is hosted by the ex-MP Robert Kilroy-Silk, one individual takes the whole pot if he or she votes to 'shaft' and the other one votes to 'share'.

There is also now a noticeable preference by young people for inanimate over animate sources of entertainment. This is evident not just in the decline of such live arts as theatre or home pastimes such as card playing or in the preference of night clubs with DJs over live gigs. Technophiliac 'Generation X' (from Douglas Coupland's 1991 novel of that name) prefer things to people: cash machines to bank cashiers (US: tellers); computers to socialising; cyber cafés to coffee houses; virtual reality to reality; the internet and technological gizmos such as pagers, mobile phones, and answering machines, to live individuals. Nor do people just prefer television and cinema to live entertainment. Within electronic media they prefer cartoons to 'real' representations of people. By the early 1980s Britain was already fertile ground for the revival of puppetry – the American Jim Henson's *The Muppet Show* was based in London. *Spitting Image* had enormous popularity on British television and was credited politically with destroying the leadership of the Liberal Party. In sum people now seem to prefer electronic representations of life to ones which purport to offer more 'real' slices of life through film or video.

Technology has proved that it can deliver the 'real world' yet people want images less 'real' than those contained in traditional representation. They prefer animated characters in television advertisements. Illustrations for a Boddingtons' Beer television advertising campaign are supplied by Dan Clowes, who is better known for his grunge illustrations. Puppets and cartoons have replaced people on hugely successful television shows such as *Beavis and Butthead* and *Crapston Villas*. Television has had huge successes with animation. Several shows have followed the age curve for children brought up on *The Muppets* and *The Simpsons*.

Cartoons have always been directed at children, but recently there have been developed television cartoon series characterised by seriousness of purpose and directed at adults. Disney's computer-generated *Toy Story* (1995) was the start of the trend. Many young people brought up on games arcades *prefer* artificially animated films to ones inhabited by humans. *The Simpsons* is more popular *per capita* in Britain than in America. Damon Albarn and Jamie Hewlett have even produced a band (Gorillaz) which is a cartoon.

Another notable change in the pattern of people's leisure is a move away from socialising at home to frequenting public places of entertainment: 'fun pubs', multiplexes (containing cinemas, bowling alley, fruit machines, and night clubs). There are regional variations, but generally the fact that British socializing took place in the pub or club made it difficult for new people to integrate into postwar British society. Asians in particular preferred to socialise at home, and this exacerbated cultural differences and separated people. In time, however, as in so many aspects of culture referred to elsewhere (body piercing, casual clothing, rap music, use of marijuana), while young mainstream people adopted immigrants' practices, young people from minority backgrounds joined the move to socialise outside the home. So young people of all ethnic origins now mix in places of public entertainment. McDonald's has had a universalising impact here. Their premises, balloons, party poppers, and so on are supplied free of charge for children's parties, and draw in all-comers. Operators of multiplex cinemas, bowling alley and night clubs (many of them multinationals, such as Time-Warner) benefit from this groundwork and cater to a young population brought up on 'canned' culture and dedicated to Britain's consumer society. Most Britons are unaware that the owner of the greatest number of pubs in Britain (4,867) is the Japanese company Nomura.

FIGURE 2.4   The Millennium Eye in London

The trend towards eating out, on the other hand, benefits local restaurateurs and will continue to do so, because of the room for growth still in the marketplace. (The French spend 45 per cent of their disposable income on food, the Americans 25 per cent, and the British only 11 per cent.)

The older generation meanwhile, which saves 13 per cent of its disposable income (against the national average of 4 per cent) continues to opt for home entertainment. Eighty-four per cent of British households have video machines and are catered for by an estimated two thousand video shops – supplying a market which didn't exist thirty years ago.

Overseas 'bars'

Lastly in this section on leisure, a revealing debate have been taking place about the influx (perhaps partly as a result of recent increases in permitted opening hours for the sale of alcohol) of Irish pubs, wine bars, and café bars on to the British high street. This trend, a 'simple' commercial phenomenon, is seen to have all sorts of other implications. Irish pubs are financially successful, but people ask: 'What are they saying about Britain? Do they suggest it is a soulless place which needs an infusion of Celtic culture?' CAMRA, the Campaign for Real Ale, resists the trend as part of a commercialising of the English institution of the pub – a dilution of authentic English values. Others are unhappy about the ideological implications of this raising of the profile of a 'minority' culture in the war for hearts and minds in relation to an Ulster political settlement. Others again are concerned that national identity is being exploited for purely commercial ends.

Some see the trend as just one more illustration of a postmodern phenomenon which uses elements of the past and elsewhere as a vocabulary with which to write the new Britain. They apply that particularly to the advent of bars such as Starbucks and Caffe Nero, which are 'themed' as American or Italian. In this context, Irishness, Americanness, or any other nationality is merely part of a benign process of internationalisation and enrichment of Britain's hitherto provinces-led culture. The nationality of the 'Italian wine bar, 'Spanish' tapas bar, 'Japanese' sushi bar, or 'American' McDonald's has only a surface significance. They suggest that the trend should be welcomed as more evidence of tolerant multicultural Britain.

However, perhaps the most significant thing is that the forum in which this nationalistic venture is being played out – the high street – is a more democratic one than Parliament, whose legislation cramps and controls people. (The postwar Labour administration, which produced a thousand pages of legislation per year, was seen as 'interventionist'. The present government produces three thousand pages per year.) People want to liberate themselves through culture and feel that cultural change can't be legislated. They suspect that laissez-faire capitalism will produce stampedes of commercial developers to out-of-town shopping centres or a situation where all high streets have more or less the same shops: Halfords, Boots, Marks & Spencer. In other words, a homogenising commercial process will take place which will ultimately dilute rather than enrich culture and cultural identity. In order to counter these forces they have only the cultural practices listed above. By exercising individual choice, they can wrest control over their lives from commercial or government agencies.

Conclusion

To sum up this chapter: the cultural ambience is not neutral, it is a plane on which warring factions contend. Education, work, and leisure are defining aspects of British cultural identity. Schools place a distinctive stamp on their pupils – a past pupil will be defined both in society at large *and* by the individual himself or herself as a *grammar school* boy or girl, or more specifically as a product of Shrewsbury School or King Street primary. This pattern is repeated in the work arena when society labels people 'owned' by particular industries or by the state as a *Ford* worker, a *civil* servant. People acknowledge these descriptions of themselves, because they also define themselves by their schools and their work functions. The rhetorical question 'How do you do?', on being introduced to

FIGURE 2.5   Strawberry picking remains a popular summer leisure activity

people, is very shortly followed by 'What do you do?' and soon thereafter by 'Where did you go to school?' So education and work are significant defining aspects of identity. As we have seen further, people will always try to take control of their lives and define their own identities through the exercise of individual choice in their leisure activities. And finally we have highlighted a number of debates which arise in relation to these issues.

❖ Exercises

1   Reading checklist
    ■ Why are public schools so called?
    ■ What is the origin of the word 'education'?
    ■ What is the difference between wages and salaries?
    ■ Are average female earnings the same as those of males?
    ■ What are 'hen' and 'stag' nights?
    ■ What is the Protestant ethic?
    ■ What is a 'glass ceiling'?
    ■ What is a wireless?
    ■ Where is the Kop?
    ■ How are soccer and cricket teams differently named?
    ■ When is the Sabbath?
    ■ What is a Merchant/Ivory representation of Britain?
    ■ Who plays the Principal Boy in a pantomime?
    ■ What is CAMRA?
    ■ Which was the last country in Europe to have a National Lottery?

2   What kinds of schools are more likely to be portrayed in films? Why is this? You might consider viewing on video some of the films referred to in the chapter: *Kes, The Belles of St Trinians, Another Country*. How do these representations differ from the school in (say) *Dead Poets' Society*?

3   Why are portrayals of work so rare in British novels or plays? Is American writing more likely to deal with work? Are British cultural forms more or less escapist than American ones?

4   Is it healthy or unhealthy to watch soap operas?

5   Discussion questions
    ■ What is the effect on individual identity of pupils attending state or private schools?
    ■ Does education always involve the imposition on one group in society of the values of another?
    ■ How is unemployment related to identity?
    ■ Does self-employment confer more dignity on workers?

- The chapter refers to the presence in Britain of McDonald's and *The Simpsons*. Are overseas influences in a culture to be welcomed or resisted?
- Should the state fund culture? If so, should it aim to encourage high or popular culture? If not, why not?
- How important are tradition and traditional ways in a culture?

Reading

Marwick, A. *The Penguin Social History of Britain: British Society Since 1945*, Penguin, 1996. Solid basic introduction.

Storey, John. *An Introductory Guide to Cultural Theory and Popular Culture*, Harvester, 1993. A very accessible book set in a British context.

Room, Adrian. *An A to Z of British Life*, Oxford University Press, 1992. A mine of information. Comprehensive and well illustrated, a useful reference source.

Giles, J. and Middleton, T. *Writing Englishness 1900–1950*, Routledge 1996. A very useful sourcebook of traditional material relating to the construction of the concept of Englishness.

Cultural Examples

Films

How to Get Ahead in Advertising (1989) dir. Bruce Robinson. Satire on the advertising and marketing professions.

Educating Rita (1983) dir. Lewis Gilbert. A working-class woman, unfulfilled by life at home with her husband, tries an Open University English course and develops a strong relationship with her tutor.

Clockwork Mice (1995) dir. Jean Vadim. Gentle drama about a young teacher starting at a Special Needs School, his relationships with pupils and staff, and his attempt to involve the children in a cross-country running club.

Another Country (1984) dir. Marek Kanievska. Speculative drama about the claustrophobic public-school life of two future British spies, Guy Burgess and Donald Maclean.

The Browning Version (1995) dir. Mike Figgis. Remake of the Terence Rattigan play about a boarding-school teacher's realisation that he and his wife have led empty, unloving lives.

Books

Muriel Spark, *The Prime of Miss Jean Brodie* (1961) Powerful story of the effects of education on susceptible young people.

David Lodge, *Changing Places* (1975). Deals with insights into human nature gained by academics from Britain and America who exchange jobs, houses, educational experiences, and much more.

Linda La Plante, *The Governor*. (1995) Drama about a women whose working environment is a prison, where she is the governor.

Bill Bryson, *Notes from a Small Island*. (1996) Idiosyncratic but informed view of Britain offered by a resident American journalist with experience of British work and leisure.

Television programmes

Boys from the Blackstuff. Sympathetic portrayal of unemployed people who work on the side, and their encounters with officialdom. Written by Alan Bleasdale.

Porterhouse Blue. Series set in Cambridge academe with David Jason and Ian Richardson – from the novel by Tom Sharpe.

Drop the Dead Donkey. Award winning weekly comedy series set in a newspaper office. Written by Andy Hamilton.

As Seen on TV. Comedy programme of very talented comedienne Victoria Wood. Includes sketches, stand-up, piano songs.

The Royle Family. Written by Caroline Aherne and starring Ricky Tomlinson. A couch-potato Salford family watch television, eat, drink, and entertain. Has won numerous awards.

The Navigators. Ken Loach drama about privatised railway maintenance workers. Mocks the jargon and short cuts of the 1990s enterprise culture.

 Websites

www.nc.uk.net/
    Official site of the National Curriculum, with information about what attainment levels are required in each of the subject areas

www.knowhere.co.uk
    This is an informative youth and leisure-oriented site – the antidote to Tourist Information

Football365@http://www.stats.Football365.co.uk
    Lots of facts here for the football-oriented

www.its-behind-you.com
    Gives an account of the evolution of pantomime through *commedia dell'arte*, mystery plays and Elizabethan masques

www.efestivals.co.uk
    An online agency containing information and booking for many UK festivals

www.liv.ac.uk/IPM/
    Institute of Popular Music at Liverpool University. Has collections and sound clips

www.leagueofgentlemen.co.uk
    Website devoted to the cult television programme. Has a scrapbook and downloads from first and second series

Chapter 3

Gender, sex, and the family

Roberta Garrett

■	The family unit	114
■	Gender and British institutions	117
■	Women and employment	120
■	Marriage and divorce	123
■	Parenting	126
■	Sexuality and identity	128
■	Conclusion	134
■	*Exercises*	135
■	*Reading*	136
■	*Cultural examples*	136
■	*Websites*	137

Timeline

1831	Infant Custody
1848	Factory Act
1861	Abolition of death penalty for sodomy
1882	Married Women's Property Act
1928	Vote for women over twenty-one
1967	Abortion made legal
1969	Divorce Reform Act (divorce by mutual consent)
1975	Sex Discrimination Act
1987	Clause 28
1993	Child Support Agency
2000	Age of gay consent lowered to sixteen

SINCE THE INDUSTRIAL REVOLUTION, rapidly changing employment patterns coupled with demographic and social movements have challenged the beliefs, laws, and customs governing notions of family and gender. As the timeline indicates, there has been a long series of legal reforms affecting sexual behaviour, kinship structures, and the social status of women.

On the one hand, these reforms were the result of progressive, humanitarian social movements such as feminism, which, in less than two hundred years, has secured rights of guardianship, property ownership, political representation, and reproductive control for British women. On the other hand, protective legislation – such as the 1848 Factory Act limiting women and children to a ten-hour working day – countered the exploitation of women workers in the newly developing manufacturing industries primarily in order to ensure their allegiance to motherhood and wifely duties. In this sense, nineteenth-century parliamentary reforms went hand-in-hand with a gradual acceptance of the state's right to directly intervene in and regulate the domestic sphere. During the 1960s and 1970s, 'permissive' legislation such as the legalisation of abortion, the introduction of the no-fault divorce, and the decriminalisation of homosexuality reversed this trend, reflecting the higher priority awarded to personal choice and freedom as opposed to public morality and duty. In recent years, the pendulum appears to be swinging back again, with legislation such as the Child Support Act, which enforced parental responsibilities by law, and calls to reintroduce more restrictive divorce laws. In the twenty-first century, there will undoubtedly be further contentious reforms in legislation concerning sexual discrimination, abortion, divorce, and sexual practice. All of these affect, and are in turn affected by, social attitudes and cultural activities. Their strongest impact, however, will be perceived in terms of the British family unit and so, when looking at trends in attitudes towards gender and sex, it is here that we must begin.

The family unit

At present, there are factors pulling in opposite directions in terms of the size of the British population. While the average lifespan has increased in the UK, British fertility rates have been steadily declining since the population boom of the immediate postwar years. A higher number of couples do not have children (20 per cent) and those that do generally have smaller families. This is largely attributed to both improvements in female education and career prospects and greater social acceptance of contraception. Childbearing is frequently postponed until the late twenties or early thirties (the *average* age of fathers at childbirth is now just over thirty) and the majority of women work outside of the home both before and after having children, regardless of marital status. Consequently, the often-quoted average British family with 2.4 children has now dwindled to 1.8: a trend which reflects the overall decline in the proportion of 'conventional' family units. Only 24 per cent of contemporary British households fall into the 'two adults plus dependent children' nuclear model, and this figure includes not only married couples but the increasing number of long-term cohabitees (who may decide not to marry for personal and ideological reasons, but also for financial ones as the average 'white' wedding in 2000 cost £13,723).

Perhaps one of the most significant shifts over the last thirty years has been in attitudes towards marriage, which, though still popular (around 75 per cent of people marry at least once), is less so than at any previous time in British history: according to the office of national statistics there were 263,515 marriages in 1999, continuing a downward trend since the peak of 426,241 in England and Wales in 1972. The decline in registered marriages has also been mirrored by a sharp increase in marital breakdown, such that if current trends continue some 60 per cent of men between twenty-five and forty will be bachelors in 2010. Four in every ten British marriages currently end in divorce, making UK rates the highest in Europe, and by 2025 divorces are set to outnumber marriages. As a result of these changes, the number of single-parent families (90 per cent of which are headed by women) has risen dramatically, comprising one in five of all family units and generating the latest in a long line of perceived threats to the fabric of British family life. It is also feared by some that this number will increase as childbirth out of wedlock rises: in 2000, 34 per cent of births took place outside of marriage, with the figure rising to 68 per cent in Liverpool, for example (the figure for Europe as a whole was 26 per cent in 1998). The percentage of new mothers aged between fifteen and nineteen has also given risen to concern, standing at 22.9, compared with 6.8 per cent in France for example.

TABLE 3.1 Divorces in the UK, 1971 and 1992 (by duration of marriage)

	1971	1992
All divorces	79,200	175,100
0–4 years	10,296	40,273
5–9 years	24,552	47,277
10–14 years	15,048	31,518
15–19 years	10,296	22,763
20+ years	19,800	33,269

Source: OPCS, NTC

If the statistics indicate a rapid decline in allegiance to the traditional family unit, these figures need to be balanced against other interrelated changes in life experience and cultural norms. For example, while the liberalisation of the divorce laws and the (albeit limited) possibility of female economic independence has undoubtedly done much to make divorce a realistic option for greater numbers of discontented married people, the extended life expectancy of both partners is also an important contributory factor. A couple who marry in their twenties are now committing themselves to stay together for the next fifty or so years, whereas a century ago, when people rarely lived beyond their mid-fifties, a lifelong marriage would have covered only thirty years. When these differences are taken into account, it appears that the length of the average marriage has stayed fairly constant over the last century, settling at around fifteen to twenty years before either death or divorce.

Ethnicity is also an important factor in accounting for different British family structures. For example, many Vietnamese and Bengali families still retain an extended family structure, while a higher than average proportion of Afro-Caribbean families are mother-led. In addition to this, the relatively low proportion of 'normal' British families does not reflect the symbolic or ideological importance of the conventional family unit, which remains strong despite its minority status. The two-parent, patriarchal family continues to be regarded by many as the most important of all social institutions, bearing the brunt of responsibility for producing well-adjusted, law-abiding citizens. And although the Conservatives have assumed the role of 'the party of family values', the family tends to occupy an elevated position within the rhetoric of all major political parties. Public discussion of the family is generally concerned with the best means of defending it and ensuring its continuation, as opposed to whether other forms of socialisation – such as communal child-rearing – might prove to be a healthier or more practical model for most people. In short, the overall desirability or legitimacy of the institution itself is rarely questioned, at least within mainstream political debate.

But as with any social institution, notions of what constitutes a healthy, normal family unit vary according to contemporary cultural practices and social concerns. In the 1970s, the 'teenage bride' became the subject of much moral concern, whereas such debates since the 1990s have instead focused on the growing numbers of single mothers. It would seem that, whether young women are for or against marriage, their marital status constitutes an on-going cause of anxiety (the insistence on and resistance to the use of Ms instead of Mrs and Miss illustrates this). In this sense, shifting conceptions of gender identity and, in particular, women's greater participation in public as opposed to domestic life, has been a key factor in generating fears about the collapse of the family throughout the last two centuries. In a similar manner, notions of the family are closely linked with debates over national identity and cultural cohesion; at all points of the political spectrum, commitment to 'the family' is frequently invoked as a source of national unity.

In attempting to understand the symbolic importance of the contemporary nuclear model, it is useful to examine its historical development. This is usually traced to the late Victorian period, when, as religious influence declined, the family took up the mantle of moral guardianship. It was expected to provide both moral guidance and social stability, or, as early twentieth-century social anthropologists put it, to function as a 'Nursery of Citizenship'. Despite being more of a cosmopolitan dynasty than a cosy nuclear group, the British Royal Family swiftly came to symbolise the ideal British family unit. Even today, the Queen is sometimes referred to as 'the mother of the Commonwealth', just as England, the imperial centre, was once viewed as 'the mother country'. The ideological importance of the Royal Family goes some way towards explaining why the recent spate of acrimonious partings and scandals blighting the present House of Windsor (most recently in 'Sophiegate', when Prince Edward's wife was recorded criticising the royals by an undercover journalist) are a cause of such consternation within the UK, but provoke only mild amusement in other countries.

Given this weight of expectations, it is not surprising that the family, as an institution, seems always to be in crisis. Nevertheless, while fears of its erosion are often exaggerated and vary according to cultural context, there is no doubt that the last twenty years have witnessed a particularly turbulent period of change in family structure and gender roles. To consider these transformations in more detail, this chapter will next examine the changing status of British women and then move on to look more broadly at attitudes towards marriage, parenting, and sexuality.

Gender and British institutions

Despite the strength and longevity of the British women's movement, many traditional British institutions remain remarkably male-dominated, although this is slowly beginning to change. We can start to examine both institutionalised sexism and the attempts to challenge it, by looking at predominately male institutions such as the political and legal systems and the Church of England. The culture of Westminster is often likened to that of a boys' public school. Not only are there very few female Members of Parliament (fewer than one in ten) but the House of Commons thrives on an atmosphere of masculine combat. Heckling, jeering, and the routine exchange of insults are so much part of the daily proceedings that Prime Minister Tony Blair, who has sought actively to promote women within the Cabinet, has repeatedly discussed the possibility of a ban on name-calling and a new emphasis on 'mature' debate (at present, only a very few insulting words, such as 'liar', are not allowed, and so not heard, in the House).

But, for aspiring female members, the macho culture of Westminster is a minor problem compared to that of getting elected, or even selected to stand, in the first place. Not surprisingly, local constituency executives nominate the candidate with the best chance of getting elected, which, given the age-old prejudices of both sexes, is less likely to be a woman. Of course, there are always notable exceptions. Margaret Thatcher's eleven-year reign proved that a female leader could be quite as confrontational and bloody-minded as any man. During her years in office, Thatcher was frequently described as both 'the best man for the job' and 'the iron lady', perhaps indicating the degree of unease and confusion produced by the presence of a female leader in a traditional male enclave (the satirical puppet show *Spitting Image* emphasised this by always showing her using a men's toilet). As it made her the first female British Prime Minster, Thatcher's election was of symbolic importance, although it may be noted that the overall number of female MPs fell during her term in office and that she herself was outspoken in her opposition to women's rights. Thatcher's appointment was shortly followed by another, no less historic female appointment, when Betty Boothroyd was made the first woman to occupy the powerful position of House of Commons Speaker – the arbiter of Commons debate.

Of the major political parties, Labour has the strongest commitment to and historical identification with feminist politics. Recent party initiatives have aimed to counter discrimination by promoting a high number of women to power-positions within the party (such as the latest Cabinet) and devising all-women electoral shortlists for some constituencies. These policies have aroused much controversy, for, while many think it necessary to take positive action to achieve equal political representation, others have argued that the policies undermine the achievements of the women they

FIGURE 3.1 During her terms in office Margaret Thatcher was described as both 'the best man for the job' and 'iron lady' (© Mike King/CORBIS)

favour. Furthermore, New Labour's pro-feminist sympathies have never guaranteed the largest share of the female vote. In fact, the Conservative Party's endorsement of strong law-and-order policies, combined with a commitment to traditional family values, appeals to a higher proportion of (particularly older) female voters.

The British legal system is one of the country's oldest, most traditionalist institutions. As such, it is often accused of gender bias in terms of proceedings, sentences, and professional opportunities. Although women are now entering the legal profession in ever increasing numbers (half of all British law students are female), they are less likely to reach the top of their profession, more often becoming solicitors than higher ranked and (generally) better paid barristers. There are few British female QCs (senior barristers, members of the Queen's Council) and even fewer female judges. It is therefore less surprising that the judiciary has come in for particularly harsh condemnation regarding its attitudes towards sexual assaults and other forms of violence against women. British judges have been accused of letting rapists off lightly and apportioning an inexcusable degree of blame to female victims. Indeed, one of the main reasons that so few sexual assaults are reported in the UK is that women feel anxious that they, and not their attacker, will be made morally, if not legally, culpable for the crime. This fear is exacerbated by well-publicised comments made by prominent members of the judiciary concerning the clothing-style and sexual history of victims. For example, one judge, Raymond Dean, summarised a rape trial in the following manner in 1990: 'As the gentlemen on the jury will understand, when a woman says no, she doesn't always mean it.' In spite of protests from many women's groups and Members of Parliament, the Lord Chancellor, Lord Mackay, refused to reprimand the judge.

Another contentious issue has been that of domestic violence. Again, the judiciary have been condemned for showing leniency towards men who perpetrate it, but have little sympathy with women who retaliate. In response, women's groups have mounted lengthy campaigns for the release of women convicted of killing violent, abusive husbands arguing that, even in cases in which the death was premeditated, years of persistent abuse amounted to provocation, and thus could not be regarded as cold-blooded murder. Interestingly, while these campaigns have proved largely ineffective, the 1995 dramatisation of a similar case in the socially conscious soap opera *Brookside* resulted in a groundswell of public opinion in favour of such women and helped to secure the release of Sara Thorton, who had served five years of her life sentence for just such a crime.

On 11 November 1992 the General Synod of the Church of England voted in favour of the ordination of women priests. This decision was the result of over a century of struggle on the part of women's rights campaigners, and ended a lengthy and divisive battle within the church. The initial demand for female ordination began in the late nineteenth century as part of the first wave of the British feminist movement. As a result of this pressure, the Church of England created the somewhat ambiguous order of 'deaconess' which entitled women to preside over certain rituals, but was not regarded as part of the holy triumvirate of bishops, priests, and deacons. The Church of England did not permit women deacons until as late as 1987, by which time Anglican church-women in Canada and the USA had been taking the priesthood for around ten years. In this respect, the Church of England was somewhat out of kilter with other branches of the Anglican Church and, indeed, the British public at large, eighty per cent of whom had been in favour of the ordination of women for some time. The fiercest clerical opposition to female ordination came, not surprisingly, from the church's influential Anglo-Catholic wing, many of whom either renounced the priesthood altogether or converted to Catholicism when the decision was announced. Since the vote was taken thousands of women have been ordained in Britain.

Women and employment

Probably the most important factor in the transformation of British gender identities has been the long-term and seemingly irreversible trend towards female participation in the paid labour force.

Women continued to enter the labour force in ever increasing numbers throughout the twentieth century, but many fears have been voiced about changing gender roles and a perceived deterioration of family life. Women's paid employment may be an accepted fact of modern life, but it is still regarded by many as an undesirable one. In the first half of the twentieth century, government policy reflected the widely held view that the female population constituted a reserve labour force, only to be drawn on in times of dire necessity. During the First World War, the vast numbers of women who were encouraged to enter the labour force had to fight bitterly to achieve the same wage as their male counterparts, a privilege which was granted to women workers during the Second World War, in which, for the first time, state-run nurseries were also provided. But, like the previous generation of women war workers, they were expected to relinquish both their jobs and their state childcare facilities during peacetime. The immediate postwar period saw a forceful reassertion of traditional roles; women were enticed back into the home as sociologists and psychologists warned of the dangers of maternal deprivation caused by the working mother's absence. Fears concerning the welfare of so-called 'latchkey kids' (those who had no mother to greet them from school) reinforced the notion that children could not be properly cared for without a home-based mother, heightening public hostility towards such women (to reinforce this, there were in 1995 several high-profile attacks in the tabloids on mothers who left their children 'home alone'). But in spite of these attitudes, women's participation in paid employment rose dramatically in the late 1950s and has continued to increase in every decade since. Shifts in patterns of employment, particularly the expansion of secretarial, administrative, and clerical occupations in the 1960s and 1970s, and the rapid growth of the service sector in the 1980s, opened up new areas of female employment. Today, nearly two-thirds of women aged between fifteen and sixty-four in Britain are in work, compared with between a third and a half in most other European countries (only in Sweden and Denmark the proportions are higher).

Coupled with the demise of heavy industry, and a subsequent drop in the male-dominated areas of unskilled manual work, for the first time ever the balance has tipped towards an almost evenly divided male and female British labour force. Moreover, there is a marked difference in the composition of the female labour force: in the first half of the century the majority of working women were either young and single or middle-aged

FIGURE 3.2 Slowly, women are entering professions that have traditionally been exclusively male (© Maggie Murray/Format)

TABLE 3.2 UK employment status by sex: % of workforce, figures are rounded

	All	Men	Women
Traditional workforce			
Full-time permanent employees	75.1	90.9	47.9
Flexible workforce			
Part-time permanent employees	24.9	9.1	44.3
Full-time self-employed	11.3	14.9	6.8
Government training schemes	0.5	0.6	0.5
Unpaid family workers	0.4	0.2	0.6

Source: 'Labour Market Trends', National Statistics Office, 2001

with grown children, whereas the greatest increase in the 1970s and 1980s occurred amongst those with partners and dependants. But these statistics can be misleading: British women are still far from achieving equality in the workplace. Despite the legacy of hard-won women's rights legislation, such as the Equal Pay (1970) and Sex Discrimination Acts (1975), women are still earning just under 80 per cent of men's pay (the 2001 annual report by the Equal Opportunities Commission found that by the age of twenty women were already earning 10 per cent less than male colleagues). In practice, equal-pay legislation is difficult to enforce and discrimination hard to prove. Women are still much more likely to be discriminated against on grounds of age or physical attractiveness, although clearly employers are no longer able to specify gender openly in a job description. The affix 'man' – as in *postman*, *salesman*, *fireman* – has been either replaced by 'person' (*salesperson*) or dropped completely (*firefighter*).

It is also the case that a small number of women are now working in previously male-dominated areas, but sex segregation persists. Female employees tend to be heavily concentrated in non-unionised, unskilled areas of work, with an overwhelming majority (81 per cent) working in service industries (e.g. as cleaners, waitresses, bar and hotel staff). The catering industry, for example, relies largely on part-time and casual labour; precisely the kind of low-paid, low-status, 'pink collar' occupations, which women with small children and limited childcare assistance are often forced into accepting. But even predominantly female skilled occupations – such as secretarial or administrative work – tend to command less pay and status by virtue of their 'feminine' associations. Probably the most serious example is that of British nurses, who earn considerably less than those in most other parts of Western Europe, chiefly because nursing is still viewed in Britain more as an extension of woman's natural 'caring' role than as a skilled profession. In addition, there is little evidence to suggest that women's increased participation in the labour force has been accompanied by a corresponding shift in domestic responsibilities. Working women continue to do the lion's share of housework, child rearing, and caring for elderly relatives. Surprisingly, this rule applies even in situations where women are the primary earners. Studies of areas of high male unemployment, such as Wearside in the post-industrial north-east, show a rise in stay-at-home husbands and working wives. But they also indicate that while husbands are prepared to perform 'light' domestic duties (such as shopping and cooking) they still draw the line at cleaning and other 'menial' domestic tasks (in May 1999, a survey by the office for national statistics reported that on average men spend 45 minutes a day on cooking and routine housework, compared to women's 138 minutes). In short, traditional gender identities persist and role reversal was regarded as temporary and pragmatic.

As we might expect, female employment opportunities are also heavily influenced by other factors, such as region, class, and race. For example, although a higher than average number of Afro-Caribbean women go on to further education, levels of unemployment within this ethnic grouping are significantly greater than amongst their white female counterparts. Predictably, the greatest career gains have been made by white, middle-class, university-educated women, who are now beginning to make significant inroads into previously male-dominated professions such as law and medicine. But even they fare badly in private industry, and despite the much-touted success of a handful of British female entrepreneurs – Body Shop boss Anita Roddick in particular – fewer than 10 per cent of British businesses are currently owned by women.

All in all, employment opportunities for British women certainly exceed those of previous generations, but they are still far from equal with those of British men. Nevertheless, if the reality of women's employment opportunity is not as rosy as it is often assumed to be, this does not diminish its impact in terms of cultural representation and notions of female identity. British advertising and television are now beginning to represent women in a much wider spectrum of roles than just girlfriend, wife, or mother. In recent years there has been an abundance of television programmes featuring women in traditionally male or 'high-powered' professional jobs (e.g. *The Manageress* about a woman football manager and *Prime Suspect* about a police Chief Inspector). These can be seen as presenting new role models or as adding a new twist to well-worn fictional formulas such as the police procedural or hospital drama series.

Perhaps as a result of these images, young women now have far greater expectations than ever before. A recent study of British teenage girls revealed that many now confidently expect to have both a career and a family, although, given present working conditions, they are unlikely to achieve both these aims.

Marriage and divorce

Prior to the implementation of the 1969 Divorce Reform Act, a legal separation required a guilty party. Adultery was by far the most frequently cited reason, and the 'wronged' wife or husband had to provide evidence that an affair had taken place. Not surprisingly, this emphasis on moral culpability heightened any existing bitterness between parties, as lurid details were dragged out in court. In fact, when divorce became available through mutual agreement (albeit after a five-, and later two-year separation) the majority of British private detective agencies went out of business as a result. From that point onwards divorce rates have soared, causing many to argue for stricter divorce laws.

FIGURE 3.3 Traditional wedding

This view was widely endorsed in the early 1990s by the Conservative government, who launched a 'moral crusade' popularly known as the 'back to basics' campaign. This initiative implored the public to stand firm in their commitment to marriage and family life, but was discredited by the disclosure of a string of sex scandals involving prominent MPs. From then on the phrase 'back to basics' became almost synonymous with sexual hypocrisy and corruption.

Those who uphold the sanctity of marriage view Britain's one-in-three divorce rate as an indictment of its commitment-shy national culture: divorced people are sometimes castigated as selfish and fickle, putting their needs above those of their children. On the other hand, while few regard it positively, many argue that it indicates a more realistic, tolerant attitude towards the breakdown of relationships. From whichever viewpoint, it is clear that, while a high percentage of the population continue to marry, people's expectations of what this entails are vastly different from those of their parents.

Until the late nineteenth century, British women, unlike those in Islamic or Hindu societies, were required to relinquish all property rights upon marriage. Divorce was virtually unheard of amongst anyone except the upper classes. Nevertheless, it was still more easily accessible to men, who had only to establish that adultery had taken place. A wife needed proof of adultery plus desertion, bigamy, incest, or cruelty to divorce her husband. It was not until 1923 that women and men could bring a divorce suit on the same grounds, and women were denied a share of their ex-husband's income until as late as the mid-1960s. Given that many had no independent means of support, divorce was clearly not an attractive or realistic prospect for large numbers of women. Even today, a woman's credit rating usually drops following a divorce while the reverse is true for her ex-husband. But in spite of this disparity, by far the majority of divorces are instigated by women, who are also much less likely to marry again. In part, the higher divorce rate is therefore an inevitable consequence of women's increased financial autonomy, but it also corresponds to more general shifts in the structure of the family and the relative importance attached to the heterosexual couple.

At least until the mid twentieth century, the dominant form of family structure was extended rather than nuclear, with parents and even grandparents, uncles, and aunts living in close proximity to their grown-up children. It was also considered normal for women and men to inhabit quite different worlds in terms of both work and social activities. Owing to the increased geographical and social mobility of the population, this often romanticised family unit has gradually disappeared and is now found mainly in soap operas based in traditional working-class communities: Albert Square in 'Cockney' soap *EastEnders* is a good example.

One consequence of the decline of the extended family has been the emergence of stronger adult friendship networks; a development explored in popular British films such as *Peter's Friends*, *Four Weddings and a Funeral*, *Bridget Jones's Diary* and *Notting Hill*. Another has been the emergence of a more 'companionable' idea of marriage. Within the contemporary companionate model, mutual respect, emotional fulfilment and shared 'quality time' have, at least in theory, replaced the old model which assumed separate spheres and female dependence. Attitudes to marriage and the family here also been influenced in recent years by greater openness about lesbian and gay relationships.

But if higher expectations and better alternatives have done much to increase the divorce rate, the financial incentives to marry are also not what they used to be. Over the last fifteen years, tax relief for married couples has been gradually reduced. Meanwhile, unemployed married people are disqualified from certain state benefits if their partners are in work. This also applies to cohabitees, but clearly it is rather more difficult to establish their domestic arrangements. As one child in three is now born out of wedlock, several proposals have been put forward to extend further the legal rights of long-term cohabitees, though plans for one-year no-fault divorces met with stiff opposition.

Parenting

Compared with other European states, Britain could hardly be regarded as a child-orientated society. There has undoubtedly been a rejection of the often harsh child rearing methods favoured in the UK a century ago, but children are still not welcomed or adequately catered for in public places such as pubs and restaurants. More serious perhaps is the fact that British nursery provision is the poorest in Europe, with only half of pre-school-age children able to obtain a place. Yet, at the same time, the family is revered and the popular media are dominated by debates about the falling standard of British parenting. We can begin to consider this paradox by focusing on two particularly contentious issues: firstly, the increase in single-parent households and, secondly, children's exposure to violence both within the family and as depicted in forms of popular entertainment.

In 1993, arguments came to a head over Britain's high proportion of single-parent families when a government minister claimed that an over-generous state benefit system was encouraging young, single mothers to 'marry the state' and embark on a 'benefit career'. This controversial statement came shortly after suggestions that teenage girls were becoming pregnant chiefly in order to secure scarce local authority housing. At the heart of this issue was not only the assumption that many young women preferred not to work, but the fear that rather than becoming single mothers through male abandonment – and thus becoming worthy recipients of state support – young women were actually choosing to live without men, in communities of single mothers. In order to lower the tax burden and reinstate traditional family values, the Conservative government considered developing a system (already operating in some parts of the USA) whereby single mothers are penalised for the birth of a second or third child. In response to these suggestions, groups such as the Association of Single Parents swiftly pointed out that, although many single parents relied on state subsidies, this resulted from difficulties in finding a decent enough job to cover childcare expenses, rather than a disinclination to work. In addition to this, it was revealed that two-thirds of lone parents had become so through divorce or separation rather than choice, and that, far from enjoying a high standard of living at the taxpayer's expense, as many as 75 per cent were surviving below the official poverty line. Due to these and other criticisms, plans to cut benefit for single parents were shelved. But in the same year, an even more explosive parenting debate arose over the establishment of the Child Support Agency.

This government-funded body was set-up to fix maintenance payments and pursue absent fathers after the discovery that fewer than one in three were supporting their children. The agency soon came under fire for fixing payment rates at an unrealistically high level, often destroying amicable agreements in the process. Critics also argued that the agency was more concerned with raising the payments of those who were already contributing rather than finding those who were not. The furore intensified after the occurrence of two well-publicised suicide cases, in which financial stress caused by the agency's demands was thought to have been a contributory factor. Eventually, a House of Commons Select Committee was formed to review the workings of the Agency. Stricter guidelines were introduced to ensure that fathers were left with sufficient funds to live on and, as was often the case, support second families.

While the single-parent and the Child Support Agency controversies highlighted the financial responsibilities attached to being a parent, there has also been a growing awareness of the widespread extent of child abuse and the long-term psychological effects on its victims. This has led to much debate concerning the difference between legitimate expressions of parental authority and malicious ill-treatment. For example, many thought that a poster campaign run by the Royal Society for the Prevention of Cruelty to Children, went too far in emphasising the damaging effects of verbal as well as physical abuse. Questions have also been raised as to how far the state is entitled to intervene in family life, leaving the social services to tread a dangerous path between accusations of unnecessary and disruptive interference and negligence.

The most serious debates about British parenting arose in 1993, after two-year-old James Bulger was abducted from a shopping centre in Bootle, Merseyside, and murdered by two eleven-year-old boys. Not surprisingly, the horrifying case caused a national outcry and much attention was given to seeking an explanation for the boys' behaviour. While a good deal of blame was apportioned to the two boys' parents, questions were also raised as to what extent the murder reflected a rising tide of British violence and how far this could be traced to the corrosive influence of violent, American 'video nasty' imports. It was suggested that the children's behaviour had been influenced by a horror film – *Child's Play* – which the pair were alleged to have watched shortly before the murder. In this respect, the Bulger case rekindled a much older debate about popular entertainment and British crime rates, centring on the wide availability of violent American videos and their moral 'contamination' of the nation's youth. As there has never been any substantial evidence to suggest that behaviour is dictated or even strongly influenced by viewing habits (despite numerous studies), other commentators looked closer to home for causes. A study authorised in the wake of the Bulger case by the Commission on Children and Violence found that the key determinants linking young, violent offenders were parental abuse and poverty rather than excessive exposure to television or cinema violence. The case has remained high-profile, and the release from prison of the two boys in 2001 was met with howls of protest from, among others, the family and friends of James Bulger. The vehemence of the reaction from sections of the community has meant that the boys will have to be given new identities and police protection once they return into society.

One of the more positive results of debates on child abuse has been the organisation of a twenty-four-hour free-of-charge phone counselling service for distressed children and teenagers – the National Childline – which began in 1993. More recently, the issue of paedophilia has been the subject of major concern. The Labour government has been under pressure to increase its published list of 'sex offenders' as many parents have demanded the right to know if paedophiles are living in their area. The issue was brought to a head in 2001 when many ex-offenders were attacked in their homes, and the assaults spread to the extent that a paediatrician was attacked by a group of people who misunderstood the meaning of the word. Subsequently, in July 2001, an edition of the satirical Channel 4 mock news programme *Brass Eye* caused a national debate over media representations of paedophilia, liberals defending the show as an attack on glib 'investigative' reporting that in fact sensationalised issues such as paedophilia and titillated viewers, while reactionary quarters, especially the *Daily Mail*, demanded that the programme's maker, Chris Morris, be prosecuted. Because the programme focused on what is currently the most controversial aspect of contemporary British morality, it met with almost hysterical responses from the press, charities, politicians, and also sections of the media, its target. A Home Office Minister, Beverley Hughes, was compelled to condemn the programme on national radio, even though she had to admit she had not seen it.

Sexuality and identity

The British are famed for both their prurience and their sexual reserve, a stereotype which, though exploited within many British cultural forms (Merchant/Ivory 'heritage' cinema, for example), probably derives less from contemporary cultural attitudes than from England's former role in the global imposition of repressive middle-class norms and values. It is certainly true that British censorship laws are still stricter than in many other European states, and that it is one of the few countries in which a government minister will be forced to resign over a minor sex scandal. But in other respects attitudes are fairly liberal. The shift towards so-called 'permissiveness' is associated with 'swinging London', the explosion of British youth culture and the legalisation of homosexuality, abortion, birth control, and divorce reform in the 1960s. The trial under the Obscene Publications Act of 1960 in which it was finally decided that

D. H. Lawrence's sexually explicit but critically acclaimed novel *Lady Chatterley's Lover* would be made available to the British public is generally regarded as something of a watershed, dividing prudish 'Victorian' Britain from permissive, contemporary Britain.

However, while the majority of permissive legislative reforms date from the 1960s (when the number of registered marriages actually increased), the social effect of this legislation was not really felt until the 1970s and even 1980s, by which time permissiveness had begun to acquire a pejorative meaning, denoting the collapse of moral authority and the traditional family unit. Aside from concerns about single mothers, absentee fathers, and rising divorce rates, the backlash against permissiveness was given a new impetus by the Aids crisis, with much attention focused on the British gay community.

Britain's first official Aids-related death, that of Terrence Higgins, occurred in 1982 and led to the establishment of what remains Britain's biggest Aids/HIV education and advice service, the Terrence Higgins Trust. The British government, however, was much slower to respond to the crisis. This reluctance was not only due to its disinclination to mount costly HIV prevention campaigns, but also related to the problems of censorship which preventative education created. Addressing the problem of HIV transmission necessitated the acknowledgement of a range of sexual practices and an extent of extra, and premarital sexual activities which a 'family-orientated' administration did not want to be seen to endorse. Only when the heterosexual risk factor became very apparent did the Department of Health launch a full-scale, five-million-pound television, cinema, poster, and house-to-house leafleting campaign in 1987. Although the Health Department's ubiquitous slogan was 'Aids: don't die of ignorance', preventative education tended to be both oblique and alarmist, stressing promiscuity as a central factor, despite overwhelming medical evidence that viral transmission was related to particular sexual practices rather than sheer numbers of partners.

The early years of the crisis produced a wave of anti-gay hysteria, exacerbated by the popular press, who were quick to identify Aids wrongly as an exclusively homosexual 'plague'. Many British newspapers actually went so far as to support such draconian measures as the recriminalisation of sodomy or the forced quarantine of those suffering from the disease. For example, speculating on the predicted growth in HIV infection, Auberon Waugh's knowingly provocative 1985 *Daily Telegraph* column asked why 'No one has mentioned what might seem the most obvious way of cutting down this figure (of 1 one million by 1990) – by repealing the Sexual Offences Act of 1967 and making sodomy a criminal offence once again'. British rates of infection have not reached these initial predictions, and in the twenty-first century such attitudes as those implied by Waugh's speculation are less common, though this is perhaps because the discussion of Aids has been backgrounded in recent years, not least because sex has become the essential ingedient of any marketing campaign. Surveys continue to indicate that, while 'safe' sexual practices have been widely adopted within the gay community since the mid-1980s, the majority of heterosexuals do not regard themselves as significantly at risk, despite the fact that new cases of HIV reached a high of 3,500 in 2000. Furthermore, the climate of homophobia created by the initial burst of Aids scare stories did much to undermine growing acceptance of the gay community. In Britain, it has never been illegal for a man actually to be a homosexual, only to participate in homo-sexual acts, while lesbianism has not been recognised by the law, supposedly because Queen Victoria refused to acknowledge its existence.

Since the 1967 Sexual Offences Act, which decriminalised homo-sexual activities in England and Wales (extended to Scotland in 1980 and Northern Ireland in 1979), a lively gay and lesbian subculture has flourished in urban areas of Britain. Soho, for example, famous for its gay-owned shops, pubs, clubs and cafés, has become one of London's biggest nightlife attractions. Moreover, the widespread adoption of the word 'gay', a term denoting positive self-identification, as opposed to 'homosexual' or more pejorative terms, suggested a growing acknowl-edgement of gay identity as an alternative lifestyle choice, rather than just a sexual preference. The growing acceptance of gay lifestyles has been apparent on television, from the first 'lesbian-kiss' broadcast in *Brookside*, through the huge popularity of the drama serial *Queer as Folk*, to the winning of the second series of *Big Brother* by a gay man in 2001. In terms of cyberspace, following the success of the digitised fantasy-figure of Lara Croft, *Gay Times* welcomed the announcement in summer 2001 that *Tomb Raider*'s manufacturer's Eidos were releasing *Fear Effect 2: Retro Helix*, featuring 'Hana and Rain', the first gay couple to appear in a computerised video game. More importantly, in September 2001 the first ceremonies for gay couples were begun in London, which has started a civil register of gay partnerships. Though the 'pacts' have no legal status, they are made formally at a ceremony conducted by an approved Greater London authority officer. Gay rights groups hope that eventually the ceremonies, after wider recognition, will lead to legislation that confers on homosexual couples the same legal rights as married people.

There remains at least one major area of concern, however: an addi-tion to the Local Government Bill of 1987 inserting the notorious Clause (also known as Section) 28. This amendment stipulated that local govern-ment authorities could not 'Promote homosexuality or publish material for the promotion of homosexuality' or 'promote the teaching in any main-tained school of the acceptability of homosexuality as a pretended family relationship by the publication of such material or otherwise'.

The Act was eventually passed, but, rather than silencing the gay community, it had the effect of mobilising and reaffirming British gay identity. The annual Gay Pride march – always the biggest, though generally one of the least publicised, demonstrations in the capital – recorded a much higher than usual attendance in the year following the introduction of the clause, and the organisers of what is now called the Gay Pride Mardi Gras in Finsbury Park, which concludes the march from Hyde Park, now aim to make London the gay capital of the world, in which they are supported by the tourist industry, less concerned with gay rights than with attracting the 'pink' pound. Ranging from 'professional' pressure groups such as Stonewall to more militant organisations such as Act Up (Aids Coalition to Unleash Power) and OutRage! (who sometimes adopt the term 'queer' to distinguish themselves from more moderate, assimilationist gay groups), there has been a resurgence of British gay activism since the late 1980s. Homophobic discrimination in the workplace is still legal, but other issues, those of the age of gay consent and of the forced exposure or 'outing' of homosexuals and lesbians, have commanded particularly high levels of public interest and will be examined in turn.

FIGURE 3.4 Organisers of the Gay Pride Mardi Gras aim to make London the gay capital of the world (© Mirror Syndication International)

Initiatives to bring the gay age of consent (which was twenty-one) in line with that applied to heterosexuals (sixteen), was part of a broader gay equality package drafted by the Stonewall group, and inspired by the European Union's social charter commitment to ending all forms of discrimination. An uneasy compromise was reached in February 1993 when the homosexual age of consent was changed to eighteen but it was finally lowered to sixteen in November 2000. At the other end of the spectrum, activists such as Peter Tatchell and OutRage! have adopted the more controversial tactic of outing allegedly gay public figures – specifically those perceived to have lent their support to discriminatory practices. Outing is often associated with the exposure of pop stars and media celebrities, but in Britain (if not in the USA) gay outing groups tend to target more Establishment figures, such as eminent clergymen or Members of Parliament. This has to be distinguished from the routine exposure of gay media celebrities more commonly practised by the tabloid press, who are also, ironically, almost unanimous in their opposition to 'political' outing. A recent example was the tabloids' revelation that Britain's most popular television comedian, Michael Barrymore, was gay. Despite being front-page news for a full two weeks, the story does not seem to have seriously damaged his career, though that of Michael Portillo was undermined by press and politicians when he ran for leadership of the Conservative Party in 2001: most people believed him to be the front runner for the office but his campaign was perhaps damaged for some members of the Party by allegations of homosexual acts. However, Portillo was in no sense politically ruined by the allegations, as his career would once have been and, a particularly vicious, homophobic press campaign can often generate a good deal of public sympathy for its victim. In fact, Britain has a long tradition of camp entertainers, many of whom both exploit and challenge gay stereotypes as a source of comedy. A recent example is that of openly gay comedian Julian Clary, whose bawdy game show – *Sticky Moments* – takes smutty jokes and gay sexual innuendo to the point of self-parody.

British attitudes towards homosexuality and lesbianism have to be considered in relation to the overall political climate. The Aids crisis increased prejudice, but current attitudes appear to be much more tolerant than before. Amongst younger age-groups in particular, the distinctions between gay and straight culture are more blurred than ever. Gay male dress codes have been widely adopted by heterosexual men, and gay clubs are now more mixed in terms of both gender and sexual orientation.

If gender roles are learnt first and foremost within the family, they are reinforced or challenged in our choice of social activities and leisure pursuits. Indeed, if the family is less central to most people's lives today, these may provide a greater source of identification. One of the clearest indications of the collapse of polarised gender identities is the slow decline of exclusively male or female British institutions such as the Women's Institute or the working men's club. Although it is often dismissed as a backward-looking, traditionalist organisation, the Women's Institute (WI) was formed in 1915 with the intention of informing and broadening the horizons of housewives, many of whom, at that time, received little or no conventional education. In fact, many of the Institute's early philanthropic patrons, such as the first chairperson, Lady Denman, were inspired by the first-wave feminist movement. But, as women's educational and career opportunities have increased, the Institute has come to be associated with one particular aspect of its work: the appreciation and preservation of traditional 'feminine' crafts such as cookery and needlepoint. Clearly, as the majority of women now work, not only do they have less time to devote to pursuing home-based crafts, but these have become less important as an indication of gender identity. Consequently, membership has fallen from 500,000 in its heyday in the late 1950s and early 1960s to the contemporary figure of 272,000. The WI is still involved in raising awareness of contemporary women's health issues, such as breast cancer, or environmental risks to children, but as membership is largely drawn from the over-fifties age-group and the Institute has little appeal for younger women, it looks set to fade away in time. Its only recent high-profile moment came when Tony Blair was given a slow handclap in 2000 by a WI meeting because he used the occasion to discuss general policy issues which the largely conservative gathering believed were not addressed to them but to members of the press in attendance.

Like the Women's Institute, the formation of working men's clubs harks back to a period in which male identity (particularly that of working-class men) was primarily constituted through the kinds of manual trades and blue-collar occupations which have receded in the post war period. With an annual membership of 350,000 around the country, working men's clubs are still popular. But most have evolved into mixed social clubs and are now only tenuously linked to the workplace. Only 2 per cent exclude women from the premises, although women are barred from participating in organisational responsibilities in 35 per cent, and as with the WI the clubs now appeal to older people. Amongst the under-twenty-five age-group, leisure activities are becoming virtually indistinguishable. Pubs, still the most popular of all British social environments, are no longer male-dominated territories, although many women still do not feel comfortable visiting one alone.

The health and fitness culture which has flourished in Britain over the last ten years has also opened up a new range of cross-gender leisure activities. Women are still less likely to compete in team sports and tend to favour fitness classes, but activities such as running, swimming, and weight training are becoming increasingly popular with both sexes. The gym, once a strictly male domain, is now frequented by almost equal numbers of men and women. Furthermore, while it is often maintained that women's participation in fitness activities is motivated by vanity and men's by health concerns, there is much evidence to suggest that British men are becoming increasingly preoccupied with appearance and body-shape. This can be understood as part of a more general shift in perceptions of British male identity, largely occasioned by the newer role models such as David Beckham or the television chef Jamie Oliver. British men have often been characterised, perhaps unfairly, as badly dressed and proudly indifferent to common standards of style, taste, and personal grooming. In the 1980s, the expansion and diversification of the menswear retailing industry, coupled with a growth in men's grooming products, revolutionised attitudes towards British masculinity. A new range of fashion and beauty products were targeted at men, and more sexualised male images began to circulate in advertising and in new men's style magazines, such as *Arena*, *FHM*, and *GQ*.

At other times such images may have carried distinctly gay connotations, but their contemporary appeal is ambivalently cross-gender. Male bodies were more crudely objectified in the new women's porn magazines, and male strippers became a regular feature of the hen party or girls' night out. It is not surprising that British men are now beginning to develop the kinds of body-image disorders, such as anorexia and bulimia, which were once confined to women. As a result of these developments, British men have finally been cajoled into spending a greater proportion of their leisure time engaged in that most 'feminine' of activities, shopping, which now takes up a fair proportion of leisure time for both sexes, augmenting more traditional male activities, such as Saturday afternoon football.

Conclusion

Today, the British population comprises 51 per cent female and 49 per cent male subjects. However, the higher numbers of women are heavily concentrated in the over-sixty age-group and do not reflect the gendered composition of the population as a whole. Recent studies also suggest that male life expectancy is catching up (it is currently about five years lower) and that over the century this imbalance is likely to be reversed in favour of men. Such predictions may be altered if all parents in the future are allowed, as some argue they should be, the right to choose the sex of their children. Either way, the gender composition of the population will undoubtedly affect attitudes towards age, marriage, children, and women in paid employment.

However, the overall picture which emerges at present is one in which gender roles are becoming somewhat more flexible and the two-parent, patriarchal family is gradually becoming less dominant. This has produced a variety of responses. Right-wing politicians and many prominent church leaders tend to blame permissive legislation and the new social movements of the 1960s and 1970s (such as feminism and gay liberation) for the decline in traditional family life and conventional gender roles. From this perspective, the nuclear family unit is evoked as a symbol of social cohesion, and its break up is regarded as the root cause of many contemporary social ills, from vandalism to drug addiction. Yet fears about the future of the family cross traditional party lines, and, while the more conservative sectors of society tend to blame liberal reforms, others have argued that, if permissiveness weakened the family, it was Margaret Thatcher's right-wing revolution that really killed it off. The rampant individualism and consumer greed associated with the 1980s economic boom are, in this version, responsible for undermining the moral values necessary to sustain family life.

Lastly, we must consider whether the decline of the traditional family has actually led to a more atomised, alienated society. There is also evidence to suggest that new, more flexible family structures and systems of community support are beginning to take its place. Single mothers, for example, often rely heavily on one another for both childcare assistance and emotional support. Similarly, while children of divorced parents are generally regarded as disadvantaged, it has also been suggested that many actually benefit from drawing on a wider support network of two families. It is also important to recognise the new range of identities which the decay of the traditional British family has opened up. For women in particular, the decline of the traditional family unit clearly coincides with greater social freedom and status, and increased financial autonomy.

Exercises

1   What is the difference between a nuclear and extended family? Do you know or can you think of other kinship structures? How do family structures vary according to (a) class, (b) ethnic background? Which, if any, is most commonly represented in popular television film?

2   What is the meaning of the following popular phrases: back to basics; Victorian values; family wage; white wedding; lie back and think of England? How did they originate, and in what sense are they specific to British culture?

3   The British blockbuster film *Four Weddings and a Funeral* featured three traditional English and one Scottish wedding. What do you think are the staple ingredients of a British wedding? What is the significance of each?

4   In recent years there has been much debate about non-sexist language. Can you think of gender-neutral alternatives for the following occupational titles: Seaman; Ombudsman; Dustman; Craftsman; Fisherman; Postman; Signalman? Do you think it is important to adopt non-sexist language?

5   Do you think 'outing' is a fair practice? Under what circumstances? Consider arguments for and against.

 # Reading

Banks, O. *Faces of Feminism*, Blackwell, 1981. An introductory guide to the development of nineteenth- and twentieth-century feminist politics in Britain.

Holdsworth, A. *Out of the Doll House: The Story of Women in the Twentieth Century*, Butler and Tanner, 1988. An analysis of popular culture, modernity and women, looking at changing British attitudes towards motherhood, marriage, sexuality, politics, and work.

Jeffrey-Poulter, S. *Peers, Queers and Commons: The Struggle for Gay Law Reform from 1950 to the Present*, Routledge, 1991. An examination of the British legal and political system in relation to its treatment of homosexuals and lesbians.

Wilson, F. *Organisational Behaviour and Gender*, McGraw-Hill, 1995. An industrially based sociological and statistical analysis of employment discrimination against women in Britain.

 # Cultural Examples

Film

Four Weddings and a Funeral (1994) dir. Mike Newell. Courtship and marriage rituals amongst the English middle class.

Notting Hill (1999) dir. Roger Michell. Ostensibly a follow-up to the above, romantic comedy about the owner of a travel bookshop and his friends in what has become the most fashionable district of London.

The World Is Not Enough (1999) dir. Michael Apted. Latest of the updated James Bond movies which knowingly flaunt their sexism.

Orlando (1993) dir. Sally Potter. Comic costume drama spanning five hundred years in the life of a gender-bending English aristocrat.

Maybe Baby (1998) dir. Ben Elton. Amiable comedy, adapted by Elton from his stage play *Inconceivable*, about a couple's attempts to have a child.

Raining Stones (1993) dir. Ken Loach. Gritty view of male unemployment and its effects on two working-class families.

To Die For (1994) dir. Peter Mackensie. London-based exploration of Aids and its aftermath amongst the gay community.

Young Soul Rebels (1992) dir. Isaac Julien. Alternative view of punk and the Silver Jubilee year, focusing on black disco and gay subcultures.

Books

Alan Hollinghurst, *The Spell* (1998). Sharply observed and often very funny novel of contemporary middle-class gay life.

Nick Hornby, *How to Be Good* (2001). Very popular social comedy centring on a modern couple attempting to save their marriage.

Kazuo Ishiguro, *The Remains of the Day* (1989). Dissection of repressive English manners centred on a 1930s butler.

Adam Mars-Jones and Edmund White, *The Darker Proof: Stories from the Crisis* (1987). A collection of short stories exploring the Aids crisis in the UK.

Timothy Mo, *Sour Sweet* (1982). Chinese family life in inner city London.

Fay Weldon, *The Life and Loves of a She-Devil* (1983). A female revenge fantasy.

Television programmes

Absolutely Fabulous. Hit comedy depicting the outrageous antics of two 1960s generation women as they reach middle age.

Byker Grove. Slightly surreal, gender-focused, comedy sketch show written by and starring three women.

Queer as Folk. First major explicit gay serial on British television.

Jake's Progress. Tragi-comic drama focused on the dynamics of a dysfunctional British family.

The Manageress. Trials and tribulations of a female football manager.

Men Behaving Badly. Post-feminist situation-comedy exploring traditional and contemporary ideas of masculinity.

The Politician's Wife. Four part drama depicting an adulterous government minister and the actions taken by his vengeful wife.

Prime Suspect. Acclaimed police procedural series centred around a female detective and exploring sexism in the British police force.

Two Point Four Children. Popular situation comedy featuring an 'average' British family.

Websites

www.theory.org.uk/ctr-que1.htm
   Site devoted to explaining and exploring queer theory

www.disgruntledhousewife.com/
   Humorous and irreverent pro-feminist site on how to conduct a male–female relationship

uk.gay.com/chat/terms.php
>   Guide to UK gay culture and on-line community

www.digitaleveuk.org/about.html
>   Site that encourages women of all ages to participate in the world of new media

Chapter 4

Youth culture and style

Jo Croft

■   Youth, teenagers, and adolescents   143

■   Going out: 'dressing up and dressing down'   145

■   Staying in: young people and the media   151

■   Sex and drugs and rock'n'roll   156

■   Conclusion   163

■   *Exercises*   170

■   *Reading*   171

■   *Cultural examples*   172

■   *Websites*   173

Timeline

16	Leave school Sex legal in UK except Northern Ireland Drive a moped Buy cigarettes Marry with parents' consent
17	Drive a car Sex legal in Northen Ireland
18	Buy alcohol Watch an 18-certificate film Marry without parents' consent Vote
26	Average marriage age: women
28	Average marriage age: men Average age of childbearing
37	Average age for remarriage after divorce: women
41	Average age for remarriage after divorce: men
60	Women can retire
65	Men can retire
73	Life expectancy: male
78	Life expectancy: female

WHEN WE ATTEMPT TO describe somebody else, or when we are required to describe ourselves (on an official form, for example), age almost always seems to be a crucial component of such descriptions. Age shapes and sets limits upon the way we live our lives in a way that we take for granted. As the timeline shows, age dictates such things as when we can leave school, when we can legally have sex (either homosexual or heterosexual), when we can drive, when we can marry, when we can join the army, when we can drink alcohol, when we can retire, and when we can vote. In an obvious sense, age is a 'fact' we cannot alter because it literally describes how long we have been alive: however much advertising campaigns for beauty products, vitamins, or health foods might try to convince us otherwise, it is something which fixes our position in society as much as, and often more than, other factors such as race, gender, or class.

Nevertheless, once we begin to consider the different ways in which age underpins the identity of any given individual, it emerges as a category which is far from being simply a biological given. The social effects of age have implications far beyond the explicit classification of how old someone is. Age, consequently, is an aspect of identity which powerfully reflects the particular character of life in any national culture, and we can learn a lot about a nation's values and cultural practices by paying attention to the significance it attaches to certain life stages. It is worth noting, for example, that – unlike the United States and many European countries – Britain has no specific legislation governing 'age discrimination'.

As the timeline demonstrates, the official landmarks of age in Britain seem to become fewer and further apart once you reach the age of eighteen, though there is a slight reversal of this trend during old age (driving licences, for instance, have to be reapplied for when you reach the age of seventy). In any case, the period between the ages of eleven and twenty-one is a time when life is most punctuated by changes in status – when the rules about what you can do and where you can go are shifting most dramatically. Therefore, in terms of understanding British cultural identities, the age-groups that fall broadly within the category of 'youth' offer some of the most interesting insights – not least because British institutions seem to subject young people to such close scrutiny. It is almost as if young people in Britain are –

consciously or unconsciously – regarded as not just guarantors of the nation's future but its soul: for, whenever anxieties surface about moral or social decline, the first target for concern is youth.

Britain is a nation which seems to attach particular importance to 'tradition'. 'Britishness' in both the upper class and the working class tends to be characterised by an adherence to 'old values', and it could be argued that the British see themselves, and are perhaps viewed by the rest of the world, as having an 'old' (established, traditional, or even ancient) culture. In consequence, it might also be claimed that, precisely because of this British conservatism, young people are regarded as both threatening and vulnerable. One of the issues which will be explored in this chapter is the extent to which British notions of social stability are explicitly associated with the stability of relationships between generations. A claim, after all, might be made that the massive changes in people's lifestyles in postwar Britain have been felt most acutely in terms of 'age relations'. 'The generation gap', juvenile delinquency, loss of community, the fragmentation of the nuclear family and disappearance of the extended family: all these much-debated social phenomena seem in one way or another to be associated with a perceived deterioration in relationships between different age-groups.

Along with the rest of Europe, Britain will soon have to cope with some drastic changes in the age distribution of its population. Over the next thirty years, the average age will increase considerably. By the year 2025 the number of pensioners is predicted by a European Commission report to rise by 43 per cent. Meanwhile the working population is set to decline by nearly 3 per cent. The number of young people under twenty will also fall, by 8 per cent. Additionally, along with that in many other European countries (France, the Netherlands, Denmark), Britain's fertility rate has fallen over the past twenty-five years, so that now it is not sufficient to maintain the current level of population (in the EU as a whole immigration of seven million people a year will be necessary to retain current levels).

The changes expressed in these figures will have profound implications. At the simplest level, when a declining workforce has to support more people it can easily lead to inter-generational tensions. Also, as the proportion of people in retirement grows, the strain on state social and health services grows. The effect of these additional expenses will be to lower people's spending power, which will in turn threaten industries which produce or sell goods. The decline in the numbers of young people may also significantly disrupt the housing market which depends on new entrants at the bottom to enable others to move up. Such changes and their likely implications will probably add to the importance attached to youth and its conduct.

It could perhaps be argued that in earlier epochs of British history less emphasis was placed upon youth as a time of crisis because there was less legislation governed by age, and hence fewer official turning points or transitions in a person's life. Age, in other words, is a component of identity which is very much tied to cultural factors such as the education system, health, or marriage practices. This is probably most acutely exemplified by British attitudes towards children in the nineteenth century: the Victorian era was a time of great sentimentality and also great cruelty towards children, when the infant mortality rate was much higher than now, and when mass poverty meant that children had to 'earn their keep' in working-class families.

In this chapter, while other aspects of age in Britain will be touched upon, the focus will be on late childhood, adolescence, and youth culture, because it is in these fast-changing periods of life that British people absorb and challenge accepted cultural identities. It is also here that the direction of present and future British identities can be apprehended, as a range of new ideas and beliefs are added to those associated with the traditional social values attaching to work, class, and the family: the staple ingredients sustaining cultural identity for older British citizens.

Youth, teenagers, and adolescents

At first glance, the terms 'adolescent', 'teenager', and 'youth' seem to mean exactly the same thing: they all refer to young people who are not children, and yet who are also not quite adults. However, there is also a sense in which these words suggest different forms of identity, different groupings of the British population. For example, 'youth' is generally used to refer to young people operating in the public sphere, as part of a social group, and most typically it is associated with boys rather than girls. We talk about 'youth clubs', 'youth training schemes', 'youth unemployment', and of course 'youth culture'. 'Adolescence', on the other hand, is a term which is more likely to be used in connection with an individual's identity – to refer to a private, psychic realm of experience, as in such common expressions as 'adolescent angst', 'adolescent diary', or 'adolescent crisis'. The term 'teenager' first emerged in the 1950s when young people were newly identified as a distinct group of consumers, and since then it has typically been associated with certain kinds of products or markets: for example 'teenage fashion', 'teenage magazines', and 'teen pop idols'. With respect to gender, we should note that the expressions 'teenage pregnancy' and 'gang of youths' suggest that 'teenage' is feminine and 'youth' is masculine. More recently, the term 'tweenager' has been coined to describe eleven, and twelve-year-olds who aspire to the lifestyle of their older siblings, and

nowadays have the pocket money to do so. While they shop for the
fashions aimed at teenagers, another term, 'kidult', has arisen to describe
adults who dress in the style of children. Both terms are predominantly
applied to females rather than males, and there is also concern expressed
about the way even younger children adopt adult habits too early, with
six-year-olds attending make-up parties and seven-year-olds wearing crop
tops and fake tattoos. Fashion is clearly no longer restricted by any age
limits, with pre-teens shopping for themselves at Gap, Tammy Girl,
Children's Next, and Miss Selfridge, their tastes dictated by pop bands such
as Hear'Say and Destiny's Child as well as magazines such as *Girl Talk*
and *Go Girl*.

The three fundamental natural events – birth, procreation, and death
– offer the most succinct summary of the human life cycle. However
universal these events may be, though, there are inevitably massive differences in the ways that they are experienced by people from one culture or
community to the next. In the contemporary context of Western capitalist
societies, patterns and levels of 'consumption' best illustrate some of these
differences. Whenever statistics are sought on the details of people's lives
(to answer the question 'How do people live?'), the most plentiful and
perhaps scrupulous sources of information are provided by market
research. In other words, the way in which money is spent and the kinds
of things that people choose to buy tell us quite a lot about the identities
of British people, and cultural formation is partly reflected in modes of
consumption. The British may not be a 'nation of shopkeepers', but, as a
capitalist nation, 'we are what we buy'.

In order to gauge how age shapes patterns of behaviour, it is important to read between the lines of facts and reports which detail how people
spend their money and their time at different stages of their lives. The term
'lifestyle' itself seems to have become inextricably linked to the notion
of choices over spending. The phrases 'lifestyle politics', or 'lifestyle magazines' therefore tend to be used (often derogatively) to refer to middle-class
preoccupations with 'consumer choice', and Britain today, where the
phrase 'everyone is middle-class now' is increasingly common if still inac-
curate, seems to be characterised as a 'consumer culture'. In this context,
the typical British teenager is viewed as the consumer 'par excellence', and
is seen by some, often older commentators, as a 'fashion victim' driven by
larger forces than personal expression. But others see the teenager as a
supple negotiator of the minefields both of contemporary style trends and
of technology. Knowing the price of a 'Big Mac' from McDonald's is sometimes the limit of an older person's familiarity with youth culture, which
is more often about empowerment than victimisation.

Famously, the 'teenager' is considered to have been an invention or
symptom of shifting consumer markets in the 1950s, both in Europe and

in North America. Many studies of British youth that have been carried out since then have focused, in one way or another, upon the way young people characterise themselves through the clothes they wear, the music they listen to, the films they watch, and the places they go to. When Richard Hoggart wrote (rather apocalyptically) about the state of the nation's youth in his well-known book *The Uses of Literacy* (1957), he summoned up an image of the British teenager being almost literally consumed by a 'Mass Culture' which in turn was linked to the saturating effects of 'Americanisation'.

More recently, social commentators have argued that it is precisely through their role as consumers of popular culture that British young people express themselves most powerfully and creatively, not least because they feel excluded by the more traditional realms of the arts. There is a widening gap between the officially sanctioned practices of 'high art' and the forms of self-expression and creativity that young people choose to explore in their everyday lives. An acute example of this is young people's use of graffiti in the UK, an art form initially borrowed from the inner-city subcultures of black Americans. From the mid-1980s onwards, complex, brightly coloured designs produced with spray-paints became a common sight on 'spare' bits of wall in many towns and cities, especially along railway tracks and under motorway bridges. Typically, these motifs would be based around a single word, name, or phrase, with obscure connotations, and an important element of the appeal of graffiti within British youth culture is that you have to know *how* to read its messages, and above all to recognise the 'signature' of the artist. For many young people, the explicit association between British graffiti and urban America seems to imbue this art form with the power to 'glamorise' mundane environments such as housing estates or shopping malls – to make these spaces both more exotic and more hard-edged. Perhaps this accounts, then, for the particular prominence of the graffiti scene in new towns such as Crawley, just south of London, where (generally) white working-class youths became minor celebrities and where police would regularly search teenagers for incriminating spray cans.

In the following sections, we will focus on the way that British young people spend their money and their time, both when 'going out' and when 'staying in'.

Going out: 'dressing up and dressing down'

It may seem a bit too easy to characterise British youth cultures in terms of fashion styles. Nevertheless, dress codes are obviously crucial keys to understanding how the lines are drawn between different identities in

Britain. After all, the way that we dress can serve either to confirm or to subvert various facets of our identities, such as our gender, race, class, and age. Clothes also reflect our perceptions of the historical epoch in which we live – how we relate to the cultural mood of the day. The postmodern preoccupations of the last decades of the twentieth century, for example, are linked to nostalgia, pastiche and what might be better described as kinds of 'fusion' or as cultural hybridity (mixing different styles of fashion, music, or anything else). Contemporary fashions conspicuously play upon these cultural themes, and styles from every previous decade have re-surfaced to evoke the spirit (or *Zeitgeist*) of contemporary Britain. 'Now' is in many ways a recycling of previous *Zeitgeists*.

One way of thinking about different subcultural groupings within young British fashion is in terms of class identities. Subcultures such as punks, hippies, crusties, bikers, and goths have tended – in one way or another – to challenge the traditional values of smart and respectable dress. On the other hand, mods, soul boys (and girls), teds, skinheads, and home-boys have usually emphasised a 'sharper' style of dress, though of course in diverse ways. This opposition between 'smart' and 'scruffy' clothes bears some relation to class allegiances in so far as dress codes which place greater value on clothes 'looking new' are more often adopted by working-class young people, while scruffier 'bohemian' styles are more likely to have middle-class wearers. But often, subcultural styles of dress confront and confound mainstream expectations about people's position in the social structure, especially in the cities.

The above is too simplistic a formula to apply to all UK youth subcul-tures, especially as these styles in themselves are not necessarily mutually exclusive, and most young people, in any case, are likely to draw on a range of possible influences. The enormous increase in the student population, for instance, is bound to affect the class delineations of subcultural style, as many more working-class young people enter a terrain which had previ-ously been a middle-class preserve.

As Dick Hebdige points out in his book *Subculture: The Meaning of Style*, black subcultures have been a central factor in the formation of many white working-class subcultural styles such as that of mods (short for moderns). Both Afro-Caribbean and Afro-American influences have been critical in shaping British youth culture since the 1950s, not least because more and more young people in Britain are growing up in multi ethnic, cross-cultural environments. In the late 1970s and 1980s, the Afro-Caribbean Rastafarian style influenced both black and white youth subcultural fashion, with red, green, and gold Ethiopian colours commonly featuring on T-shirts, hats, badges, and jackets. Today, more than ever, black subcultural styles tend to lead the way in British street fashion, espe-cially those derived from the Afro-American Rap scene: the 'home-boy' look of very baggy jeans, big hooded jackets, and baseball caps is almost ubiquitous among teenage boys, especially the under sixteens. 'Clubwear' styles (for example tight lycra, shiny fabrics and bright colours) also seem to be influenced strongly by black street fashions. Perhaps most significantly, Asian youth culture in Britain seems to draw very much on Afro-American and Afro-Caribbean subcultural styles (as in the music of Apache Indian). The influence of the European club scene has also affected British styles, as clubs in the UK often try to recreate the atmosphere of Ibiza or Ayia Napa, and the ambient sounds of European bands such as Air (amid the eclectic Anglophone Euro sounds of, say, Aqua, Daft Punk, and Kings of Convenience) have eroded the deep-seated British aversion to pop music from the Continent, previously denigrated as 'Europop' (the title of a parodic song by the Divine Comedy). Identifications and cultural allegiances in Britain are now much more complex, in other words, than is suggested by traditional models of assimilation.

When considering what people wear, we need also to think about where they go, as the two are usually connected. In 1994, 34 per cent of adults in Britain visited a pub at least once a week. However, for young

FIGURE 4.1 Black London punk

FIGURE 4.2   Female London punk

people between the ages of eighteen and twenty-four, the figure was much higher at 64 per cent. So, it is perhaps not surprising that UK pubs seem to be becoming more overtly geared towards a youth clientele, as increasing numbers of them, and particularly pub chains, introduce competitions, quizzes, and games areas. Nevertheless, pubs still have a unique status in British culture as places where people of different ages and, to a lesser extent, different classes, are likely to socialise together, particularly with the introduction of sports screens to show live football matches. British soap operas such as *Coronation Street* and *EastEnders* have long played on the pub's function as a place where lots of different kinds of people could plausibly meet up. This, in turn, has led to complaints from television monitoring groups that soap operas might encourage viewers to drink more alcohol, because characters are so often portrayed having a drink in their 'local'.

Since the 1990s, it has been argued, clubs rather than pubs are the focus of many young people's social lives. The growth of the 'rave' scene in Britain (which began with 'Acid House' parties in the late 1980s) has meant that dancing has again become a central activity, as it had been in the 'dance halls' of the 1950s and early 1960s, and the discos of the 1970s. In contrast to these earlier dance scenes, though, alcohol has tended to be a peripheral element of contemporary UK dance culture. Instead, rave puts much more emphasis on taking drugs such as Ecstasy, the effects of which tend to be cancelled out by alcohol. People dancing constantly for several hours are more likely to drink fluids, especially bottled water, to avoid dehydration and to restore energy levels, which no doubt accounts for the cultish popularity of the soft drink Lucozade in the rave scene. Traditional drinks have also re-marketed themselves to appeal to a new generation, and so the latest Lucozade adverts are cartoons featuring Lara Croft (a far cry from the medicinal advertising in the 1970s that simply stressed 'Lucozade aids recovery'). Lucozade now also comes in a variety of types for different lifestyles: Lucozade Energy, Lucozade Sport, Lucozade Low Calorie and Lucozade Solstis.

At the outset, a key element in the appeal of raves was their illegality: events where thousands of people would come together were often publicised by enigmatic flyers, and by messages transmitted on pirate radio stations such as Kiss. The countercultural status of raves could be compared to 'blues parties' or 'shebeens', which became particularly popular in Afro-Caribbean communities in the 1980s. Like raves, these parties blurred the boundaries between private gatherings and public events in so far as they tended to be held in 'unofficial' or even squatted venues, with entrance by informally sold tickets or invitations. Like raves, blues parties were associated both with a specific type of music (reggae and ragga), played through enormous sound systems, and with drugs (cannabis) more than with alcohol – though cans of beer or other alcohol would usually be sold or included in the entrance price.

Significantly, though, raves were one of the key targets of the Criminal Justice Act (1994), and this no doubt partly accounts for the decrease in their popularity now, their place increasingly being taken by big ('legitimate') clubs such as Cream and The Ministry of Sound. More than anything, however, these shifts in the popularity of different venues reflect the fast-moving, changeable nature of British youth culture: new scenes or styles quickly transmute from 'subculture' to 'mainstream' trends, and with equal rapidity they also fade from favour or disappear altogether. This ebb and flow in subcultural activity informs most young people's cultural identities in one way or another, but this is by no means to suggest that everybody's lives follow the same patterns. For instance, even though clubs and parties might well represent a central (and glamorous) social activity in 1990s Britain, many young people on a 'night out' will still often 'start the proceedings' by visiting a pub. The more traditional activity of 'pub crawls' – on which lots of different pubs are visited in one evening – also persists in Britain, particularly among students, and groups of 'laddish young men' (such as the members of a rugby team or the groom and his mates on a 'stag' party).

Since the 1980s, traditional features of pubs such as bar billiards have often been superseded by CD or video juke boxes, and wide-screen televisions tuned to MTV, or Sky Sport. And yet, whether or not loud music is played in pubs, most of them still retain the same function, especially in the countryside where pubs are not vying for clientele in the way they are in the cities. The pub remains *the* primary leisure institution for white British culture but is generally much less popular among Afro-Caribbeans and Asians. It could be argued that pubs are bound up with British ideas of 'rites of passage', in so far as a young person's 'first legal drink in a pub' is often treated as a landmark. Growing concern about under-age drinking has meant that more attention is paid to young pub customers providing proof that they are over eighteen, and the major companies that run pubs have introduced their own ID cards. It is perhaps not surprising therefore that, since the late 1970s, increased emphasis has been put on eighteenth birthday celebrations, rather than twenty-first birthdays.

In large cities, especially northern ones such as Liverpool, Manchester, or Newcastle, there is a whole ritual which revolves around 'going out on the town' on Friday and Saturday nights. Long queues form as hundreds of people gather around the pubs, clubs, and wine bars – young women often dressed extremely glamorously in thin-strapped, backless evening dresses, gauzy tunics, or very short skirts, and young men in more casual (but nevertheless immaculate) shirts and trousers. In the context of 'a night out on the town', the stereotype of the British love of queuing acquires another significance. The more popular clubs, for instance, sometimes hire 'queue spotters' who look out for particularly stylishly dressed 'punters' – the best dressed may well be allowed to go to the front of the queue, while those guilty of certain 'fashion crimes' (for example wearing white socks or the 'wrong' kind of shoes) may not be allowed in at all. Like the film lines curling around corners in the heyday of cinema going, these queues of clubbers function as a kind of social scene, a place to meet your friends, to flirt, or to compete with your peers. Young people also might end their evening in another queue, waiting to buy chips or a kebab, or standing in line for a taxi.

This kind of weekend spectacle is not often regarded as being part of any specific subculture, apart from what might be broadly described as 'clubbing', and yet it is still governed by a distinct set of codes – for example, in many cities, Friday night is girls' and boys' night out but Saturday night is for couples. One of the most striking aspects of these weekly events is the disregard most of the young people appear to have for the weather – the rule seems to be that jackets or coats are not worn even

FIGURE 4.3 Haçienda clubbers: now closed, the Haçienda in Manchester, alongside Cream in Liverpool, and Heaven in London, was one of the foremost night-clubs on the dance and rave scene (© S.I.N./CORBIS)

on freezing winter nights (this is also a question of money as it is a luxury to buy an impressive coat or jacket which will only be 'checked', hung away, at the club). Perhaps most noticeable, though, is the fact that men and women tend to go out not with boyfriends or girlfriends, but with their 'mates' of the same sex. For women especially, this seems to be an important element in the way they choose to dress – the flamboyance and overtly sexual nature of the outfits that many young women wear are apparently in some way legitimated by the fact that they are dressing up 'for fun', rather than explicitly to attract men. Indeed, it is often said that women on these occasions are 'dressing up' for other women, that an integral part of the ritual is be identified as part of a female subculture and to gain the approval of other members of that social group. None of these so-called 'rules' or codes of dress is clear-cut, however.

Staying in: young people and the media

On average, people in Britain spend four hours watching the television or video every day, which is more than in any other European country. These days, after talking about the weather, it is accurate to say that television programmes provide a favourite topic of conversation for British people (according to market research, 46 per cent of the population discuss television programmes with their friends or family). In many ways, television now seems to be at the hub of 'the British way of life', offering a structure and rhythm around which people may shape their leisure time. Nowadays, the success or otherwise of major national holidays such as Christmas and Easter is far less likely to be talked about in terms of the quality of church services, than the quality of programmes on television. Now, in fact, there is a mood of nostalgia about the 'good old days' of family viewing on television, especially in connection with Christmas, and weekend nights are crammed with 'Top Ten' shows and compilation programmes about the 1970s and 1980s. In the 1950s through to the 1970s, there was actually a regular programme broadcast from a theatre in Leeds called *The Good Old Days* which simulated a night out at the music hall in Edwardian England (complete with audiences in fancy-dress Edwardian clothes, singing along with the performers). Today, equivalent viewing slots are more likely to show archive footage of old television shows, and now there are several satellite television stations such as UK Gold which are entirely devoted to re-runs of 'classic' British programmes. So, whereas thirty years ago older people might sentimentally reminisce about 'happier' times when the family would make their own entertainment – singing songs around the piano or playing charades people these days are more likely nostalgically to recall 'the golden age of television' during the late 1960s and early 1970s – a time when adults and children could supposedly sit together to watch favourite programmes (such as *The Morecambe and Wise Show*, *Dr Who*, or *The Generation Game*), comfortable in the knowledge that it would all be 'good clean fun'.

A traditional British Christmas has been characterised (or caricatured) through images of the family, ranging across three generations, sitting in front of the television after Christmas dinner, watching the Queen's Speech at 3 pm and then a re-run of a film such as *The Sound of Music* or *The Wizard of Oz*. It is important not to underestimate the status of these televisual myths in relation to the attitudes British people themselves express about national identity, and as a corollary of this, it is often the case that anxieties about social decline are most readily articulated in terms of 'falling standards' and 'dumbing down' on television. The concept of 'family viewing' is a central stake in debates about the role of the BBC, a public-owned institution known to the country as 'auntie' (suggesting its cosy, nanny-like persona – one programme which shows out-takes from BBC television series is called *Auntie's Bloomers*). In an attempt to recapture the 'all-round' entertainment of twenty or thirty years ago, the BBC now has nostalgic television shows such as *The New Generation Game* and panel shows such as *A Question of TV* or *It's Only TV, but I Like It* which celebrate celebrities' knowledge of television's 'good old days'.

Young people nowadays watch more television than preceding generations. However, as far as television programmers and advertisers are concerned, 'youth audiences' are potentially the most elusive segment of the population in Britain, for, although television may play an influential role in the identities of British young people, they generally spend less time watching television than people over twenty-five or under twelve (that the older generation are expected to stay in explains the prevalence of nostalgia shows on Saturday nights). British youth, implicitly, are less likely than any other section of the population to be seen as inhabitants of the domestic environment. In response to this, there has been a growing movement towards 'youth television' in Britain, which aims to 'catch' young people either before or after they go out socialising. Youth television was famously pioneered in the 1980s by the Cockney television producer Janet Street Porter and sometimes satirically referred to as 'Yoof television'. The kinds of programme that fall into this category tend to have a fast-moving magazine format with young, fashionably dressed presenters, often speaking in 'non-standard' English. A peak-time viewing programme such as *Blind Date* also targets a youth audience, not least because it is shown on Saturdays, fairly early in the evening so that people can watch before they go out 'on the town' (to increase the programme's cross-generational appeal, it also occasionally sends middle-aged or older people on 'blind dates').

Other television programmes which seek to reflect youth lifestyles, such as *Around the World in 80 Raves*, *Banzai*, *Euro-trash*, *Bondi Dreams*, *Temptation Island*, *So Graham Norton*, and repeat showings of *Top of the Pops*, are broadcast later at night, working on the assumption that they will be watched by young people returning from a night out. Another way of interpreting 'youth television', though, is to argue that it is watched in a different way: less as a central activity than as a backdrop – more akin, say, to having the radio turned on than watching a film at the cinema. This is reflected in the success of reality television shows in the new century, especially those that can also be 'watched' on the internet twenty-four hours a day, such as *Big Brother*. The rise in reality television (*Castaway*, *Human Zoo*, *Survivor*, *The 1900 House*) has been perceived in numerous ways, from 'dumbing down' to the fulfilment of Andy Warhol's prediction that 'in the future everyone will be famous for fifteen minutes', but its main effect has been to place 'ordinary' people, rather than actors or celebrities, on television, and so to encourage young viewers (participants are rarely over thirty-five) to make assessments of themselves and their peers in relation to a set of 'real personalities' they might themselves easily know or even be. Students are also notoriously likely to celebrate kitsch shows broadcast during the day, and will make an afternoon programme such as *Watercolour Challenge*, in which three contestants leisurely paint the same landscape, regular viewing. The late afternoon schedules are also currently stocked with innumerable quiz shows, such as *Fifteen-to-One*, *Countdown*, and *The Weakest Link*, which can appeal to anyone wishing to unwind from the day, and arguably reflect the traditional British love of games.

However, whereas youth television seems to anticipate (or fantasise about) an audience which is caught up with the demands of a hectic social life, other activities such as computer games (which now generate more profits than films), reading, or listening to music suggest a more solitary vision of the teenager at home. Uncommunicative teenagers playing with their Gameboys or listening to their Walkmans acutely exemplify this. The 1990s saw the emergence of a whole new range of concerns about the state of the nation's youth which focused upon the dangers of children and adolescents inhabiting private fantasy worlds, accessed through computers. Jokes and anecdotes are commonplace about the technology 'generation gap', whereby children are deemed to be more adept than their parents at operating machines such as videos and computers (many television advertisements play on this discrepancy). However, the internet has rendered such jokes a little more sinister, in that they suggest a loss of parental control. Above all, fears seem to centre upon the fact that the internet enables children to communicate not only with other children but also with adults, without supervision. The much-publicised emergence of chatrooms, as well as pornographic and paedophilic 'pages' on the World Wide Web, has created a mood of pessimism about what might otherwise have been greeted more optimistically as a communication system which encourages the breakdown of many traditional boundaries, including those between different ages and generations. In terms of computer games, since the early 1990s 'shoot-'em-ups' such as *Quake* and *Duke Nukem* have acquired a cultish popularity, particularly with teenage boys. Unlike surfing the internet, playing these games involves no human communication, and so is an activity which seems to provoke different anxieties in some adults because it is deemed to be anti-social and introspective, plunging the player into a fantasy world.

Aesthetically and thematically, computer games have a close relationship to comics and magazines. Since the mid-1980s, comics – especially 'graphic novels' – have spawned a whole subcultural scene, and most British towns now have a specialist comics shop (Forbidden Planet, for instance, is a nationwide chain of shops). Virgin Megastores, which principally serve as music outlets, also sell comics and magazines aimed at this cultish readership, thus suggesting further subcultural cross-overs between computer games, music, movies, and comics. However, when people in Britain talk about 'teenage magazines', they are most likely to be referring to publications aimed at girls – for example magazines such as *Just 17, 19, Sugar*, and *Looks*. This is significant in that adolescent femininity in the UK tends to be associated – more than any other aspect of youth culture – with stereotypical consumerism. While things have definitely moved on since the days when British teenage girls were represented almost solely in terms of 'teenybopper' culture – screaming at popstars, or gazing at posters on their bedroom walls it is still the case that young women are more explicitly identified as a 'market', even one enfranchised with 'girlpower', rather than as a series of subcultures. Surveys about how much money is spent on clothing and footwear in the UK actually tell a very different story. For instance, around 6 per cent more money is spent on clothes and shoes by young men over fifteen than by young women in the same age group. The point to make here, perhaps, is that the cultural activities of British young women are interpreted less positively, in that women are more likely to be stereotyped as passive consumers (of clothes and popstars) than as creative participants in a subcultural scene.

Many parents tend to expect their children to buy and enjoy the same magazines as they did (though none of the most popular five magazines read by men, for example, is the same in 2000, headed by *FHM*, as it was in 1980). Shifts, as with music and youth fashion styles, are almost always perceived negatively by older generations. In the 1970s, *Jackie* was by far the highest selling magazine for teenage girls, selling an average of 605,947 copies per week in 1976. More recently, this pole position has been taken up by *Just 17*, which had a readership of 941,000 in 1994, selling primarily to the under-seventeens, to whom the magazine is now *J17*. Comparing the content of *Jackie* in the 1970s with *Just 17* creates some sense of the kinds of changes which have taken place in the lives of British teenage girls over the last twenty years. The most notable, and perhaps optimistic, difference is that teenage girls today seem to be far less exclusively associated with a private, domestic space (the adolescent girl, in her bedroom, dreaming about love). *Jackie* by and large used to be concerned with 'romance', whereas contemporary teenage girls' magazines focus much more on actual, often sexual, relationships (most are dominated by their 'problem pages' where readers' questions are answered). The magazines use the same terminology that their readership does, considering attractive girls 'honeys', boys 'hotties', and a whole raft of phrases meaning *fashionable*: 'heavy', 'mint', 'hectic', 'phat', 'quality', 'rinsin'. Far more attention is also now paid to music and fashion, which can be interpreted in a number of ways. These preoccupations would seem to confirm the idea that the British adolescent girl's identity is almost wholly shaped by her status as a consumer. However, it could also be argued that these features imply that young women now participate more actively in the public domain – they are no longer 'stuck in their bedrooms'. Above all, perhaps, the images of British young women offered by contemporary teenage magazines suggest cultural identities which are far from straightforward in so far as they often negotiate conflicting concerns between sexual relationships and autonomy.

In 1996, two new television programmes, *Pyjama Party* and *The Girlie Show*, appeared under the auspices of late-night youth television. These shows were supposedly an attempt to counter the 'laddishness' of many 1990s television shows aimed at young adult audiences. However, with their emphasis on sexual outrage, such programmes offer a vision of young women in Britain which is a far cry from the 'cropped hair and dungarees' of 1980s feminism. Features such 'wanker of the week', where the behaviour towards women of one well-known male personality is 'exposed', or a section of the show where women audience members offer up their boyfriend's soiled underpants for public scrutiny, suggest a vogue for countering and parodying traditional 'girlie' gossip and confession. Though such shows are less common in 2001, their features have been incorporated into other programmes rather than rejected, indicating the extent to which some of their assertive approaches have become mainstream. Today, there is some concern over 'ladette' louts, once epitomised by brash television personalities such as Denise van Outen and Zoe Ball (now married to Fatboy Slim), whose hedonistic lifestyle is driven by increasing levels of financial independence. The consequence is that some hotels and restaurants refuse to accept bookings from all-female parties, where once they would have thought twice about all-male groups. Some pubs now ban 'hen' parties and, reportedly, holiday companies claim that Britain's new wave of ladettes, young women with a love of binge drinking and brazen behaviour, are exceeding the antics of male 'yobs' in terms of noise, abuse, and violence. Another recent cultural phenomenon is 'excessorexia': supposedly, because of the aspirational character of life in the twenty-first century, one person in five in Britain is thought to be obsessed with wanting more than they already have. A phenomenon which may be related is the 'Quarter life' crisis, a tendency for young fast-living urban professionals to suffer a mid-life crisis twenty years too soon.

Overall, the crucial point to make about youth culture is its speed of change and its difference from more mainstream representations of British identity, whether those of children at school or adults at work. Youth identities are more commonly associated with pleasure and leisure, but they are crossed by other crucial factors in cultural positioning discussed in this book: gender, ethnicity, region, and class.

Sex and drugs and rock'n'roll

It is both clichéd and true to say that the lives of young people in the UK in the postwar era have been characterised on the basis of the rather unholy trinity of 'sex and drugs and rock'n'roll'. This concluding section will therefore focus on these three aspects because they are associated more closely and apprehensively with British youth culture than any others.

Although the poet Philip Larkin suggested that 'Sex began in 1963 . . .', anxieties about the sexual mores of the younger generation certainly preceded the so-called sexual revolution of the 1960s. Nevertheless, sex is undoubtedly a realm of contemporary British life where the mythical 'generation gap' is felt particularly keenly, and this is no doubt exacerbated by a perceived difference between what is sexually common now and what was acceptable forty years ago. Nostalgia is now expressed with peculiar intensity in relation to notions of childhood innocence, whereby today's children and teenagers are regarded both as more vulnerable and as more sexually 'knowing'.

Whereas a hundred years ago, fears were rife about the social dangers of adolescent masturbation, since the 1970s the key areas of concern surrounding British young people have been the role of sex education, the availability of contraception, HIV, teenage pregnancy, sexual abuse, and homosexuality. In Britain's increasingly secular climate on the other hand, the issue of 'sex before marriage' or cohabitation is no longer hotly contested, and 70 per cent of women now cohabit before marriage.

More than anything, carnal knowledge seems to be the central stake in debates about young people's sexuality. Since the 1980s, for instance, UK campaigns and initiatives such as Childline and Kidscape have increased public awareness of childhood sexual abuse. The fact that these issues are now more openly discussed has sometimes been taken as an indication that the British nation is being overwhelmed by an epidemic of paedophilia. However, this is not the case, and it is probably much more accurate to say that British people are now less inclined to draw a veil of silence over these kinds of problems. Social Services policy, as well as the less official influences of magazine problem pages and television shows such as *That's Life* (in which Esther Rantzen launched Childline) have been key factors in bringing about this shift. Changing attitudes towards child sexual abuse in the United States have also been extremely influential in the UK, especially with the increasing popularity here of American talk shows, such as *Oprah*.

Until the 1980s, the general perception in Britain had been that sex would inevitably be subject to fewer and fewer restrictions for each subsequent generation. However, concern over HIV and Aids has obviously put paid to this vision of an unstoppable machine of sexual liberation, and this has been compounded by wider knowledge about sexually transmitted infections such as chlamydia, which by 2010 may affect one in five women between the ages of sixteen and twenty-four and, if untreated, can cause infertility. It could even be argued that many young people today have more restricted sex lives than their parents had as teenagers. It may be the case that British young people have less sex with fewer partners than teenagers did in the 1970s and early 1980s, the heyday of the contraceptive pill.

Certainly there are more fears about sex, and unwanted pregnancy no longer necessarily represents the worst possible scenario for sexually active teenagers. Campaigns to educate people about 'safer sex' have meant an increased openness about referring to sexual practices which fall outside the scope of 'straight sex' (for example, dressing up or using 'sex toys'), and the idea of conventional sex as being the only kind has ceased to dominate.

Glossy media representations of sex are far more likely nowadays to play on fetishistic imagery, and, where earlier advertising used to appeal to men almost exclusively along the lines of 'buy the car, get the girl', marketing often now seeks to associate products with erotic experimentation. As if, perhaps, to distract attention away from the fact that sex is now more circumscribed by risks, contemporary British youth culture seems to place a premium upon the idea of imaginative sexual practices, and is perhaps less ready to equate 'experience' (that is of penetrative sex) with sexual pleasure and knowledge. Teenage magazines such as *Just 17* are littered with slogans such as 'to be sussed is a must', and most young people in Britain over the age of eleven (and often younger) now know what a condom is. Since the late 1980s, numerous youth projects have been set up in Britain to educate young people about safe sex, workers often distributing free condoms as well as leaflets. 'Condom buses' have even been enlisted in the service of health education, a phenomenon which plays on the mythically clean-cut images of British teenagers 'having fun on buses' featured in the early 1960s film *Summer Holiday*, and the children's television series *The Double Deckers*.

Sex, for British young people today, is double-edged. Talking about sex, listening to other people talking about sex, reading about sex, and even watching sex on the television or video has become progressively easier. In a sense though, actually having sex is becoming more complicated, not least for teenagers. In 1996, controversy erupted about the content of magazines aimed at teenage girls in the UK after a Tory backbench MP, Peter Luff, made an unsuccessful attempt to introduce a 'Periodical Protection Bill'. Luff's main objection to magazines such as *Just 17*, *TV Hits*, and *Bliss* was that they encourage young girls to be obsessed with sex because they deal with sexual issues too explicitly. What is most telling about the debates which surrounded Luff's crusade is the polarisation of the arguments. For some people, childhood is in danger of becoming entirely eroded, while for others young people can never know too much.

Drugs are another area of life where the 'generation gap' appears to be wide. In postwar Britain, youth subcultures have always been associated with the use of particular (usually illegal) drugs: mods with amphetamines ('speed'), hippies with cannabis ('dope', 'pot', 'blow', etc.) and LSD ('acid'), ravers and clubbers with Ecstasy. Today though, drug use has become fairly mainstream among the UK youth population, and it is estimated that more than 50 per cent of young people will have tried at least one illegal drug by the time they are eighteen (while more than half of all students say they are regular users of cannabis, according to the Office of National statistics in 2001, 30 per cent of all fifteen-year-olds in England have tried the drug). The drugs scene has now been characterised, rather ambiguously, as being about 'recreational drug use', rather than as a small alienated enclave of drug addicts, as in the past. This is a shift indicated by the increasing calls to legalise soft drugs, at least: a wave of pressure which resulted in the experiment in 2001 of police being officially told in Lambeth, which includes Brixton, to turn a blind eye to cannabis use, effectively decriminalising the drug for the first time. An ICM poll at the same time showed that 65 per cent of people in Britain think that prosecution for cannabis possession should be the police's lowest priority (yet, in 2000, 97,000 people were prosecuted for precisely that offence). Cannabis has most recently been associated with the latest strand of club culture, Chill Out, where rooms are set aside for clubbers who want to relax on sofas and scatter cushions watching cool images on large screens and listening to ambient sounds, by bands such as Groove Armada and Zero 7. Especially since Thatcher's generation of children – born between 1979 and 1990 – are now aged between about twelve and twenty-three, an apolitical consumerism appears to have taken hold of British youth for an earlier generation raised on CND marches and anti-Vietnam protests, hippie love-ins followed by punk rock anarchism (on a recent Radio 4 programme, the gathered audience voted overwhelmingly that it was 'Better to have been young in the 1960s than the 1990s'). However, the young in Britain seem yet again to fulfil their role as 'sophisticated' consumers who make discriminating choices from, in this case, a whole menu of intoxicating substances. In his book *Street Drugs*, for instance, Andrew Tyler argues that 'value for money' influences the decisions young people make about using drugs: 'They will judge a pint [of beer] against, say, the psychoactive clout of a £2 LSD blotter.' This may account for the fact that, while overall alcohol consumption rose by more than 30 per cent between 1961 and 1991, pub and club sales of beer have dropped by more than a quarter since 1979. Drinks with a relatively high alcohol content, including alcoholic lemonades such as Hooch, and fruit cocktails such as 20/20 seem to be aimed, by and large, at a youth market which appears to prioritise both 'cheapness' and 'coolness' and a guaranteed 'high'. In the twenty-first century, the high-energy fizz drink has become the staple beverage alongside bottled water, but with the added attraction that drinks such as Red Bull serve as mixers for vodka, which has become the trendy spirit, as witnessed by the high number of vodka bars, with names such as Revolution, that have sprung up in British cities.

Set against this image of British youth as adept 'recreational' users of drugs are the media portrayals of young people either as hapless victims or as crazed addicts. Such representations do not offer an accurate overall perspective. In the 1980s, there was a huge increase in heroin (or 'skag') use among British working-class youth, especially in urban areas, and this 'skag' culture was often the target of sensationalist news stories. Heroin was, somewhat exaggeratedly, rumoured to be as easy to get hold of as tobacco in some cities, and was undoubtedly a major cause of rising property crime. Although there has been no drastic change in the numbers of people using heroin in the UK since the 1980s, media attention has almost completely shifted towards other drugs. In the early 1990s, concern was focused upon the possibility of a cocaine ('crack') epidemic, and numerous stories were run in the press and on television about crack-related crime in the United States. However, while crack has become more common in Britain, particularly in inner-city areas, the spotlight has shifted once again: Ecstasy (which first appeared on the British drugs scene in 1988) prompted a number of media-led moral panics in the mid-1990s, based around the widely publicised deaths of teenagers using the drug (the most notable case being Leah Betts's death in 1995 on her eighteenth birthday). Though fewer than sixty people died in Britain from Ecstasy use between 1988 and 1996 (that is less than 1 per cent of alcohol-related deaths of young people), national publicity has focused on this drug in particular (even though, in 2000, 20 per cent of pupils excluded from schools were suspended for drinking alcohol on the premises and one in four deaths of young men aged between fifteen and twenty-nine is alcohol-related). One of the most commonly expressed concerns is that British parents no longer 'know what their children are doing', and the relative novelty of Ecstasy seemed to exacerbate older people's sense of estrangement. However commonplace drugs may be, within the social lives of many young people in Britain they are seen as both alien and threatening to much of the British population over forty, even those who were teenagers in the 1960s.

Most British youth subcultures have been aligned, at some stage, with a particular type of music. Consequently, as delineations, cross-overs and fusions between different styles of pop music have become ever more complicated, so too have the criteria distinguishing one subcultural scene from another. Rock'n'roll music certainly no longer is (if it ever was) a single unifying symbol of youth rebellion. At one level, it is almost as if British pop music has become so diverse that the differences between music scenes now seem to be blurred and indistinct. The 'tribalism' of the 1960s and 1970s, whereby musical taste was often inextricably bound to much broader allegiances, seems to be fading in the 2000s. Music nevertheless still plays a critical part in the construction of identities for British youth, but in more fluid ways. In 1978, British fifteen-year-olds may well have used musical taste as a means of declaring themselves to be punks or mods. Today, fifteen-year-olds are probably more likely to say that they like 'a bit of jungle, house, techno or garage' than to use music to ascribe a specific subcultural identity to themselves, and the proliferation of music styles, giving rise to new forms such as Ghetto tech and Colombian drum'n'bass, means that musical fashions are changing more quickly than in the past. The phenomenon of Britpop in the mid-1990s is a good example of this historical shift in the constituency of youth subcultures in so far as bands such as Oasis, Pulp, and Blur were not closely linked to a fixed subcultural identity, despite their associations with 'mod' style. This contrasts with bands of the late 1970s such as The Jam which inspired a much more distinctly 'mod' following.

The 'serious' end of popular music in the twenty-first century has become far more diffuse, though bands such as Radiohead, Coldplay, and Travis manage to play songs that would have fitted into airplay lists in the 1970s and still be enormously successful. Now that the first rock stars (for example Bob Dylan, Paul McCartney, and, soon, Mick Jagger, who appeared on the cover of *Saga*, the journal of the over-fifties, in September 2001) are turning sixty, there is an increasing tendency to see rock both as 'over', in the sense that 'rock bands' are to an extent passé, and having in some sense 'won' the battle over popular music: to have become a part of

FIGURE 4.4 Crowd at U2 concert: Irish group U2's album *The Joshua Tree* was recently voted 'Best album of all time' by viewers of the VH1 satellite music television channel in Britain (© Douglas Kirkland/CORBIS)

the mainstream, such that even the Prime Minister, Tony Blair, used to be in a band. The music scene more generally has diversified into a battery of trends, such as alt.rock, trance, ambient, garage, trip hop, the new acoustic movement, and so on, though the most common word on the scene continues to be 'fusion', suggesting again that old categories such as 'rock' are fast becoming outdated. This would be evident at the annual Knebworth music festival, for example, which twenty years ago would have provided a stage for bands such as Led Zeppelin and Genesis, but which in 2001, only five years after Oasis's famous performance crowned the summer of Britpop, played host to a cluster of groups from the cream of UK dance culture, capped by a performance from Jamiroquai, a band who fuse 1970s funk with New Age mysticism.

An article by Gavin Hills in *The Observer* in February 1996 argues that the ascendancy of the dance music scene in Britain 'could signal the end of youth culture'. However exaggerated such a claim may be, there does seem to be a definite shift in Britain since the 1990s away from the oppositional youth subcultures of the previous three decades, and, following the success of Take That, Boyzone, and the Spice Girls, mainstream British pop has leant heavily towards manufactured, choreographed bands of slim and pretty dancing singers who espouse a distinctly upbeat, celebratory view of teenage life, from S Club 7 and Steps, to Hear'Say, the group created by an enormously popular television show in 2000 called *Popstars*. Hills describes 'the dance generation' as multiethnic, unisex, and intergenerational. This broadly optimistic vision of the 'dance generation' can be linked to what the American writer Douglas Coupland describes as 'Generation X': a postmodern, post-industrial grouping of people who embrace the idea of diversity and who do not strictly fall into a specific age-group. 'Generation Xers' are associated with a more flexible attitude towards clothes, music, and peer groups as markers of identity.

At the turn of the millennium, age seems to be a less rigid, though perhaps no less significant aspect of British cultural identity. This can be seen as a positive effect of the fact that Britain has become a far more diverse culture since the Second World War. However, it can also be seen as an effect of more negative cultural changes, brought about by mass unemployment in the UK: transitions between life stages are now much less stable for many people because the 'adult' status formerly incurred through work is no longer guaranteed. The labour market as a whole is much less stable, and British cultural identities are generally far less securely rooted in the jobs that people do. At some level, youth culture in Britain may well still be based around 'sex and drugs and rock'n'roll', but it's also worth bearing in mind that 'rock'n'roll' is rhyming slang for 'the dole'.

Conclusion

To conclude, we will look briefly at two aspects of culture which are in many ways opposed to each other: fashion and New Age culture (you will find out more about the New Age in relation to religion in a later chapter). Both are associated with youth, but both also in fact stretch across the generations and provide intriguing case-studies for analysing the production and consumption of contemporary British identities.

A recent morning television programme focused upon the 'street style' of young people in Britain. The discussion emphasised the flexibility, eclecticism, and originality of British fashion and, above all, the refusal of most stylish British teenagers to be 'slaves' to the dictates of the cat walk or the high-street fashion chains. While the newsagents' shops in Britain are filled with row after row of women's magazines giving the latest tips about 'what's in this season', the British seem to maintain a rather ambivalent attitude to the very concept of 'fashion'. There is a sense, of course, in which this ambivalence can be linked to British conservatism or reserve – to the nation's reputed resistance to anything new. However, there is another, equally important, strand to the way in which many British people seem to approach fashion, which is the almost mythical 'eccentricity' of the British (or perhaps more precisely the English). In fact, the most famous of British designers – Vivienne Westwood, Red or Dead, Katherine Hamnett, and Paul Smith – are often characterised specifically in terms of their eccentricity and their lack of conformity with the broader trends of the global fashion industry. There is even a clothes company called English Eccentrics. 'Reserve' and 'eccentricity' are attributes which are famously associated with 'the British character', and as qualities – albeit stereotypical ones – they possess a particular resonance in relation to British fashion, not least because they seem almost to cancel each other out. 'Classic' British clothing, of course, is characterised by muted colours (especially brown, navy blue, and green), sensible or comfortable tailoring, fabrics such as wool or corduroy, and the obligatory, 'understated' string of pearls for women. Above all, perhaps, this style of dress is associated with an upper-class lifestyle of 'hunting, shooting, and fishing' (as well as sailing), readily mythologised through media representations of the Royal Family striding over moors, walking dogs, and so on. It is probably not surprising then, that these kinds of clothes tend to conjure up conservative, non-urban identities (and often Conservative with a capital 'C'), though they are far from being the exclusive preserve of the aristocratic, landowning echelons of British society. Rather, the 'wax jacket and brogues' way of dressing seems to be identified with what we might call an 'aspirational lifestyle' (compare 'young fogies', *Country Life*, Marks & Spencer etc., and shops for women such as Laura Ashley). Perhaps most significantly, this 'classic' style of

British dress has been readily exported and is almost certainly more popular with young people abroad than it is with their British contemporaries. In 2001, British cultural stereotypes, from bulldogs and pony club rosettes to skinheads and Sloane Rangers, are being parodied on the catwalk, not just by British fashion designers such as Luella Bartley but by others such as Roberto Menichetti, the Italian ex-design director of Burberry, or the Spanish designer Desiree Mejer of Fake London.

Often, the way people dress in Britain is explicitly informed by distinctions of social class, and yet certain articles of clothing have much more ambiguous class connotations. The 'cloth cap' for instance (which is typically made of woollen cloth, in a small check pattern) is associated both with traditional working-class men (especially in northern working men's clubs) and with upper-class gentlemen (especially out shooting etc.). In a far more specific and self-conscious way, clothes such as Burberry rain-coats, and even 'deerstalker' hats, have crossed certain cultural divides in so far as they were adopted in the late 1980s and early 1990s as part of black street fashion – a gesture which seemed at the time both to mock the complacency of white 'Home Counties' style and to challenge the monopoly of designer sportswear in black Afro-Caribbean fashion itself. In a way, this tendency within British fashion to play with or parody familiar images of British tradition represents a central element in the dress codes of several youth subcultures in Britain: for example teddy boys, Wigan soul, skinheads, and punk.

In the last few decades the Doc Marten boot or 'DM' has probably exemplified the shifting, playful moods of British fashion more than any other single item of clothing. Skinheads in the late 1960s adopted DMs as part of a dress code which seemed to be an exaggerated version of the clothes worn by manual labourers (drainpipe Levis, Ben Sherman check shirts, and braces). A particular brand of work boots therefore acquired a significance far beyond the bounds of its initial function, and by the late 1970s the divisions and subdivisions between different subcultures such as punks and rudeboys were marked out not only by haircuts and music but by the way people wore their DMs (the number of holes, the colour, customized versions). As part of a more general impetus among feminists in the early 1980s to reject the trappings of a 'stereotypical' femininity, DMs became more and more popular with young women, especially students, who tended to adopt a kind of 'proletarian' look of baggily prac-tical clothes – overalls and donkey jackets – as a gesture of rebellion against both sexism and the materialistic excesses of the decade. Now, the Doc Marten boot seems to have entered yet another phase, having been adopted, briefly, by the catwalks of international fashion houses at the beginning of the 1990s. The omnipresence of the DM in high-street chains of shoe shops has robbed it of much of its potency as a symbol of nonconformity

FIGURE 4.5   Boot store in Camden market

and nowadays it's as likely to be worn to school by a middle-class eleven-year-old (or by a schoolteacher for that matter) as it is to be worn by an 'indie' musician or an anarchic art student. Even the Pope has a pair. You can now buy velvet or silver or brocade Doctor Martens but somehow they seem to have lost the power to shock, acquiring instead the more dubious accolade of a British 'design classic', which of course is readily exportable and hence less likely to be popular in Britain. At the other end of the spectrum are Jimmy Choo shoes, founded in a workshop in Hackney in London, but now bought in bulk by stars such as Cameron Diaz and Jennifer Lopez.

Mainstream street looks are today probably most influenced by idolised figures such as David and Victoria Beckham. David Beckham's hairstyle changes, from floppy to shaved to mohican and so on, also inspire countless imitations, and not just among football fans. Beckham is indeed a role model for many young boys, but there have been countless newspaper articles from the late 1990s onwards speaking out about the downturn in boys' fortunes generally, and their lack of positive role models in particular. Much of this concern is based on statistics such as the following: boys are five times more likely to commit suicide than girls, and four times more likely to be addicted to drugs or alcohol; boys are nine times more likely to be sleeping rough; girls outperform boys at every level of education and now outnumber boys at university by a ratio of three to two. The concern over such figures has grown, and the causes of boys' disaffection have been variously diagnosed as a general 'crisis of masculinity', as poorer communication skills and an inability to express feelings, a macho culture that is anti-education, the lack of male teachers in primary schools, and a new 'post-feminist' imbalance between perceptions of girls and boys. The social results are supposedly football thuggery, an increase in violent crime, the spread of drugs, and more playground bullying, but there is no consensus over the way to give boys more confidence and a sense of purpose. A related concern is that over the phenomenon of 'dumbing-down', a general accusation made by older generations against the shift towards a post-literate visual culture, in which theoretical abstractions and analytical complexities appear less and less in the media. An example of this could be considered even at the level of the differences between the film *Planet of the Apes*, made in the late 1960s, and the 'remake' in 2001. The first was noted for its commentary on contemporary race relations and the nuclear threats of the Cold War, but the producer of the remake, Richard Zanuck, explained in the *Sunday Times* in August 2001 why the new film was different: 'There are social crises going on. But they've resulted in an audience that wants pure entertainment; that wants to go in and not have to think too much; that wants to enjoy itself for a couple of hours. That doesn't mean that it's a dumb audience, but you go in for escape. In the 1960s, the audience was more accessible to thought-provoking subjects. It's just a sign of the times.' The argument seems to hinge upon whether one considers aspects of culture, from news reporting to summer movie blockbusters, to be more accessible and inclusive than they were, losing their overly didactic and 'improving' elements, or increasingly crass and simplistic.

Finally, we need to note how youth culture can become softened and anaesthetised, but also transformed and diffused. It has now become a kind of truism that more or less every town or even village in Britain is bound to have its resident punk, a figure as much a part of the repertoire of stock British types as the bowler-hatted city gent. Like most myths though, this scenario of 'a punk in every high street' represents only a very partial truth, one which fails to register the complex differences between particular communities and the constant mutations in the ways different subcultures identify themselves. Elements of punk can be found in various British subcultures, the most notable probably being New Age travellers. Crucially though, the style of clothes worn by many New Age travellers or the early 1990s phenomenon of 'Crusties' also draws very heavily on a hippy aesthetic – ethnic clothes, beads, and bangles. New Age hair styles similarly seem to draw on a range of cultural references such as dreadlocks (Rastafariansim), bright hair dye (punk), shaved (skinhead), mohican (Native American/Hari Krishna/punk), and shaggy, matted long hair (hippy). Any subcultural identity can of course be dissected into its component parts of 'key' motifs and symbols, but the example of New Age/Crusty subculture in Britain today also acutely demonstrates how problematic such checklists of cultural identities can be, not least because contemporary British cultural identities seem to be so enmeshed and hybrid – often self-consciously playing with or parodying the styles they adopt. New Age/Crusty subculture was perhaps the most recent indication of an extra-social trend that did not react or rebel from within mainstream culture but sought a mode of life outside society, and has consequently been portrayed negatively and ignorantly in most media. People tend to get lumped together according to very superficial criteria, and what is interesting about the phenomenon of New Agers/Crusties is that certain marginalised elements of the population which may have previously formed far more distinct groupings, such as hippies, travellers, political activists, the urban homeless, and young unemployed people from both urban and rural communities, came to be bracketed together, albeit in an impressionistic way. In fact, the very vagueness of the boundaries which surrounds this subculture suggest that the label of 'Crusty' or 'New Age traveller' is more likely to be invoked as a derogatory /disapproving term in 2001 to describe scruffy youths or homeless people.

FIGURE 4.6   Goth and punk clothes store in Camden market

Despite the fact that such disparate kinds of people might potentially be described as 'Crusty' or 'New Age', there seem to be marked regional differences between the north and south in that towns in the north are far less likely to have any conspicuous 'Crusty' culture. The south-west, on the other hand – particularly old rural cities such as Bath and Winchester – has large highly visible 'Crusty' communities, which crystallised in the 1992 'Summer of Crusty' and especially the free but illegal rave that May at Worcestershire's Castlemorton common, attended by twenty thousand people.

In September 2001, the Archbishop of Westminster, leader of 4.1 million Roman Catholics in England and Wales, declared that Christianity 'has almost been vanquished' in Britain and that people now increasingly gain their 'glimpses of the transcendent' in music, green issues and especially New Age movements. Indeed, New Age culture seems to combine spirituality with green politics and music in a way that speaks to the young in a more positive way than any other movement since that of the hippies in the 1960s.

Though many people who identify with New Age lifestyles may originally come from urban areas, there are several reasons why the subculture is generally associated with more rural areas. In the 1980s, a group of travellers known as 'The [Peace] Convoy' received a lot of coverage in the British media, partly owing to clashes with police over access to the ancient standing stones at Stonehenge in Wiltshire. A festival had been held annually over the summer solstice period at Stonehenge and had come to acquire the status of an 'alternative' to the well-known Glastonbury Festival, which had first taken place in 1970. Whereas Glastonbury has developed into a much bigger, more organised event, with an entry fee and big-name bands, Stonehenge remained steadfastly 'unofficial' – a free festival with a greater emphasis upon drugs and anarchism – until in 2000 unrestricted access was allowed for the first time on the solstice, and again on 21 June 2001 an estimated eleven thousand Crusties, ravers, pagans, and others partied peacefully all night to see the dawn. Both Stonehenge and Glastonbury festivals seem to offer strangely powerful conjunctions between modern folklore and the ancient myths of pagan Britain. Events such as 'the Battle of the Beanfield' at Stonehenge in 1983 and the more recent road protests at Twyford Down and elsewhere highlight a conflict of interest between those who claim institutionally to speak in the name of a national heritage and those who might make another, very different kind of claim to be protectors of an ancient land. Some of the campaigners who fought unsuccessfully against the construction of a bypass at Twyford near Winchester in the early 1990s called themselves 'the Donga' tribe and protested not only against the destruction of the landscape but also against what they believed to be the desecration of a sacred site – the tombs of King Arthur's legendary knights. Although archaeologists working in the area disputed the existence of these tombs, the road protesters' political campaign nevertheless remained tied to a mystical vision of the ancient kingdom or law of the land being destroyed by invasive industrial machines (graffiti on the road builders' equipment read 'Earth Rape'). As part of a slightly more recent road protest, campaigners near Newbury literally took to the trees to prevent the felling of centuries-old woodland. These tree camps obviously served a very practical purpose, but in doing so also conjured romantic images of Robin Hood and his merry men in Sherwood forest.

In such a way, the most recent cultural practices, and their representations in the press, will often draw on some of the oldest, and in many ways most powerful, British identities available. For example, when the New Labour government was first elected in 1997 it tried to capitalise on people's perceptions of a national rebirth after seventeen years of Conservative rule, by pushing the idea of 'Cool Britannia', a pun on the patriotic song 'Rule Britannia'. Tony Blair, a younger prime minister than Margaret Thatcher or John Major in all ways, but especially in his youthful 'presidential-style' image which in covert ways implied comparisons with the rejuvenation the USA felt when John F. Kennedy was elected, sought successfully to chart a populist 'third way' between left and right politics, but his much-publicised soirées with rock stars such as Noel Gallagher and television personalities such as Harry Enfield soon began to fade from the limelight as many of his newfound celebrity friends started to abandon him and the 'Cool Britannia' label became quickly out of date by Blair's second term of office. Blair has been more in touch with youth culture than previous prime ministers, showing himself to be a 'new dad' when his fifteen-year-old son Euan was found by the police lying drunk on a London street (leading to the latest playground word for drunk to be 'Euaned'). However, in this chapter overall, we have seen how Britain's youth since the 1950s continues to generate a varied range of subcultures, most of which in the 'noughties' seem uninterested in political stands or in politicians such as Blair. This proliferation of styles and trends means that the images and assumptions of fifteen years ago can no longer be applied to the way teenagers and youths see themselves today, just as today's styles and identities will be changed or discarded in a decade's time.

❖ Exercises

1   How important do you think age is within British culture? Would you say that the differences between age groups are becoming more or less distinct?

2   What kinds of music do you associate with the following British youth subcultures? Name specific bands or artists where possible.

- Hippies
- Goths
- Skinheads
- Crusties
- Bikers
- Rastas
- Rudeboys

3   Why do you think Britain has produced such distinct subcultural styles and groupings? What, if anything, does this tell us about British culture as a whole?

4   What do the following phrases mean? Comment upon the possible insights they offer into British attitudes towards age.

- 'Mutton dressed as lamb'
- 'Put out to pasture'
- 'Trying to teach your grandmother to suck eggs'
- 'Toyboy'
- 'One foot in the grave'
- 'Whippersnapper'
- 'Wet behind the ears'
- 'Darby and Joan'
- 'Long in the tooth'
- 'Cradle snatcher'
- 'Pushing up the daisies'

5   Discuss the implications of the term 'ageism'. Is it possible and/or desirable to avoid ageism in contemporary British society?

6   To what extent do you think that young people have more in common with the youth of other nations and cultures, than with older people from their own country?

Reading

Griffin, Christine. *Representations of Youth: The Study of Youth and Adolescence in Britain and America*, Blackwell, 1993. Academic analysis of youth and its influences across the Atlantic.

Hebdige, Dick. *Subculture: The Meaning of Style*, Routledge, 1979. Influential review of youth and alternative culture.

McRobbie, Angela. *Feminism and Youth Culture: From 'Jackie' to 'Just 17'*, Routledge, 1991. Looks at the effects of the feminist movement on magazine contents and on teenagers.

Redhead, Steve. *The End of the Century Party: Youth and Pop Towards 2000*, Manchester University Press, 1991. Short and often sweeping, but still a punchy cultural politics review of rap, rave, and youth culture.

Thornton, Sarah. *Club Cultures: Youth, Media, Music*, Blackwell, 1995. An exploration of subcultures across the main areas of youth activity and performance.

 # Cultural Examples

Films

Summer Holiday (1963) dir. Peter Yates. The archetypal 1960s British teenager, Cliff Richard, goes to France on a London bus with his friends, singing all the way (worth comparing with the subculture of Nicholas Roeg's *Performance* (1970), starring Mick Jagger).

My Beautiful Laundrette (1985) dir. Stephen Frears. Urban realist film, with touches of magic realism, looking at sexuality and racism in the 1980s 'enterprise culture'. Focuses on the relationship between two youths – one Asian, one white working-class.

Jubilee (1978), dir. Derek Jarman. Anarchic, decadent depiction of punk subcultures in the Queen's silver jubilee year, 1977.

The Great Rock'n'Roll Swindle (1980) dir. Julien Temple. Portrait of the punk rock group the Sex Pistols.

Scum (1980) dir. Alan Clarke. Brutal portrayal of life for young men in the Borstal system.

Quadrophenia (1979) dir. Frank Roddam. Film about mod culture, featuring Sting and based on an album by *The Who*.

A Clockwork Orange (1971) dir. Stanley Kubrick. Futuristic cult film about gang violence, withdrawn by the director following supposed 'copycat' brutality and only recently re-released after his death.

Rita, Sue and Bob Too (1986) dir. Alan Clarke. Realist portrayal of sexual relationships between two northern working-class teenage girls and an older man.

Books

Irvine Welsh, *Trainspotting* (1993). Grim, darkly humorous novel about heroin subculture in Edinburgh. Made into a film in 1995.

Colin MacInnes, *Absolute Beginners* (1959). Cult novel about swinging teenage life in London. Also made into a film in the 1980s.

Richard Allen, *Skinhead* (1970). Teen-novel about violent youth subculture.

Sue Townsend, *The Secret Diary of Adrian Mole 13¾* (1982). Bestselling humour about growing up in Thatcher's Britain through a schoolboy's fictional diary.

Maude Casey, *Over the Water* (1990). Teenage novel about the problems of growing up as a second-generation Irish immigrant girl in the UK.

Leonore Goodings (ed.), *Bitter Sweet Dreams* (1987). Anthology of writings by a cross-section of British teenage girls.

Hanif Kureishi, *The Buddha of Suburbia* (1990). Growing up in and around London, in the 1970s, between different ethnic cultures.

Nick Hornby, *Fever Pitch* (1992). Amusing account of growing up as an obsessive football supporter.

Television programmes

Trigger Happy TV. Twenty-first-century fast-moving 'candid camera' sketch show with hip indie soundtrack.

The Young Ones. Anarchic, surreal 1980s comedy about student life in a shared house.

Live and Kicking. Saturday morning programme with music and competitions.

Top of the Pops. Long-running chart music show.

Bad Ass TV. Late-night black youth programme, with music and outrageous stories.

Websites

www.indiemusic.co.uk
> The Penny Black Music record shop's site provides in-depth knowledge and obscure information

www.theory.org.uk/
> Ultra-cool social studies and cultural theory site

www.youthwork.co.uk/websites/weblinks08.html
> Links for finding out about UK youth culture

www.dotmusic.com
> Lowdown on the British pop scene from Craig David to the Spice Girls

www.confused.co.uk
> Hip online spinoff from *Dazed and Confused* magazine

Chapter 5

Class and politics

Frank McDonough

- The upper class   179
- The middle class   183
- The working class   187
- Social change   191
- The nature of politics   192
- Party politics   195
- Voting behaviour   199
- Conclusion   203
- *Exercises*   205
- *Reading*   205
- *Cultural examples*   205
- *Websites*   207

Timeline

1911	House of Lords Reform Act
1924	First Labour Government
1940	Churchill PM
1945	General Election: Labour elected
1948	National Health Service
1951	General Election: Conservatives elected
1955	General Election: Eden PM
1956	Suez Crisis
1959	Gaitskell failed reform Clause Four General Election: Macmillan PM Third consecutive Tory victory
1964	Labour victory
1967	Devaluation of the pound
1973	Britain joined EEC
1979	Winter of Discontent General Election: Thatcher PM
1981	Urban riots
1982	Falklands War
1990	Poll Tax riots Thatcher ousted from office
1992	Fourth consecutive Tory victory
1994	Police Act
1995	Leader Tony Blair elected PM
2001	Second consecutive Labour victory

IT WAS ONCE COMMONPLACE to portray Britain as a class-ridden society. Class was a staple part of the British way of life. Each class had unique characteristics. The upper class had stately homes, aristocratic backgrounds, and posh accents; the middle class, semi-detached houses, suits, and bowler hats; the working class, common accents, fish and chips, and council flats. This produced a society divided between 'Us' (the workers) and 'Them' (the rich and the bosses). Pubs always had a 'public bar' and a 'lounge'. Even railway carriages were divided into First, Second, and Third class compartments.

In recent years, many writers have begun to speak of the 'decline of class' in British society. The term 'classless society' has become commonplace. The rise of Margaret Thatcher, the daughter of a Grantham shopkeeper, and John Major, the son of a garden-gnome salesman, to the post of Prime Minister has been seen as evidence that anyone can rise to the top in British society, whatever their social origins.

The credit for this transformation is mostly given to Margaret Thatcher, Prime Minister from 1979 to 1990. Accordingly, many political commentators have suggested that the 'Thatcher Revolution' removed class from the political landscape, by shifting power through government reforms away from the Establishment, the bureaucrats and the trade unions to individual consumers and the free market. Many of Margaret Thatcher's reforms were delivered in the rhetoric of 'empowerment of the people'. Parents were encouraged to become school governors and take control of their schools as teachers faced the imposition of a National Curriculum to ensure that children in both state and private schools received a core course of study. The Community Charge (Poll Tax) was designed to recoup money for local amenities more evenly across the total adult population. It was also promoted to make local authorities more accountable to local people, but revenue-raising limits were effectively imposed by the Treasury. Privatisation ended up turning public utilities such as gas, electricity, telephone, and water into private monopolies. Nevertheless a large number of commentators have argued that the Establishment (monarchy, Church of England, Oxbridge and the BBC) no longer exists. The middle-class bureaucrat is made to work much harder, often implementing reforms which are designed to 'get government off the backs of the people'. The working class has retreated from collective action towards domestic pleasures. The only source of collective working-class unity today is the purchase of a weekly National Lottery ticket. Even the railways now have only two classes: first and standard.

'Hurricane' Thatcher seemingly blew class off the face of British society. Many writers now view Britain as a socially fragmented society, with life revolving around the individual, his or her family, and the idea of a better life through home ownership and consumer goods. And under Tony Blair, there has simply been more of the same. But pronouncing the death of class is premature. A recent wide-ranging survey of public opinion found 90 per cent of people still placing themselves in a particular class; 73 per cent agreed that class was still an integral part of British society; and 52 per cent thought there were still sharp class divisions. Thus, class may have become culturally and politically invisible, yet it remains an integral part of British society.

One unchanging aspect of a British person's class position is accent. The words an individual speaks immediately reveal her or his class. A study of British accents during the 1970s found that a posh voice sounding like a BBC news reader, usually spoken by a person from the south-east of England, was viewed as the most attractive voice. Most respondents said this accent sounded 'educated', 'soft', and 'mellifluous'. The accents placed at the bottom in this survey, on the other hand, were regional city accents: Liverpool (Scouse), Birmingham (Brummie) Newcastle (Geordie) and London (Cockney). These accents were seen as 'harsh', 'common', and 'ugly'. No great prejudice was expressed against well-spoken Scottish and Irish accents. However, a similar survey of British accents in the USA turned

FIGURE 5.1 Labour Party poster, at 2001 General Election, depicting Conservative party leader William Hague with Margaret Thatcher's hair style and ear-rings

these results upside down and placed Scouse and Cockney as the most attractive and BBC English as the least. This suggests that British attitudes towards accent are, to a large extent, based on ingrained class prejudice. Can it be mere coincidence that British people (including working-class people themselves) reserve their most negative comments for accents associated with areas containing large groups of working-class people?

In recent years, however, young upper middle-class people in London have begun to adopt fake Cockney accents (estuary English), in order to disguise their class origins. This is another sign of class becoming invisible. A good example of the desire to hide a privileged background is displayed by Nigel Kennedy, the brilliant violinist. He adopts the accent of a 'Cockney lad' even though a national newspaper reported that he was the product of a very 'posh' middle-class family. However, the 1995 pop song 'Common People' by Pulp puts forward the view that though a middle-class person may 'want to live such as common people' and 'sleep with common people' they can never appreciate the reality of a working-class life.

In the power stakes, however, if you want to get ahead in Britain then you would be well advised to lose a regional accent. A recent example of the importance of accent to upward mobility is Mandi Norwood, appointed editor of *Cosmopolitan* magazine at the age of thirty-one. When she began her career in journalism she had a Geordie accent. Her London friends advised her to drop it, if she wanted to get on. In a couple of years she admits to 'speaking like Lady Di'. From that point on, her career went swiftly upward. Even more significantly, a recent survey of recruitment managers of major corporations found that, although the majority of them knew it was wrong to discriminate against people because of a regional accent, they did. Despite all the talk of a classless society, it is still possible to divide British society into three broad classes – upper, middle, and working – even though the nature and composition of each class have undergone change.

The upper class

The traditional upper class was always closely associated with the aristocracy. They lived in stately homes and had their character shaped on the playing fields of Eton. They were an hereditary elite whose wealth and position were based on property and title. These were both used to gain substantial political privileges. For example, the House of Lords, an unelected second chamber, had a veto over House of Commons legislation until 1911. However, during much of the twentieth century the power and position of the aristocracy were steadily weakened. As long ago as the 1930s Noël Coward commented that the 'stately homes of England' were 'rather in the lurch.' By the 1960s the aristocracy were lampooned by Harold Wilson, the Labour Leader, as the 'Grouse Moor tendency'. The House of Lords was further slimmed down by the Blair government. Peers were invited to choose from among their number, who were to continue in office. Other 'life peers' were appointed, and effectively the Upper House became an advisory body to the Commons rather than its master. Hence, over time the aristocracy have been gradually replaced by a new upper class of businessmen who emerged with 'gentlemanly characteristics' and settled in London and the south-east. These 'gentlemanly capitalists' have come to dominate the financial and political heart of British society. By the 1980s Denis Healey, a leading Labour politician, was able to suggest that Margaret Thatcher had transferred power from the 'aristocracy to estate agents'. This shift in power was bemoaned by many of the old guard, including Alan Clark, son of art historian Lord Clark, who in his *Diaries* famously accused Tory minister Michael Heseltine of having 'bought his own furniture'.

Wealth however can never replace 'breeding'. The *Sunday Times* publishes an annual 'Rich List' showing whose wealth is rising, falling, or static. This gives a snapshot of both how rich the country is (the thousandth richest person on the list was worth £400 million) and how wealth and power are shifting. Most of the 2001 top ten have family wealth (Duke of Westminster, Lord Sainsbury, Sir Adrian and John Swire). The remainder are mostly self-made business people. Sports personalities, pop stars, and other 'mavericks' appear further down the list. Millionaires such as the footballer David Beckham and the singer Posh Spice will eventually become part of Britain's elite, but not yet.

TABLE 5.1 The *Sunday Times* rich list, 2001 (million pounds)

1	Duke of Westminster	4,400
2	Hans Rausing	4,200
3	Bernie & Slavica Ecclestone	3,000
4	Lord Sainsbury	2,900
5	Joseph Lewis	2,200
6	Bruno Schroder	1,750
7=	Nadhmi Auchi	1,700
7=	Terry Matthews	1,700
9	Philippe Foriel-Destezet	1,600
10=	Mark Dixon	1,400
10=	Sir Adrian and John Swire	1,400

Source: The *Sunday Times*, 22 April 2001

Hence, most writers would put wealthy families involved in the control of major banks, insurance companies, pension funds, and stocks in the City of London at the core of the modern upper class. These families still pass on wealth from generation to generation and enjoy a dominant position in society. But the nature of the modern upper class is very complex. Most vast family businesses are becoming increasingly global and are run by a highly paid managerial elite, often dubbed 'City Fat Cats'. The modern upper class is not as visible as the former owners of the stately homes of England who sought to impose standards and demanded deference. The new upper class is much more culturally invisible. Highly paid managers, PR people, and the Conservative Party now represent their interests. It has been shown that a numerically small number of powerful families wield enormous power over the business life of the City of London. The Conservative Party has increasingly become the party of this City business elite, and downplays its past association with the monarchy, the Church of England, and aristocracy. Many of Margaret Thatcher's reforms in the 1980s, including sharp reductions in the highest rates of personal and company tax, the removal of exchange controls, City deregulation, the expansion of the private sector through privatisation, and the weakening of trade unions, have clearly benefited the business elite. The result is an upper class which has never been more wealthy. A recent study, for example, showed the top 1 per cent of wealth owners possessing 33 per cent of the nation's total wealth. Tony Blair's Labour government, with its 'Third Way', unlike previous Labour administrations, is at least as friendly to business and the upper class as was its Tory predecessor.

Thus, the modern upper class is still based on individuals with a common background and close social contacts. Power is still kept in the family. For example, 45 per cent of bank directors with a listing in *Who's Who* could boast a father with a previous entry. Moreover, 75 per cent of bank directors had attended fee-paying public schools and 50 per cent had been to Oxford or Cambridge. Furthermore, a study of the top 250 companies in Britain recently revealed multiple directorships in the hands of a few wealthy families.

Hence, the upper class is largely made up of wealthy families. It is not exceptionally large. In 1986, for example, 43,500 people (less than 0.1 per cent of the population), held 7 per cent of the nation's wealth – or £740,000 each – while the wealthiest 10 per cent in Britain owned 50 per cent of all marketable property. Yet the numerical smallness of the upper class only serves to add to its exclusivity. It is a self-selecting elite, closed to outsiders – and money cannot buy someone into it. Networking is much more important. Contacts occur so frequently within the upper class because of their common background. The first point of entry is family background. The second is a public school education, privately

FIGURE 5.2 Houses of Parliament

funded by parents. The ethos of British fee-paying public schools such as Eton, Harrow, and Rugby is geared towards life long friendship. At boarding schools, pupils live with each other during school terms. This allows the development of extremely close social friendships between pupils and their families. This is followed by an Oxford or Cambridge education which expands the networking process still further. It is quite remarkable to note that, though public school pupils account for only 5 per cent of the total school population, they take over 50 per cent of Oxbridge places. A public school and Oxbridge education, therefore, moulds an integrated elite.

However, the question of whether the upper class acts in unison is extremely difficult to answer. There are clearly powerful families who wield power in the City of London, and have influence over both the Conservative and Labour Parties. Yet, the increasingly competitive nature of business suggests that conflicts of interest are likely to develop between elements within this ruling group. Equally, the close networking ethos of the upper-class business elite is able to make life difficult for the 'new rich' such as Richard Branson (owner of the Virgin group of record label, airline, radio station, cola), Alan Sugar (business tycoon behind Amstrad and chairman of Tottenham Hotspur), and Anita Roddick (creator of the Body Shop). These brilliant entrepreneurs, who have truly gone from 'rags to riches', are still considered 'outsiders' within the upper class. This partly explains why Richard Branson decided to withdraw his Virgin group from the stock market because he feared its independence was being compromised by powerful City groups. The turn of the new century spawned a rash of dotcom millionaires People such as Martha Lane-Fox and Brent Hoberman became rich overnight through the stock-market flotation of their company Lastminute.com. A year later they were relatively poor (£25 million) as the bubble burst and Lastminute.com joined 'the 90 per cent club' of those companies which lost most of their value.

For all the talk of an 'enterprise culture', much of British business is dominated by companies set up well over a hundred years ago. Upper-class families who own these companies have enormous power over investment, markets, companies, and shareholders. The fate of any 'self-made' business person ultimately lies in their hands. Hence, the upper class, such as the public schools, may be small in size but its members occupy positions of leadership in the major businesses in Britain. The upper class uses its wealth to confer social advantages and to retain a privileged position for its future generations. The closeness of the upper class ensures over-representation by this group in all the key positions in society. For example, 65 per cent of Conservative MPs in 1987 had been to a fee-paying public school. Equally, many of its members have made accommodations with the ruling Labour administration. Thus, the upper class can be seen to be a relatively closed, coherent and self-recruiting elite. It may have become an invisible elite in cultural terms but its underlying power and influence have never been stronger.

The middle class

In recent times, it has become fashionable to be a middle-class hero. This was not so in the 1960s. In those days, the lifestyle of the middle class was derided in pop songs such as 'Semi-Detached Suburban Mr Jones' by Manfred Mann and 'Matthew and Son' by Cat Stevens. These songs suggest that a suburban middle-class lifestyle is boring and repetitive. In the 1970s, prejudice against a conformist life continued. The popular television comedy show *The Fall and Rise of Reginald Perrin* portrayed the dull life of a middle-class executive who takes the same route from his semi-detached house to work each day. At work, Reggie grows tired of life with equally dull people, at home he despairs of his boring relatives whose idea of fun is to drink prune wine and visit a safari park at the weekend. To break free of this middle-class Alcatraz, Reggie Perrin fakes his own suicide and disappears.

In the 1980s, however, Reggie Perrin came back from the dead to find the boring middle-class lifestyle that he escaped had become, of all things – fashionable. Everyone aspired to own a dull semi-detached house in the suburbs and go to work in a dull job in the City. A middle-class hero suddenly became something to be. The coffee morning became the 'in thing'. Everyone wanted Gold Blend coffee at these events. Indeed a sequence of advertisements featuring the burgeoning romance of a couple whose close relationship blossoms over several cups of coffee became extraordinarily popular – so much so that the last advertisement featuring the 'Gold Blend Couple' drew a larger audience than popular soap operas such as *EastEnders* and *Coronation Street*.

Even 1960s rebels were falling over themselves to become respectable. Roger Daltrey, the lead singer of The Who, had sung in the 1960s hit 'My generation', 'I hope I die before I get old.' Yet in the 1980s he had got old, and was now telling everyone in the middle class it was a jolly good idea to get a credit card. Even Mary Whitehouse, the much derided campaigner against television sex and violence suddenly found herself going around for regular cups of coffee at number 10 Downing Street with Margaret Thatcher. This seems to indicate that a crucial, yet ignored part of the Thatcher Revolution was to elevate the coffee-club brigade almost into a government think-tank. Everyone was 'tuning in and turning on' not to LSD but to *This Morning* with Richard Madely and Judy Finnegan, who reigned until 2001. This popular daytime television show featured, of course, a special interlude known as 'Coffee Time'. No doubt Reggie Perrin was wishing he had never returned from the grave.

Even so, it is difficult to pigeonhole the middle class neatly. Much definition of the middle class still revolves around the differences in their employment situations. A common assumption these days is that the middle class is extremely fragmented. However, there is general agreement that most middle-class people fall into one of four broad categories. The first is the higher professionals – doctors, lawyers, architects, accountants, and business executives. They may lack the power and wealth of the upper class but they are certainly a distinct group. Higher professionals value education, training, and independence. They have all been to university and in most cases have post graduate and professional qualifications. They have generous pensions, holidays, expenses, sick pay, and considerable freedom within their own job. It is quite noticeable that family members of this group tend to follow their parents into a professional career. For example, 64 per cent of the sons of higher professionals end up in similar jobs, while only 2 per cent end up in a manual job. This low level of downward mobility suggests a high level of shared values concerning hard work and educational attainment which are passed on from generation to generation.

However, this higher professional group is not a completely closed elite. In 1972, for example, 28.3 per cent of male professionals were the sons of manual workers. Even so, one recent study showed that 34.5 per cent of top professionals had a father from a similar background. There are clearly difficulties for a working-class person finding 'room at the top', to quote the title of a well-known 1957 novel. Indeed, the novel's leading character, Joe Lampton, shows the difficulties that an upwardly mobile member of the working class faces when entering the world of the upper-middle class. Joe Lampton is portrayed as a ruthless opportunist who marries upward to a life of boredom and soul-destroying disillusionment – the underlying moral being that working-class people who wish to rise can do so only by acquiring the moral scruples of vipers. Oddly enough, this powerful image of educated working-class people 'selling out' and feeling ill at ease 'above their station' has acted as an effective weapon to prevent talented members of the working classes ever wanting to find any 'room at the top'. This may explain why only 6.5 per cent of the very top professionals had fathers with semi-skilled or unskilled manual backgrounds. Indeed, in many of the top professions the proportion of those whose father came from a manual background is exceptionally low. Hence, the medical profession, merchant banking, and the judiciary are largely Joe-Lampton-free zones.

The second major group in the middle class comprises salaried professionals (sometimes known as 'The Salatariat'). This group includes university and college lecturers, school teachers, local government officials, civil servants, and social workers. They too have all attended university, and often have post graduate and professional qualifications. In most cases, they have modest pensions and some freedom over their own job. Yet they have nowhere near the same level of salary autonomy enjoyed by higher professionals.

The largest group in the middle class comprises routine white-collar workers. A great deal of white-collar work takes place at a desk and is heavily supervised. It is very much a nine-to-five job with little freedom. Clerical work is now becoming female-dominated. In 1911, for example, 21 per cent of clerks were women. Today the figure is 78 per cent. Some clerical jobs such as secretaries or telephone operators are almost totally held by women. Many now work part-time. Oddly enough, 50 per cent of clerical workers now view themselves as part of the working class. However, there is little evidence of clerical workers flocking to join old working-class bastions such as trade unions. They do not exhibit an 'Us' and 'Them' view of themselves and their employers. In general, lower-middle-class employees use their jobs to improve the quality of their lives through consumer goods, foreign holidays, and entertainment.

The final group in the middle class is the self-employed. They became the 'stars' of the 1980s in cultural terms. These small businesspeople and shopkeepers have more control over their working lives than clerical workers. They view themselves as middle-class. Yet they work exceptionally long hours, have no career structure, and must finance their own pensions. In many cases, they earn less than a routine clerical worker.

The self-employed have always been the staunchest supporters of the Conservative Party. Advertising, which is really an art concerned with influencing public opinion, focused a great deal of its energy in the 1980s on popularising the self-made business person, epitomised perhaps by the television impressionist Harry Enfield's character Loadsamoney: a loud-mouthed 'Essex man' who flourished a roll of banknotes to emphasise his rising social status. This was the era when it was fashionable to 'go it alone'. A famous car advertisement featured a man who gives up a steady job to start his own business and drives a Renault car which 'takes your breath away'. Another introduced us to 'Vector Man,' who did not just know his own mind, he knew his own bank account and told his bank manager so. He was not stupid either. Even at the height of the brief 1980s boom, he wanted a free overdraft facility. Many similar advertisements portrayed high-flying businesswomen who told insurance sellers and bankers where to get off. These women would give up everything except their Volkswagen and their Gold Blend. This climate in which 'greed was good' and 'lunch was for wimps' made the self-made person a hero. It clearly had benefits for the Conservative Party. Lord Young, architect of the 'enterprise culture' promoted by the Department of Trade and Industry during the 1980s, recently confessed that much of the promotion of self-employment in the 1980s was 'social engineering'. Of course, the great financial crash of 1987 brought all these dreams of 'rags to riches' down to earth. The housing market crashed. No doubt Vector Man's bank

FIGURE 5.3 May Day protest against consumer capitalism: dissent is sometimes expressed against the Western political system as well as within it
(© Rune Hellestad/CORBIS)

manager is telling him what sort of repayments he wants on his bank account these days. The Gold Blend couple have doubtless switched back to ever-reliable PG Tips. Never has a revolution been as dependent as the Thatcher one on the strength of public relations and coffee, and the effects of that revolution were felt throughout the 1990s.

The working class

Oddly enough, it is the working class, at the bottom of the social pile, who have been most closely examined as a class. More ink has been spilled about them than about any other group in British society. They have been portrayed in novels, plays, films, and television documentaries. Endless sociological surveys on working-class life and numerous government reports have been produced. Unfortunately, most of these studies have been conducted by members of the middle class. For example, George Orwell in *The Road to Wigan Pier* (1937) views the plight of the unemployed working class of the 1930s through the eyes of a bourgeois intellectual. Many films contain the idea that 'it's grim up north' for a member of the working class. (*Private Eye* parodies this with a cartoon series 'It's Grim up North London'.) Even the television series *Our Friends in the North* (1996), produced as part of a 1990s 'acceleration of nostalgia' for the 1960s, repeats many of the old stereotypes about traditional working-class life in the north. Richard Hoggart, an eminent writer on working-class life, has been accused of being over-critical of the life from which his education had allowed him to escape. Hence, what we know of the working class is more often than not what the middle class think about it.

In the 1950s, there was a traditional picture of typical, usually male, members of the working class. Such people left school without any qualifications to find a job as a manual worker. They had a regional accent and a trade-union membership card, and lived in a close knit community of 'two-up-two-down' terraced houses owned by a landlord or the council. They enjoyed a pint 'down the local pub', a bet, and a trip to the football match. The chip shop was the central aspect of local cuisine and the Sunday roast dinner was a national ritual. They always voted Labour and enjoyed a shared experience. Of course, the working-class woman was depicted as a wife who always stayed at home to look after the kids with very few leisure activities, except perhaps the bingo. The working class saw themselves as 'Us' and the middle and upper classes as 'Them'.

Even in the 1950s it was already being suggested that this traditional picture of working-class life was undergoing change. The sweeping victories of the Conservatives in General Elections in this period led many writers to speculate whether improved wages, living conditions, education, welfare, and consumer goods had led the working class to no longer feel part of the 'lower orders'. It was even suggested that as workers became more affluent they ceased to feel a close affinity towards the Labour Party. The idea that a classless – 'You Never Had it So Good' – consumer society had emerged was widespread. It seemed as though the working classes were looking forward to their next consumer purchase and not some grand socialist revolution. Many books, novels, and films reflected the idea of a new working class emerging. *Saturday Night and Sunday Morning* (1960), which examined the life of an affluent worker within a traditional working-class community in the late 1950s, is a prime example. The film portrays the life of Arthur Seaton, a young lathe-operator from Nottingham who, though highly paid, is dissatisfied with the parochial attitudes and restricted cultural activities of the working class. He proclaims with rugged individualism: 'I'm Me, and nobody else; and whatever people say I am, that's what I'm not, because they don't know a bloody thing about me.' This rugged individualism leads Arthur to have contempt for his new-found affluence, which is mostly spent on drink, women, and fishing. Significantly, he is indifferent to politics.

A flood of studies appeared in the 1950s and 1960s to examine whether affluent workers had ceased to feel close class solidarity. The most prominent example was a detailed study of Ford car workers. This showed that affluent workers had grasped the idea of a better life through consumer goods and spent a great deal of time on 'domestic pleasures'. Yet these studies concluded that in cultural terms the majority of affluent workers did not aspire to be middle-class. They still saw being a member of a trade union and voting Labour as extremely important expressions of their class identity. Even so, these affluent workers placed a better life for their family as a greater priority than the struggles of the labour movement. This tends to indicate that the advent of a consumer society and improved standards of living were already leading to a more individualistic approach to politics among the working class before the 1980s, and that has certainly continued into the new millennium.

It is, however, the years since Margaret Thatcher came to power in 1979 which have reopened the debate over the 'embourgeoisement' of the working class. Previous assumptions about the working class are being discussed once again. The Thatcher years are being viewed as a period of cultural transformation which has produced an increasingly fragmented working class. There are few who would doubt that the working class has changed. The crux of the traditional picture of working-class life suggests a shared experience. In 1979, male manual workers formed a majority of the workforce and most belonged to trade unions. Today nearly 50 per cent of the present workforce is female or from an ethnic minority. The membership of trade unions has fallen from 13 million in the 1980s to less than 7 million today (of which 39 per cent are female). In the 1970s, trade unions were seen as having the power to bring down governments. Yet this power has been all but extinguished by successive trade-union reforms during the 1980s. Trade-union leaders who enjoyed national fame in the 1960s and 1970s are now unknown figures. In the 2001 General Election, Arthur Scargill, President for life of the National Miners' Union stood against the official Labour candidate Shaun Woodward, former Conservative MP and member of the wealthy Sainsbury family, in the working-class constituency of Wigan. Scargill was trounced. This shows how rapidly Britain has changed since the union heyday of the 1980s. Many former steel, coal mining, and dock areas have become industrial wastelands. Many have even been turned into industrial museums. In 2000, there were seventy-six unions representing only 6.8 million workers. Membership figures for some of the largest unions are given in Table 5.2.

However, the greatest new division within the working class is the gap between the employed and unemployed. The living standards of those in full-time jobs have improved, but the plight of the unemployed has worsened. For a start, unemployment has increased rapidly. From 1951 to 1979, unemployment never rose above 1.5 million. Under the Tories from 1979 to 1997 it was as high as 3.5 million and rarely below 2 million. A great many male unskilled workers fell down a black hole of despair with no job, little hope, and no future. They became walking museum exhibits. These changes led to talk of the development of an 'underclass' in Britain

TABLE 5.2 Membership of selected major unions, 2001: thousands (1994 membership in parentheses)

Amalgamated Engineering and Electrical Union	727	(835)
UNIFI (formerly Banking, Insurance and Finance Union)	171	(141)
General, Municipal and Boilermakers' Union	694	(835)
Graphical, Paper and Media Union	201	(224)
Manufacturing, Science, Finance	416	(516)
National Association of Schoolmasters, Union of Women Teachers	184	(138)
National Union of Teachers	201	(169)
Transport and General Workers' Union	872	(949)
Union of Construction, Allied Trades and Technicians	123	(136)
Union of Shop, Distributive and Allied Workers	310	(299)
UNISON (formed by merger of NALGO, NUPE & COHSE[1])	1,300	(1,458)

1 NALGO = National and Local Government Officers Association, NUPE = National Union of Public Employees, and COHSE = Confederation of Health Service Employees

Source: *The Lifestyle Pocketbook*, NTC Publications, 2001

which is cut off from the consumer society and is poor and politically apathetic. In 1979, only 6 per cent of the population qualified for maximum social security benefits. Today 19 per cent do so. Homelessness for many is 'the big issue' – this conviction spawned a publication of that name sold largely to fund its vendors.

Alongside the growth of poverty have come riots in very poor urban areas such as Toxteth (Liverpool), Moss Side (Manchester), Handsworth (Birmingham), and Brixton (London). Despite the undoubted affluence of some areas of Britain, in 2001 there were riots in deprived areas of Oldham, Bradford, and Burnley. (Coincidentally or not, of the three best (far-right-wing) British National Party results in the General Election of 2001, two were in Oldham. The third was in Burnley.) Street begging and the 'cardboard cities' of homeless people in London and other major cities are other symptoms of a new harsher climate. Even diseases such as diphtheria and tuberculosis are making a comeback. This 'underclass' is excluded from the 'flash' car, the Vector bank account, and Gold Blend coffee. Many of the new poor go to 'car-boot sales' where people sell second-hand goods, usually from the back of a very ancient car which really does 'take your

FIGURE 5.4   Legalise cannabis: after years of protest, possession of cannabis has been all but decriminalised (© Adrian Arbib/CORBIS)

breath away'. In many areas of inner-city Britain, crime has risen to record levels, drug addiction resembles the American inner city, and unemployment is over 60 per cent. A recent study showed that one household in five now has no adult in any sort of employment. The growth of one-parent families in Britain is faster than in any other European country. Contrary to the 1950s image, the working-class woman of the 2000s is often depicted as an unmarried single mother living on a council estate.

Social change

This out-of-work underclass is divided from those in work. Indeed, a 1992 earning survey showed that the average manual worker's full-time pay was £268 per week, compared to £248 for the average clerical worker. Nevertheless, there has been a sharp decline in number of male manual workers, a group always seen as the core of the traditional working class. Between 1951 and 1981 the number of manual workers fell from 15.6 million to 13.3 million. In 1951, 70 per cent of the workforce was made up of manual workers. In 2001, they made up only 27 per cent of workers.

Few doubt that the lifestyle and cultural activities of manual workers have changed. The majority of manual workers still in work own their own homes, have a car, a fridge, a washing machine, a television, a telephone, and inside toilets and bathrooms. They now go abroad on holiday and their diet does not revolve around the fish and chip shop any more. The number of foreign restaurants in working-class areas has increased rapidly. Formerly exotic fare such as naan bread, Australian wine, pasta, and hummus are now sold in the majority of supermarkets.

The greatest revolution, however, has been in housing choice. In 1950, over 80 per cent of skilled and unskilled manual workers lived in private rented or council-owned properties. In 1988, 72 per cent of skilled and 55 per cent of semi-skilled manual workers owned their own home. A recent opinion survey showed that 90 per cent of manual workers who lived in council property would like to buy their own homes. Since 1981, 33 per cent of all council tenants have bought their council houses.

The modern working-class manual worker spends less time with workmates at the pub (increasingly the preserve of youth) or the football match (increasingly attended by the middle class) and much more time at home. The growth of DIY superstores and encouragement from television programmes has led to more working-class men spending time making their homes more attractive. Industrial change has radically altered many former working-class communities which depended on heavy industries such as coal mining, shipbuilding, dock work, railways, and steel making. New industries have tended to be located long distances from where workers live.

An additional change in the traditional pattern of working-class life has been in the role of women. A majority of working-class women are now going out of the home into either part-time or full-time work. Thus, female members of the working class are actually much less home-centred than ever before. Of course, much of this work is poorly paid and part-time. Nevertheless, more opportunities exist for women in expanding service sectors such as retailing, banking, and insurance, and, over 30 per cent of households now boast a female breadwinner. Hence, working-class women are much less reliant on males. This has resulted in more all-female social activities outside the home. A recent example is the popularity of male groups of strippers, the most famous being the Chippendales, who are viewed by women as sex objects. The idea of a working-class woman accepting a traditional housewife role is declining. The novelty of the house husband has emerged in the working class. There is also evidence that an unemployed male is increasingly being seen as a poor marriage partner – hence the sharp increase in one-parent families.

It seems that the majority of working-class people aspire to higher levels of consumer spending. The power to withdraw one's labour has been eroded – and replaced by the power to buy goods. This has led to a climate in which 'we are what we buy'. Working people have become more money-centred, family-centred, and individualistic. House and car ownership in working-class areas has become a symbol of rising status.

However, this cultural revolution has not completely led to the working class no longer feeling working-class. When account is taken of what working-class people say about class, we find they still do not feel middle-class. They still believe that class has a detrimental impact on their life. They still consider class to be an important part of British life. Accordingly, working-class people still see themselves as part of a particular class and few believe they live in a classless society. However, a great many of the modern working class are politically apathetic.

The nature of politics

There are numerous organisations which agitate for political change outside the formal channels of government power. Some prominent examples include Greenpeace and Friends of the Earth which are concerned with environmental matters, the Campaign for Nuclear Disarmament (CND), which agitates for the adoption by the government of a nuclear-free British defence policy, the National Farmers' Union (NFU), which lobbies government on behalf of the agricultural community, the Confederation of British Industry (CBI), which represents the interests of big business, the Trades Union Congress (TUC), which lobbies on behalf of workers, and Shelter,

which speaks on behalf of the homeless. British pressure groups are prolif-
erating at a rapid rate and enjoy the support of people whose ordinary lives
are nowhere near as radical. Yet these groups are primarily interested in a
single issue rather than a broad range of policies. They all seek to influence the government in London.

It is clear that the dominant mechanisms of power still reside with
the Parliament at Westminster. Many writers would suggest that the power
of central government has never been stronger. Equally, the power of local
government and pressure groups has never been weaker. In 1979, when
Margaret Thatcher took office, she promised to end the 'enlarged role of
the state'. But this bold claim never really came true. In 1979, the state was
responsible for 43 per cent of the economy and in 2001 the state was *still*
responsible for 43 per cent. Indeed, Britain is the most centralised state
among all the major Western industrial democracies. Power has increasingly been concentrated in the hands of the Prime Minister and the Cabinet.
The power of central government has been extended since 1979. In the
1994 Police Act, the police, previously organised on a local basis, were
brought under the control of the Home Secretary. In 1988, British universities came under central research and teaching regulation for the first time.
British schools now have a National Curriculum. Regional health authorities have been abolished and the National Health Service is now under the
control of the Health Secretary. The power of local government has been
dramatically weakened from 1979 to the present. Local authorities no
longer have the right to build homes. The introduction of rate-capping
(limits imposed by the government on the amount of money raised through
local taxation) has turned local councils into little more than the agents of
central government. Until 1999 London was the only major world capital
without an integrated local government agency. (The government then
reluctantly granted limited autonomy to a new London administration
under the mayor Ken Livingstone.) Other centrally controlled agencies
have appeared, including the Child Support Agency, the Student Loans
Company, and the National Rivers Authority. Even the National Lottery,
though privately managed, is under central government control. It was
partly to address the accusation of centralisation that Tony Blair's government pressed ahead with a programme of political devolution. Assemblies
were set up in Edinburgh and Cardiff, where locally elected representatives
could look after the interests of the people. This has been welcomed by
members of those assemblies, naturally, but others complain about the
costs of another layer of administration, and say that the amount of real
power devolved is limited.

In theory centralisation should enable the government to deal better
with national emergencies such as the 2001 foot and mouth crisis. In practice the experience for rural Britain was catastrophic, with government

seeming more inclined to manage the news rather than handle the disease. Over 3.5 million animals had been slaughtered and burnt by mid-year; meat was being imported from countries which had endemic foot and mouth and had vaccinated, which the UK government itself refused to do.

Oddly enough, not since the days when the monarchy dominated Parliament has power been so centrally controlled as it is from Westminster today. Yet, since the English Civil War in the seventeenth century, the power of the monarch over Parliament has dwindled. It has always been claimed that the British monarch reigns but does not rule, whereas the American president rules but does not reign. Today, Queen Elizabeth II remains the head of state but is little more than a ceremonial figure-head. She even pays income tax. The actual power of the Queen over Parliament is reflected in the State Opening of Parliament, which takes place each November. At this ceremony, a messenger of the monarch (Black Rod) has the door of the House of Commons slammed in his face, to symbolise Parliament's independence from the monarchy, before MPs decide to listen to the 'Queen's speech', which outlines the legislative programme of the government for each year and is written by the Prime Minister.

The whole ceremony may seem to be one of those peculiarly silly British rituals. Yet it emphasises the way power has shifted from the monarch to Parliament, which is made up of two Houses. The less important of these is the House of Lords. This is an unelected body based on hereditary and life peers. Until 1911 the House of Lords had a veto over government legislation. These days it acts as a body which gives advice on government legislation. The Labour government has reformed its membership – hereditary peers are reduced to 92, elected by their fellows, and the remaining 524 life peers are nominated (but see below).

The dominant political forum is the House of Commons. In 1992, this was composed of 651 MPs. Each MP represents a particular part of Britain known as a constituency and is elected at General Elections held every four or five years. The growth of the power of the House of Commons has been accompanied by an expansion of the electorate through various parliamentary reform Acts (today people can vote at eighteen) and the growth of organised political parties with leaders, national organisations, and competing policies. After a General Election, the party leader who wins a majority of seats in the House of Commons forms a government from members of her or his party. The Prime Minister selects a Cabinet, which is composed of ministers individually and collectively responsible for carrying out the legislative programme of the government. The dominance of the Prime Minister and the Cabinet over the British system has led to charges that the British political system is an 'elected dictatorship' of the Party leader (and the leader's closest associates) and an Opposition leader (and Shadow Cabinet organised on a similar basis).

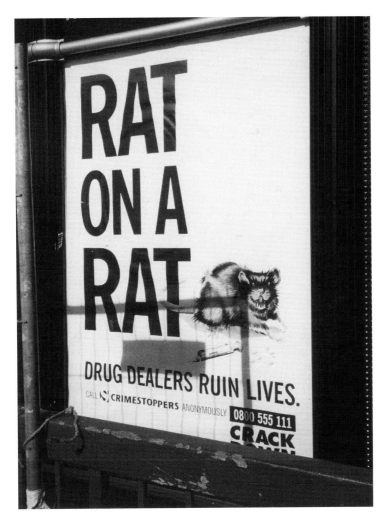

FIGURE 5.5   The government's 'war on drugs' remains a high priority and when Prince Harry was caught smoking cannabis in early 2002 he was splashed across all the news headlines for the first time

Party politics

The two main parties in Britain are the Conservative Party and the Labour Party, and they have dominated elections since 1918. From 1950 to 1970, a total of 92 per cent of votes went to the two major parties. Even in 2001 the Conservative and Labour Parties took 73 per cent of the votes cast.

The Conservative Party emerged in the 1830s from the 'Tory' grouping in Parliament. In the later nineteenth century, under the leadership of Disraeli, the party was concerned with defending traditional institutions such as the monarchy, the aristocracy, and the Empire. Disraeli also popu-larised the idea of 'One Nation' Conservatism. This suggested that the Conservative Party was the only true national party which could rise above class and special interest groups to represent the people as a whole. After 1918, and the creation of a mass electorate, the party has constantly and successfully adapted its policies to suit prevailing trends in British society. In the 1930s, the party started to shed its aristocratic image and was led by businessmen. In the 1950s, the party accepted Labour policies such as nationalisation and the welfare state. This led many commentators to speak of Britain from 1951 to 1979 as having a consensus politics in which there was very little difference between the two major parties. Under Margaret Thatcher, the party moved away from 'One Nation' Conservatism towards a set of policies aimed at business, the consumer, and the upwardly mobile. Thus, the Conservative Party, once the party of the Establishment and the classic aristocratic, stiff-upper-lipped ruling class, became associated with the business and commercial sections of society. However, the legacy of Margaret Thatcher's conviction politics for the long-term electoral appeal of the Conservatives remains uncertain. Since her fall from power in 1990, the party has been greatly divided on the way forward. However, it is always dangerous to write off political parties. Labour were in opposition for eighteen years from 1979 to 1997, and after they failed to win the election against John Major in 1992 at a time of Conservative unpopularity, people said they were finished. They returned to power in 1997 with a landslide which led to a mood of national euphoria. People delighted in iconic television moments of Tory minister Michael Portillo losing his seat and independent MP Martin Bell winning Tatton. The Conservatives went away to lick their wounds having lost safe seats up and down England and every seat in Scotland. Its leaders claimed that the low turnout cost them votes. They said people had abstained from voting because of despair with the political process not because they disliked the Tories. However, a *Today* programme poll three months after the election found that, of one thousand people who had not voted, 53 per cent said they would have voted Labour and only 19 per cent Tory. So the Tory case was even worse than it seemed. In 2001, they held a damaging leadership election which went to Iain Duncan Smith, and are now in disarray.

In the 2001 General Election, Labour's majority was only slightly reduced, and they seem as secure as ever, but conceivably at some point in the future the Conservatives also will return from their wilderness. Over time the Conservative Party has been the most consistently successful British political party, and even at a low point in 2001 had more actual party members (318,000) than the party in power, Labour (311,000).

The Labour Party is Britain's second major party. It was formed in 1906 from the Labour Representation Committee (LRC) with the financial backing of the trade unions to represent the interests of the working class. In 1918, the party made a firm commitment to the 'common ownership of the means of production'. The first Labour government came to power in 1924. By 1929 the Labour Party had replaced the Liberals as one of the two major parties. The Labour Party gained a spectacular victory in the 1945 General Election. This government introduced several important social reforms, most notably, the National Health Service, the social security system, mass education, and the nationalisation of several leading industries. The party won power again under Harold Wilson from 1964 to 1970 and was in office again from 1974 to 1979. However, while the Labour Party has established itself as one of the major parties, until 1997 it had never ruled for longer than five and a half years. Labour had spent the majority of time in opposition. The failure of the Labour Party to dominate politics was attributed to its image as a party of the labouring working class in major industrial cities. The close link with the trade unions also put off many voters. This may explain why the party had difficulty in winning support from non-union members and from those living in affluent middle-class suburbs or rural areas.

However, under Tony Blair, the Labour Party attempted to ditch its old 'cloth-cap' image. The party constitution now gives greater powers to individual members. The former dominance of the trade unions over the party is downplayed. In 1995, the party revised Clause Four of its constitution and thus ended the historic commitment of the party to state ownership. The party is now portrayed as 'New Labour', but it is probably a change in personnel rather than policies which has led to greater electoral success for the party. The 1997 Labour government contained more women ('Blair's Babes') and minorities than hitherto, and this has evidently contributed to its effectiveness.

The success of Labour under Tony Blair is also attributable to his having controlled the unions and the left wing, and brought about fiscal stability while reducing unemployment. He has had a highly successful PR machine and his press secretary Alistair Campbell is credited with managing the information flow ('spin') to the government's advantage. This has meant timing the release of bad news to coincide with national distractions, or repeating news of allocations of money to the National Health Service.

Some commentators fear that Blair has cultivated a presidential style and undemocratically seeks to bypass Parliament. For example, Britain's involvement in the 'war on terror' in Afghanistan was undertaken without discussion in the House of Commons. When 'President' Blair set about reforming the House of Lords, formerly made up of unelected, hereditary peers, he set up a Royal Commission chaired by Lord Wakeham. This reported in January 2001 and proposed that the new Lords should have about 550 members. Most would be appointed by an independent committee, but a 'significant minority' would be elected from the regions. The Conservatives were suspicious of Labour's plans, because the House of Lords has always been a Tory stronghold. (Even after the first phase of reform, the Conservatives have 223 peers, compared with Labour's 200.) The then Tory leader, William Hague, said that Blair intended to 'get rid of the hereditary peers, stuff it with a load of people from the Labour Party and then forget about it'.

Mr Blair continued with his plans. In April 2001, the first tranche of 'people's peers' (a term spin-doctored from Downing Street) was appointed. The fifteen people chosen by the House of Lords Appointments Commission all have an Establishment background and include seven knights and three professors. Four of the fifteen were women and four were from ethnic minorities. But nine lived in London or the south-east, and only one, Victor Adebowale, chief executive of the Centrepoint charity, was under forty.

In November, the government produced a White Paper which proposed that only 120 of the six hundred members of the new Lords would be elected, well short of the 190 suggested by the Wakeham commission. The proposals included the removal of the remaining 92 hereditary peers. Thus, only a fifth of the new chamber would be elected by the public, another fifth nominated by an appointments commission (set up by the Government) and the majority appointed by political parties. Furthermore the new chamber was expected to be only a 'revising and deliberative body,' in which the Prime Minister reserved to himself the right to put forward a 'limited number of holders of very high office' for life peerages. The struggle continues.

Meanwhile, in popular culture, the Labour government has been given an easier ride than previous administrations. However, Rory Bremner performs telling impersonations of Blair on television, and he is also caricatured as a vicar in *Private Eye*'s fortnightly feature, *St Albion Parish News*. The vicar sanctimoniously preaches complaisancy to 'the parishioners', whilst sideswiping colleagues. Spoof letters from fellow MPs John Prescott or David Blunkett are ruthlessly 'edited' by Mr Campbell and prayers are invoked for '[Clare] Short who has been suffering from panic attacks, causing her to say things she must deeply have regretted'. Such satire, however, reaches only a limited audience.

The third largest party is the Liberal Democrats. This was an amalgamation of the old Liberal Party and the Social Democratic Party, the latter being a breakaway group from the Labour Party, formed in 1981 by the 'Gang of Four' (Roy Jenkins, Shirley Williams, Bill Rogers, and David Owen). The Liberal Democrats advocate policies based on freedom of the individual and support for the adoption of proportional representation at elections. However, in spite of its desire to 'break the mould of two-party politics' it remains a minority party which draws support from voters dissatisfied with the two major parties. This may explain why its most spectacular victories are in by-elections in single constituencies. Thus, the Liberal Democrats are a party of protest rather than a real alternative for government. The image of the party is moderate and appeals predominantly to middle-class people, often in rural areas. In 2001, they had fifty-two MPs, including their Scottish leader Charles Kennedy.

The other parties represented in parliament are the Ulster Unionists, who largely campaign on the question of Northern Ireland remaining part of the UK, the Scottish Nationalist Party, which demands independence for Scotland, and Plaid Cymru, which makes similar demands for Wales. There are all manner of small fringe parties who have no representation in Parliament. The most prominent examples are the Socialist Workers Party (SWP), which advocates a socialist society on the principles of Marx and Trotsky, the Green Party, which champions environmental policies, the National Front, which advocates 'Britain for the British', and the Monster Raving Loony Party founded by 'Screaming Lord Sutch' which advocates free ice cream and at a by-election in Bootle, Merseyside, in 1990 actually gained more votes than the Conservative candidate.

Voting behaviour

The most important part of political activity for the average person is voting at elections. The way people vote has become the subject of enormous discussion. Between 1951 and 1966, over 90 per cent of voters strongly identified with and voted for one of the two major political parties. Table 5.3 gives an indication of the current two-party dominance in the

TABLE 5.3 General Elections: number of seats (% of the vote in parentheses)

	1992	1997	2001
Conservative Party	336 (42.8)	165 (31.4)	166 (31.7)
Labour Party	271 (35.2)	419 (44.3)	412 (40.6)
Liberal Democrats	20 (18.3)	46 (17.1)	52 (18.2)
Welsh and Scottish nationalist parties	7 (2.4)	9 (1.7)	9 (2.7)
Northern Ireland parties	17 (2.3)	18 (1.8)	18 (2.8)
Turnout	77.7	71.4	59.4
Overall majority	21 (Cons)	179 (Lab)	167 (Lab)

Source: *The Times*, 9 June 2001

House of Commons. The three major parties between them accounted for 90.66 per cent of the votes cast in 2002.

The 1992 election was the fourth consecutive victory of the Conservative Party. However, the Liberal Democrats, who polled nearly six million votes, were hampered by the 'first past the post' system. This system gives a seat to the candidate who wins the most votes in each constituency instead of giving a number of seats to each party based on their percentage of all votes, as is the practice in systems with proportional representation. Not surprisingly, the Liberal Democrats favour the adoption of a proportional representation system and the Conservatives are the strongest supporters of the present system.

It has long been claimed that in Britain class is closely related to voting choice at elections. At the 1964 General Election, for example, there was a two to one chance in favour of a person from a manual working-class background voting Labour and a four to one chance in favour of a person from a non-manual middle-class background voting Conservative. The major anomaly for pollsters has been to explain why 33 per cent of the working class do not vote Labour. Indeed most Conservative election victories have included at least 30 per cent of votes from the working class. The classic example of the working-class Tory in popular culture used to be the character of Alf Garnett in the popular television comedy series

FIGURE 5.6 Political party fliers: beside Labour's emphasis on basic priorities such as education and health, the Conservatives' attempt to fight the 2001 election on the issue of the Euro proved a poor decision despite many British voters' scepticism about European integration (© Alistair Daniel)

Till Death Us Do Part. He voted for the Conservatives because he thought they were patriotic and well-born. He wanted to be ruled by what he saw as his betters not his equals. At the 1987 election, Neil Kinnock, the Labour leader, was castigated by working-class Tory voters in opinion polls for 'not sounding or looking like a Prime Minister'.

However, many writers have suggested that class voting is in decline. The result is a growing apathy with both major parties, accompanied by an upsurge of support for centre and fringe parties. In the six General Elections since 1970 the share of the votes of the two major parties has fallen from 92 per cent to 72 per cent. It seems that more and more people are willing to vote for the Liberal Democrats, or the Scottish, Welsh, and Irish nationalist parties. At by-elections, the share of the vote for numerous fringe candidates has grown enormously. The number of 'floating' voters who switch their votes to different parties at each election has also grown. Nowadays most people are less attached to any political party than ever before. In 1964, 48 per cent of voters said they identified strongly with one party. But in 1992 this figure had fallen to 21 per cent. This growing apathy may also explain why the number of non-voters has increased. This is especially true of the eighteen to twenty-four age group. In the 1992 General Election, less than 40 per cent of such people bothered to vote at all. After a century of around 75 per cent of the total electorate turning out to vote, in 2001 the figure was 58 per cent. In fact, it was widely reported that more people voted in polls to eject people from the house in *Big Brother* than did in the 2001 General Election.

This apathy may also be linked to the fact that the public standing of politicians has never been lower. They have become figures of ridicule. On *Spitting Image*, a comedy show which uses caricatured puppets, leading politicians have been portrayed in negative and often ludicrous terms. Indeed many politicians have complained about the images presented of them in the programme. Some of the most memorable images include Kenneth Baker (Conservative), who was depicted as a slimy, crawling snail, Norman Tebbitt (Conservative) who was portrayed as a leather-clad Cockney 'bovver boy', Roy Hattersley (Labour) as a spluttering fool, David Steel (Liberal Democrat) as a fawning dwarf, Tony Blair (Labour) as an overgrown schoolboy, and Peter Mandelson (Labour) as a slimy half-worm, half-snake. This programme has served to hold up politicians as figures of ridicule rather than admired leaders.

Another reason for the low public standing of politicians has been the reporting of their sexual activities outside Parliament. A long list of political sex scandals has been eagerly discussed in the tabloid press during the past few years. Indeed, coping with a daily diet of new allegations of political sleaze has become a central aspect of British political life. The popular tabloid press has a mighty appetite for such stories. All the participants in such scandals are offered enormous sums of money by news-papers to 'tell all'. For example, when it emerged that the Liberal Democrat leader Paddy Ashdown had once had an affair with his secretary, he was dubbed by the *Sun* newspaper as 'PADDY PANTSDOWN'. Similarly, the *News of the World* bought the story of an unemployed actress who had had a torrid affair with the Tory Cabinet Minister David Mellor. It was revealed that Mellor had made love to her wearing a Chelsea Football Club shirt. Not surprisingly, he was forced to resign. Norman Lamont, the Tory Chancellor of the Exchequer, created a scandal by renting out his basement flat to a 'bondage-queen'. The reporting of the sad and lonely death of a Tory MP who had asphyxiated while engaging in an obscure sexual activity which involved a plastic bag and an orange seemed to plunge the standing of politicians to an all-time low. This climate of sleaze, heated up by the tabloid press, has no doubt contributed to the growth of political apathy among voters.

It seems that, even for those who do vote, single issues are playing a vital part in voting choice. During the 1992 election campaign, voters put the Labour Party well ahead on all the 'caring' issues such as social welfare, the NHS, education and unemployment. Yet the majority did not trust Labour on taxation and keeping inflation down and so voted for the Conservatives again. This suggests that the key issue at the election was the 'pound in your pocket', indicating that the likely victor at future elec-tions will be the party which allows the consumer greater economic stability and more opportunity to consume. In practice, this is likely to mean the party which keeps tax down and inflation low. Thus, the slump in Labour's fortunes from 1979 to 1992 can be put down to offering policies which were unattractive to the consumer's needs. Hence, a user-friendly leader who deals in 'sound bite' politics, such as Tony Blair, may prove popular with these volatile single-issue voters who have ceased to be aligned to any party.

Another factor which was noticeable in the four election victories of the Conservatives from 1979 to 1992 was the growth of stark regional differences. At the 1983 General Election, for instance, the Labour Party, excluding London, won only three seats south of the Midlands. Most of Labour's seats were won in big inner-city areas with high proportions of working-class people. At the 1992 election, the Conservative Party held fewer than ten seats in Scotland and Wales put together. In fact, the Labour vote in many of its working-class heartlands has increased from 1979 to 1992. In Wales, 69 per cent of the working class voted Labour. However, Labour has lost the support of the working class in the south of England: only 30 per cent of voters there chose them in 1992. Thus, the Conservative dominance at elections since 1979 has been in the expanding working-class Tory vote in the Midlands and the south of England. This strongly suggests

FIGURE 5.7 This political cartoon by Schrank parodies the efforts of the Conservative Party (leader William Hague aided by such figures as Margaret Thatcher and Michael Portillo) to stall the Labour Party's attempt to drive Britain into Europe (Tony Blair and Chancellor Gordon Brown in the car) (© *The Independent*)

Margaret Thatcher's hard-core support came from areas which were not part of industrial Britain in the first place. The yuppie lifestyle of the 1980s was also largely based in the south of England. Hence, the class composition of the south has produced a situation in which, in three-cornered fights between the Conservatives, Labour, and the Liberals, it was the Tories who were able to come out on top in 1979 and 1992. By adopting their commitment to consumerism, Labour's Blair was able to reverse those victories in 1997 and 2001.

Conclusion

For the reasons cited above, pronouncing the death of class in British society does seem premature. The stark regional differences between the affluent south and the more impoverished north suggest that Thatcherism represented a rather narrow class appeal. In fact, Margaret Thatcher never won more than 44 per cent of the vote at any General Election, while in 1950 the Labour Party polled 51 per cent. The link between class and politics has not been completely broken. It seems that the overwhelming majority of manual workers still vote for the Labour Party. Yet this group, owing to the decline of manufacturing industry, has fallen within the workforce. Class position still remains the best way of establishing long-term voting patterns. At the 1987 General Election, 48 per cent of working-class voters chose the Labour Party, while only 15 per cent of salaried professionals did so. The self-employed are still the staunchest Conservative Party voters. The Liberal Democrats are most strongly supported by salaried professional and white-collar members of the middle class. What has probably happened is that the size of the classes has changed. This has resulted in the middle class growing in size in certain geographical locations in the Midlands and the south and the size of the working class has fallen owing to the decline of heavy manufacturing industry in the north, Scotland, and Wales.

Finally, to trace a couple of intersections between this chapter and two others, we may ask the question: in which political party were women and members of ethnic minorities to be given the fairest chance of advancing themselves? One of the complaints made against Margaret Thatcher was that she 'never did anything for women'. This may well be so in terms of legislation, membership of her cabinets, and furtherance of the interests of those traditional families where women did not work outside the home. Yet many others have argued that Thatcher certainly offered a powerful role model for women.

The Labour Party under Tony Blair tried to increase the number of its prospective parliamentary candidates who were women. However, all-women shortlists for seats at Westminster were judged to be illegal in 1995. The proportion of women and ethnic minority MPs in different political parliamentary parties is extremely low. The earlier attempt to introduce 'black sections' in local constituencies was shelved after heated debate. However, individual MPs, including Diane Abbott, Bernie Grant, Paul Boateng, and Keith Vaz have raised the profile of ethnic minorities in Britain. These four were all elected Labour MPs in 1987 (the first black representatives in Parliament for sixty years) but it was not until 1992 that a Conservative MP, Nirj Deva, was elected from an ethnic minority.

For the future, perhaps the most significant aspect of contemporary politics is the fact that the next generation, Britain's young people, seem alienated not just from allegiance to individual parties but from the whole democratic process. Hence their cultural identity is formed far more by consumer considerations and single-issue politics than by a belief in the potential for party politics to bring about change for the better.

Exercises

1   Offer a definition of upper, middle and working class.

2   To what extent do British people vote along class lines?

3   What is your understanding of the voting systems: 'first past the post' and 'proportional representation'? Which offers the better model on which to base a system for electing a government?

4   How have British class attitudes and styles changed since the 1950s?

5   Name some British people from a range of occupations. Can you place them in terms of class?

Reading

Hutton, Will. *The State We're In*, Jonathan Cape, 1995. Wide-ranging, accessible review of Britain's political economy in relation to its competitors.

Jenkins, Simon. *Accountable to No-one: The Tory Nationalization of Britain*, Hamish Hamilton, 1995. Book about the privatisation and commodification of Britain, and the Conservatives' shift to centralised control.

Marr, Andrew. *Ruling Britannia*, Michael Joseph, 1995. Popular account of recent British government.

Radice, Giles (ed.). *What Needs to Change*, HarperCollins, 1995. Compendium of views of people in politics, social sciences and the arts, including film maker David Puttnam and Prime Minister Tony Blair

Cultural Examples

Films

Damage (1992) dir. Louis Malle. Cold film about a British politician's love affair and subsequent family crises (an updated fictional treatment of the theme found in *Scandal*, Michael Caton-Jones's 1989 film based on the early 1960s Profumo Affair).

Betrayal (1983) dir. David Jones. Harold Pinter's love-triangle play about British middle-class manners and infidelities.

The Ploughman's Lunch (1983) dir. Richard Eyre. Concentrates on a cynical reporter to give a critical analysis of British morals during the Falklands War.

Life Is Sweet (1991) dir. Mike Leigh. Light, poignant comedy, typical of the director's films, about the British lower middle class and working class.

Books

John Braine, *Room at the Top* (1957). Portrays the social ascent of a young man whose education and marriage make possible his upward mobility.

David Caute, *Veronica, or the Two Nations* (1989). Critique of Thatcherism taking its title from a novel by Disraeli.

David Hare, *The Secret Rapture* (1988). Allegorical play about morals, materialism, and politics in 1980s Britain. Also made into a film in the early 1990s.

Television programmes

Spitting Image. Very influential topical programme in which prominent public figures, from royalty to politicians to television personalities, represented by grotesque puppets are held up to ridicule.

Yes, Minister. Comedy series about the opposition between government and the civil service in which an MP, seeking change and votes, and his Private Secretary, seeking continuity and bureaucracy, try to out-manoeuvre one another. Every episode illustrates the political, and supposedly British, art of compromise.

House of Cards. Fictional series about a manipulative Conservative MP seeking power whose skill at political evasion and double-dealing was compelling, and whose typical hypocritical expressions such as 'You might think that, but I couldn't possibly comment' and 'I have no ambitions in that direction' became catch-phrases.

The New Statesman. Comedy series about an obnoxious but successful ultra-right-wing Tory MP.

Have I Got News for You. Topical satire on the week's news with Angus Deayton, Ian Hislop, and Paul Merton.

Music

Pulp, *Different Class* (1995). Album of vignettes about class politics, drug culture, and British social attitudes.

Blur, *The Great Escape* (1995). A series of comments on British life from the opening track on 'Stereotypes', through a song on the 'Country house' to 'Top Man' (a clothes shop).

Billy Bragg, *Workers' Playtime* (1988). Named after a postwar radio programme broadcast from a factory canteen, this, like all Bragg's albums, is a collection of love songs and political anthems such as 'Waiting for the Great Leap Forwards', 'Tender Comrade' and 'Rotting on Remand.'

The Clash, *The Clash* (1977). Archetypal British punk featuring songs such as 'White Riot', 'London's Burning', 'Career Opportunities', 'I'm So Bored with the USA', and 'Police and Thieves'.

Websites

www.news.bbc.co.uk
> Contains in-depth coverage of contemporary issues with lots of links to background stories.

www.statistics.gov.uk
> These deal with thirteen areas of British life; economics, employment, etc.

www.labour.org.uk www.libdems.org.uk www.conservative-party.org.uk
> Web addresses of the main UK political parties.

www.the-times.co.uk/ www.telegraph.co.uk/ www.guardian.co.uk
> www.independent.co.uk/
> These broadsheet newspapers offer daily comment and analyis which reflect and inform the culture.

Chapter 6

Ethnicity and language

Gerry Smyth

■   Varieties of English   213

■   Gaelic, Scots, Welsh   217

■   New languages, new identities   223

■   Conclusion   232

■   *Exercises*   236

■   *Reading*   236

■   *Cultural examples*   237

■   *Websites*   238

Timeline

1066	Norman Invasion from northern France
1362	English legally recognised
1603	Death of Queen Elizabeth I
1616	Death of Shakespeare
1707	Union of England and Scotland
1800	Union of Ireland and Britain
1870	Welsh banned for teaching
1947	Gaelic banned on Northern Ireland road signs
1955	Churchill wanted slogan: 'Keep Britain White'
1958	'Race' riots in Notting Hill
1965	Race Relations Act
1968	'Troubles' start in Northern Ireland
1976	Commission for Racial Equality
1977	Advisory Council on Race Relations
1983	Black sections in Labour Party
1991	Census questions on ethnicity

Asurvey carried out in a number of London schools in 1980 found that only 15 per cent of pupils spoke what their teachers considered to be standard, or 'correct' English. The rest spoke twenty different varieties of English from the British Isles, forty-two dialects of overseas English, and fifty-eight different world languages. Another survey of the same period found that there were at least twelve languages in Britain which could claim over a hundred thousand speakers. To some people, such linguistic diversity might seem surprising in the homeland of arguably the world's most successful modern language. These statistics, however, are indicative of the multitude of ways used by the citizens of modern Britain to communicate.

These languages, moreover, are closely linked with the ways in which people perceive themselves and their role in British society. For although the United Kingdom is a state, many people within this state think about themselves, their families, and their local communities in quite different ways. One way of describing these individuals and the groups to which they belong is in terms of 'ethnicity'. Ethnicity is a highly complex and contentious concept. For the purposes of this chapter however, it can be defined as the patterns of behaviour, cultural values, and political affiliations shared by certain individuals who come together to form a group within a larger population.

According to the National Statistics agency, in 1999–2000 the 56.93 million people in the British Isles included 3,830,000 people from ethnic minorities (having risen from just over 3 million in the 1991 census). The largest ethnic minority populations are found in inner London (25.6 per cent) and West Midlands Metropolitan County (14.6 per cent), and the smallest in the rural areas of Scotland (1.3 per cent), Yorkshire (0.9 per cent) and Northumberland (1 per cent). Because many of the references in this chapter are drawn from Liverpool (in the metropolitan county of Merseyside), and because the area of Inner London offers an extreme example, the statistics in Table 6.1 (not including Northern Ireland) are supplied for comparative purposes.

Additionally, the United Kingdom comprises four separate indigenous populations, one very large – English (approximately 48 million) – and

TABLE 6.1 Comparison of ethnic populations

	Inner London	Great Britain	Merseyside
Total persons	2,504,451	54,888,844	1,403,642
White	74.4	94.5	98.2
Black Caribbean	7.1	0.9	0.2
Black African	4.4	0.4	0.2
Black Other	2.0	0.3	0.3
Indian	3.0	1.5	0.2
Pakistani	1.2	0.9	0.1
Bangladeshi	2.8	0.3	0.1
Chinese	1.1	0.3	0.4
Other Asian	1.8	0.4	0.1
Other	2.3	0.5	0.4

Source: Census, 1991

three small: Scottish (5 million), Welsh (3 million), and Northern Irish (1.5 million). What all this means is that there is a large number of people in the United Kingdom – around 20 per cent (12 million people) of the total population who do not have a straightforward relationship with the political state in which they live. In recent years, this problematic relationship between the state and its ethnic and regional minorities has become the subject of one of the most important debates in modern British life, and in this chapter I want to examine some of the practices, attitudes, and strategies which have emerged around this debate.

Ethnic and regional identity can appear in many forms. Historians, sociologists, and anthropologists have discovered, however, that one of the most important ways in which ethnic groups identify themselves is through language. Not only is language the principal conveyor of symbols, ideas, and beliefs which are of importance to the ethnic group, very often the language becomes a powerful possession in itself, something to be protected and preserved as the main badge of ethnic identity. Much of the time, then, the alternative allegiances which constitute ethnic identity emerge specifically as tensions about language and the social status and cultural possibilities of different accents, dialects, and vocabularies.

The recognition of ethnic status has significant legal, educational, and social implications. But ethnic status, going back to our definition, also has important sociological and psychological implications for the kind of person the individual understands himself or herself to be – that is, for an individual's identity. The point of departure for what follows is that a significant part of our individual identity is constituted through language – the language the world uses to communicate with us, and the language we use to communicate with the world. Putting this all together, then, these issues of ethnicity, identity, and language are going to be our main areas of focus in this chapter. Specifically, I want to examine three interrelated issues – the usage and status of: (1) 'standard' and 'non-standard' forms of the English language and implications for English and British identity; (2) other indigenous British languages – Welsh, Scots, and Gaelic – and the challenge to the domination of English; (3) non-English languages brought to Britain by immigrants and other groups, such as Chinese and West Indian.

Varieties of English

In the nineteenth century, the notion of 'correct', 'good', or 'pure' English became something of an obsession for many literary critics, philosophers, and educationalists. The result of this anxiety was the invention of an ideal form of the English language, covering aspects of grammar, vocabulary, pronunciation, and so on, but also importantly linked to ways of acting, kinds of belief, and systems of value. Such an ideal was needed to support Britain's self-image as a great industrial and imperial power, and to measure various kinds of linguistic deviance. The fact that this ideal or 'standard' English was an invention did not appear to worry those who used it to condemn the linguistic 'errors' made by the vast majority of the British population. It must have seemed strange to a person from Northumberland or Somerset for example, regions with dialects evolved over a thousand years and completely immersed in local history and local geography, to be told that the way they spoke was wrong – according to the arbitrary rules invented by certain intellectuals and scholars! In the twenty-first century, it has been most commonly argued that in most social situations an upper-class accent is a disadvantage and there are actually now speech coaches who will help 'posh' people lose their accents, whereas thirty years ago everyone else was trying to acquire them. This has to be linked to the perception that class is nowadays more about celebrity than breeding, especially as many of the prestigious events on the social calendar, and the magazines that cover them, will now be overrun with the famous as much as the aristocratic, the only connection between the two groups being that both are comparatively rich.

The question of the correct way to speak and to write English continued to exercise a very great influence in British life throughout the twentieth century. Many people even today adhere to the model of standard English (or 'Received Pronunciation' as it is sometimes called) invented in the nineteenth century, believing it to be the real or true English language, a fixed linguistic structure against which deviations and mistakes can be measured. These people remain anxious about what they consider to be falling standards in spoken and written English, feeling that this is in some way related to Britain's wider economic, cultural, and political status. Letters are written to the 'quality' newspapers (such as *The Times*, The *Independent*, the *Daily Telegraph*, and *The Guardian*) and to the British Broadcasting Corporation (BBC), both radio and television, about bad practices in spoken and written English. In the early days of broadcasting, the 'BBC accent' was the hallmark of correct spoken English, and news-casters are still seen as 'custodians' of the language. But in recent years this 'BBC accent', such as its close relation 'the Queen's English', has in itself become a minority form; one of the few people likely to be heard speaking 'the Queen's English' is the Queen herself, in her Christmas Day speeches to the Commonwealth (and even she has been accused of loosening her speech in recent years). The clipped pronunciation and mannered voice of Prince Charles, as well as his constant use of the impersonal pronoun 'one' – as in 'one feels one's responsibilities' – is also somewhat of a throwback to an earlier stage in Britain's linguistic history. Although versions of the 'BBC accent' still exist – for example, in some sports commentary such as tennis, cricket, equestrian events, or in some arts programmes – it is now more likely to be used for satiric or ironic purposes. To an extent, this debate has been won by the pluralists, and been replaced by a new concern over written English. Here, rules and standards are far more deeply ingrained, but the need to write 'correct English' is coming increasingly under pressure as new technologies such as the internet and text messaging encourage compressed forms of expression. A growing informality is apparent, fuelled by the diversity of 'Englishes' among different ethnic and regional communities, despite concerns in some quarters that, for example, it is possible for a student to gain a first-class degree without being able to write grammatically correct English to the standards upheld by their parents' generation. The counter-argument is that visual culture is taking over from written culture and that a 'post-literate' society will be a more rounded one in terms of its creative thinking, less hung up on words, more capable of thinking in terms of ideas and images.

Adequate command of English still constitutes a major part of modern British education, even for those who do not speak the language regularly at home or outside the classroom. One way in which the fixation with the language manifests itself is in the debates surrounding the educa-tional significance of William Shakespeare. Of course, to anyone familiar with it, Shakespearean language can hardly be thought of as a viable means of communication in the twenty-first century. Nevertheless, Shakespearean language is felt by many to represent the pinnacle of British cultural achievement, and it is widely argued that in his poetry and plays Shakespeare captured the essence of English (though not British) identity.

To those taking this line, it therefore appears obvious that young British people, of whatever ethnic origin, should become familiar with Shakespeare's work so that they can appreciate the history and the society of which they are now a part. Drawing on these opinions, a 'Shakespeare industry' has become established, linked in many significant ways with other major industries such as publishing, leisure, tourism, and heritage.

On the other hand, some people claim that Shakespeare's relevance is only historical, and that modern education should be dealing more with students' contemporary practices, values, and beliefs. Both in terms of theme and language, it is argued, Shakespeare has limited significance for those from different ethnic backgrounds possessing important cultural and linguistic traditions of their own (it was, for example, widely questioned in 2000 whether Shakespeare's works should remain standard texts in British schools). The same could also be said of certain sections of the indigenous British population which have traditionally been excluded from the high cultural institutions where 'Shakespeare' has been enshrined for so long. During the 1980s one cultural critic claimed that a television soap opera such as *Coronation Street*, set in contemporary Salford and detailing the experiences of a community of working-class people was of far greater interest and significance to millions of people throughout Britain than anything by or about Shakespeare. This was because the themes, language, and accents of *Coronation Street* were closer to what most British people experienced in their daily lives. This is a contentious argument, as it might be seen to deny people from working-class or ethnic backgrounds access to a valuable cultural experience. The emphasis on regional accents was underscored by the decision of the French government, in an agreement with the BBC, to help French schoolchildren improve their English by broadcasting programmes such as *Open All Hours* (set in the north), *EastEnders*, and *Only Fools and Horses* (both featuring Cockney accents and estuary English) in teacher training colleges and secondary schools. The launch of the initiative, in a Paris school in September 2001, was scheduled to coincide with the European Day of Languages.

Regional variations in accent, vocabulary, and pronunciation, as practised by the characters in *EastEnders* or *Coronation Street*, are of great importance in British life, as well as having an important bearing on the question of standard English. Some of the more easily distinguishable accents are those of Cornwall, the West Midlands, Tyneside, Northern Ireland, and Clydeside, although to a sensitive ear there are dozens of separate regional accents in Britain, and hundreds of minor linguistic peculiarities which set one region, one town, even one village, apart from another. The city of Liverpool, for example, has a very strong and recognisable accent, known as 'Scouse', deriving from a mixture of Lancashire, Irish, and Welsh influences, and those speaking with this accent are referred to as 'Scousers'. One version of 'Scouse' was brought to national and world attention by the success of The Beatles in the 1960s. The phrases, slang, and inflections which characterised the speech of The Beatles however, were but one version of what is in fact a highly complex set of linguistic practices operating within the city of Liverpool.

One factor influencing all the varieties of English in contemporary Britain is the economic and cultural domination of the United States. Especially since the end of the Second World War, the issue of American influence on British life has been hotly debated. Some people fear that sharing a language with the most culturally successful nation on Earth will erode Britain's own linguistic identity and also accounts for Britons' woefully poor grasp on other European languages, while others argue that the global dominance of English ensures Britain's continuing cultural vitality. It does seem that, through exposure to popular music, cinema, and computer technology, British people are becoming more and more familiar with the various speech patterns of the USA, even learning to differentiate between them (for example, Southern drawl, New York nasal, Californian rising intonation). Distinctive American rhythms, intonations, and slang are becoming common throughout Britain, not only in pubs and clubs but to an increasing extent also in more formal contexts such as education and the media. Much British popular music since the 1960s, for example, is heavily influenced by American styles. Against this, part of the attraction of groups such as Catatonia (Wales), The Proclaimers (Scotland), or Blur (London) is hearing the singers using their local accents. At the same time, it is clear that English, albeit American English, remains the dominant language of diplomacy and of popular culture, and it could be argued that this has given British people cultural and economic opportunities they might otherwise not have had.

All the issues raised in this section have important implications for the question of British identity. The ways in which the English language is used continue to be of great importance, for those who adhere to standard English as well as for those who accept and rejoice in the latest slang words and phrases. The number of official or authoritative bodies who accept that language is a constantly changing and vibrant part of culture is increasing. For example, dictionary compilers are more likely to include recent slang words than they used to be. The *New Compact Penguin English Dictionary* has entries for 'pants' (awful), 'manky' (dirty or rotten) and 'dis' (to show disrespect), but there are new words appearing in playgrounds all the time. A 2001 survey of seven- to fourteen-year-olds listed scores of buzz-words, ranging from the familiar such as 'wicked', 'radical', and 'dingbat', to the less common, such as 'savage' or 'vicious' (for excellent), 'trev' (a designer-clothes wearer), 'minging' (ugly or disgusting), and 'talk to the hand' (because I'm not listening). Unsurprisingly, television shows provide many new catchphrases, from the 'whazzup' of Budweiser commercials to the 'boyakasha' of the *Ali G Show*. 'Doh!' is among the young the most popular expression of stupidity these days, and it is therefore interesting to note that in 2001 Homer Simpson was voted Britain's most popular comedy character (pushing Basil Fawlty into second place). Other words, of course, fade out of fashion: only the over-thirties would call anything 'brill', 'ace', 'fab', or 'naff', though the success of the Austin Powers films has given 'groovy' a new lease of life. Pop music also changes language from month to month, so 'bootylicious' (Destiny's Child) and 'teenage dirtbag' (Wheatus) are currently in, but probably not for long. Rhyming slang is also increasingly common in young street culture, though its connections with Cockney are far off, and the emphasis is on using celebrities' names in a way that makes the commonplaces of everyday teenage life more interesting. Some recent examples are: 'Britney Spears' for beers, 'Wallace and Gromit' for vomit, and 'Brad Pitt' for shit.

The possibility of a single, ideal English language was always remote, both because of its artificiality and because of the active role played in cultural life by accent and regional variation. But such an ideal is becoming less and less viable, given both the speed with which language circulates in the technological age, and the number of British people for whom the English language is deeply problematical. With regard to this latter group, I now want to discuss those non-English languages which are, nevertheless, indigenous to the British Isles.

Gaelic, Scots, Welsh

Before modern technology made travel and the spread of information so much quicker, it was possible for people from different parts of the British Isles never to hear the English language spoken. From the influx of European invaders and migrants who began to come to the islands around two thousand years ago, a great number of distinctive local dialects, as well as a smaller number of discrete languages, emerged. But as English evolved into the successful international language it is today, these other, mainly Celtic, languages tended to be marginalised. For many people, this predominance of the English language is a problem in that it deprives individuals and communities of a distinctive local cultural inheritance. Instead it collapses all history and all possible experience into a homogenous yet spurious Britishness. A character of James Joyce's describes a conversation at his school in Ireland with his teacher, who is an Englishman:

> The language in which we are speaking is his before it is mine. How different are the words *home*, *Christ*, *ale*, *master*, on his

lips and on mine! I cannot speak or write these words without
unrest of spirit. His language, so familiar and so foreign, will
always be for me an acquired speech. I have not made or
accepted its words. My voice holds them at bay. My soul frets
in the shadow of his language.

(James Joyce, *A Portrait of the Artist as a Young Man*
[1916]: Penguin, 1977, p. 172)

For many minority language speakers, Joyce manages to capture in this
passage the social and personal frustrations of being caught between a way
of speaking which is specifically attuned to local experience and local
history and an all too 'familiar', too dominant language such as English,
in which they are expected to communicate.

Gaelic is the language of the Gaels, Celtic invaders from Europe who
came to the British Isles in the second and third centuries before the beginning of the Christian era. Gaelic rapidly became the principal language of
Ireland, and later it was also widely spoken on the west coast of Scotland
where many Irish Gaels emigrated in later years. (The census of 1991
showed that out of a Scottish population of 4.9 million, 1.4 per cent –
about seventy thousand people – spoke Gaelic in some form.) Gaelic
remained the first language of Ireland until the middle of the nineteenth
century, when the Great Famine (1845–8) decimated the population.
Death, mass emigration, and the association of Gaelic with poverty and
backwardness combined to marginalise the language, so that, by the time
the southern part of Ireland gained partial independence from Britain in
1922, Gaelic was spoken only in small pockets (called Gaeltachts) in the
north and the west of the island.

This marginalisation did not go unopposed, however. During the
1890s a cultural movement known as the Celtic Revival became very influential throughout the British Isles, and this movement was closely linked
with the idea of political independence for Ireland. An important part of
its programme was the restoration of Gaelic as the first language of Ireland.
This was felt to be necessary because, going back to the introduction to
this chapter, language was seen as the crucial element of a distinctive identity, and therefore it was not possible for Irish people to achieve real
freedom if they continued to speak English.

In 1992, the Northern Ireland Office spent £1.2 million promoting
Gaelic projects, and although this is only a fraction of the amount spent
on Scottish Gaelic and Welsh, it has been welcomed as official acknowl-
edgement of the importance of Gaelic for the cultural health of the
community. The city of Belfast has bilingual schools, a Gaelic newspaper
(called *Lá*, meaning 'Day', which began publication in 1981), and a (very
small) number of Gaelic radio and television programmes broadcast by the

BBC and independent stations. While use of the language is now declining in the south, voluntary Irish classes flourish throughout Northern Ireland. All this activity is encouraging for Gaelic supporters, although whether the language can truly escape its sectarian heritage and help resolve the political divide in Northern Ireland remains a hotly debated question.

One of the most interesting British languages, precisely because of the debate as to whether it is a distinct language or merely a dialect of English, is Scots. Scots is descended from the Northumbrian dialect of Old English, and at one time forms of the language existed in all the non-Gaelic regions of Scotland, including the remote Shetland and Orkney Islands. By the sixteenth century one particular form of Scots supported a highly developed cultural and political tradition entirely separate from England. At that point, however, a number of factors combined to force Scots into decline, the most important of which was the union of the Scottish and the English crowns in 1603. After the abolition of the Scottish parliament in 1707, Scots, like Irish Gaelic in the nineteenth century, began to be rejected as a sign of cultural backwardness, and the ruling classes attempted to purge their speech of any remnants of the old Scots tongue. Despite interest in what came to be known as 'Lallans' (Scots for 'Lowlands', as opposed to the mostly Gaelic-speaking Highlands) amongst some poets and novelists of the eighteenth century, the language survived only among the peasantry and, after the industrialisation of Scotland during the nineteenth century, among the urban working class. Scots was under constant threat throughout the twentieth century because, unlike Scottish Gaelic, most people do not regard it as a separate language but as a deformed version of English, or as an artificial dialect invented by the romantic writers of the eighteenth and nineteenth centuries. Both of these misconceptions add to the stereotypical notion of Scots that tends to be reproduced in the popular imagination as the 'sign' of Scottishness – words such as 'wee' (small), 'braw' (fine, good), 'lassie' (girl), and so on, as well as a heavily inflected accent when speaking English. Mr Scott, from the original *Star Trek* series (played by an American actor, James Doohan), possesses probably the most famous, and least convincing, Scots accent in popular culture. The comedian Gregor Fisher, who plays the part of working-class Glaswegian Rab C. Nesbit in a BBC Scotland television series of the same name, is the nearest one will find outside Scotland to a genuine Scots speaker on television, though it would be very difficult for anyone who did not speak English as a first language to understand the characters in the programme. One of the dominant Scots forces in British culture today is the resurgence of indie bands from 'north of the border': groups such as Belle and Sebastian, Arab Strap, The Reindeer Section, and Adventures in Stereo have brought back the idea of Scottish pop which flourished in the early 1980s, when the Postcard record label launched groups such as

Orange Juice and Aztec Camera (more well known Scottish popstars are Fran Healy, the lead singer of Travis, and Sharleen Spiteri, the lead singer of Texas). The health of this new movement was acknowledged in 2001 by the English band Spearmint, who recorded a track called 'Scottish Pop': a song that compared the feeling of being in love to the joy of listening to the new Scottish bands. (Welsh pop groups are also flourishing, from the 'idiosyncratic' Gorky's Zygotic Mynci to the mainstream Stereophonics and Manic Street Preachers, or the slightly less well known Super Furry Animals, who in 2000 released a CD in Welsh, *Mwng*, which quickly became the best-selling Welsh-language album ever.)

Scots receives little institutional support in the 1990s. It is not recognised for census purposes, and, given the success of Welsh and Scottish Gaelic in competing for what funds *are* available from central government and the BBC, this situation is unlikely to change in the near future. As with the Gaelic language in the Republic of Ireland, it is only amongst a relatively small number of historians, critics, and writers that Scots is still valued; indeed, this intellectual support confers on Scots a sort of cult

FIGURE 6.1 Bagpipe player in Edinburgh

status, granting the language a vogue somewhat at odds with its shrinking working-class base. The familiar argument is that, despite its impoverished condition, the language articulates a way of life, a way of thinking about the world, a way of being Scottish, that cannot be adequately expressed in English. This argument is rejected by many, however, and not only by those 'Unionists' who maintain that Scotland's future depends on remaining an English-speaking region of the United Kingdom. The revival of Scots is also dismissed by many nationalists (seeking separate national sovereign status for Scotland) and devolutionists (seeking an autonomous Scottish parliament while remaining part of the United Kingdom) who feel that, given its history of strong cultural and political independence, Scotland does not need the support of an artificially resurrected language. This latter understanding of the relationship between language and national or ethnic identity is in marked contrast to the feelings underpinning the most successful non-English language of the British isles: Welsh.

Like Scotland, since the nineteenth century Wales has had great difficulty in asserting its cultural independence from England. Before the Education Act of 1870, which prohibited teachers from using Welsh as a medium of education, about nine out of ten people spoke the language. As with all the minority languages mentioned so far however, Welsh became stigmatised as the language of the poor and the backward, and, when the southern part of the country began to industrialise, it was only in rural areas such as the counties of Gwynedd and Dyfed in the north and west that Welsh managed to survive.

Since the 1960s, however, a new attitude towards the language has become evident. The rise of Welsh political nationalism has encouraged a pride in the Welsh language and in recent years the ability to speak Welsh has become a highly prestigious attribute. This pride has manifested itself in many ways, but the basic impetus is towards the conversion of Wales into a fully bilingual country.

Many people began in the 1960s by abandoning anglicised names in favour of Welsh ones, while for those who had not yet mastered the language, it was possible to assert a Welsh identity simply by using the heavily inflected Welsh accent. Once over the border, all road signs are now given first in Welsh and then in English, as are most job descriptions, and the language has had great success at all levels of education. Welsh programmes represent well over 50 per cent of the country's radio and television output, and the success of the annual Eisteddfod festival adds to the sense of an autonomous nation supporting a distinctive national culture. Although the number of Welsh-speakers as a whole dropped from 19 per cent to 18.7 per cent between 1981 and 1991, the number of speakers aged between three and fifteen rose from 17.7 per cent to 24.4 per cent, a real rise of 21,000. This augurs well for the future of the language, and is in marked contrast to Scottish Gaelic where the highest percentage of speakers are aged sixty-five and over. However, some Welsh nationalists argue that the success of the language has been achieved at the cost of a coherent political programme, and that central government support for various cultural initiatives does not represent a relinquishing of power, but merely a way of redistributing it.

We should remember that Welsh is reviving, not revived, and in the industrialised south, Swansea, Cardiff, Glamorgan, and the Rhondda valley, where over half the population lives, Welsh is still to all intents and purposes a foreign language. Even so, the relative success of the language has been difficult for many English people to cope with. One recurring image is that of the English tourist feeling intimidated and offended by their exclusion from the Welsh conversations of local bilingual communities. Stories such as these reflect more, perhaps, on the insecurity of English people who hold an idea of Britishness specifically invented to incorporate the various identities of the British Isles under one, English-led, banner (some controversy was sparked by Parliament repeatedly appointing non-Welsh-speaking Secretaries of State for Wales, including John Redwood, who ran for Leader of the Conservative Party in the early 1990s). For it hardly seems strange that Welsh people should wish to converse in their own language, nor that in the absence of political self-determination this should represent a valuable means of identification for them. In autumn 2001, it was suggested that an unofficial citizenship examination for English people planning to move to Wales would be a test of their ability to pronounce Llanfairpwllgwyngyllgogerychwyrndrobwllllantysiliogogogoch, the longest place name in the world after the Maori names of some towns in New Zealand. The town's county council clerk argued that newcomers needed to mix in with the community more, and that pronouncing the town's name correctly would be a good start, especially for people who had moved from England. Local people in fact, however, refer to the town as Llanfair PG, rather than calling it by its full name, which in English means 'The church of St Mary in the hollow of white hazel near the rapid whirlpool by the church of St Tysilio of the red cave'.

It may be that, given time and the global domination of American English noted in the last section, Gaelic, Scots, and Welsh will suffer the fate of other non-English languages of the British Isles such as Cornish (from Cornwall) and Manx (from the Isle of Man), ceasing to be living languages, preserved only in the artificial confines of the library and the university. Welsh appears to be in a reasonable state of health, but Gaelic and Scots must give cause for concern to their supporters and speakers. It might be wondered why, having being so neglected for so long, Britain's non-English languages have aroused so much interest in recent years. Certainly there has been concern about the fate of Gaelic, Scots, and Welsh since the beginning of the twentieth century, but one could argue that it is only since Britain's non-indigenous ethnic minorities began to work for proper recognition of their distinctive cultural heritages that the islands' Celtic minorities have begun to see their languages in a new perspective. I will now turn to those non-indigenous languages.

New languages, new identities

Since the end of the Second World War (1945), immigration has become an issue of increasing public and political concern in Britain. Not only that, but the very terms in which the question of immigration is considered are also highly charged. If you reread the previous two sentences, you will see that the words I have used at the beginning of this discussion of immigration and ethnicity are 'issue', 'concern', and 'question'; other terms invariably found when this subject is raised are 'problem', 'solution', 'answer', 'debate', etc. For many people, such language is itself part of the 'problem' in that it only allows immigration and ethnicity to be discussed as anomalies in an otherwise efficient system, anomalies that 'we' – that is, the established indigenous population of Britain – need to resolve. Being constituted a 'problem' or an 'issue' or a 'cause for concern' even before their arrival in the country has serious implications for the way in which migrant ethnic communities perceive their relations with the state and with Britishness generally. More recently, political commentators have observed that, aside from cultural benefits, only by welcoming migrants will European countries be able to increase their long-term rate of growth and also pay for the pensions of those currently in work.

People have been migrating to and from Britain for centuries, and as long as this has been so, native and immigrant have been constantly reviewing their mutual relations. In 1596 the parliament of Queen Elizabeth I issued an edict limiting the number of black people entering England. This may be seen as the first of a large number of measures taken by British governments in an effort to define exactly what kinds of people have had the right to enter Britain and claim citizenship. The years since 1945 have seen numerous Immigration and Citizenship and Race Relations Acts, all in an effort to supply British identity with a legal and constitutional basis. Over this more recent period, two opposing attitudes appear to be at work. If, as some commentators suggest, increased population mobility is becoming a characteristic contemporary experience, then cultural and political systems which used to construe immigration and ethnicity as 'problems' may no longer be applicable. Such systems indeed, it is argued, were never acceptable in the first place. On the other hand, with the breakup of the Soviet Union, the reunification of East and West

Germany, and the growth of Europeanism, the issue of borders and national and ethnic identity has become very important throughout Europe. Britain, as we have already seen, has its own internal borders and identities, a situation which has led to its unique political constitution. The exact nature of Britishness, however, has become even more complex in the decades since 1945 with the influx of a new range of ethnic identities, and the subsequent emergence of new ways of being British.

There have been well-established black, Chinese, and Indian communities in Britain since the nineteenth century, especially in London and some of the bigger seaports such as Liverpool and Cardiff. The postwar period has seen the arrival of people from many geographical backgrounds – West Africa, the Caribbean, Hong Kong, India, Pakistan, and so on, countries and regions known as the 'New Commonwealth' (as opposed to the 'Old Commonwealth' of Canada, Australia, and New Zealand). Traditionally, the most positive response in mainstream Britain to immigration from the New Commonwealth has been mild interest in the possibility of viewing exotic cultures at close hand. Asians, for example, have been 'contained' by mainstream British culture in terms of the 'colourful' or 'alternative' practices – food, clothes, music, religion, and philosophy – brought from their homelands.

The multitude of identities brought by immigrants from the Indian subcontinent are frequently collapsed into one exotic 'brown' identity which can then be more easily accommodated by modern 'multicultural' Britain. The Indian restaurant and the Pakistani newsagent or corner shop are established parts of British life, and certain other stereotypical traits and practices – yoga, the Sikh and Muslim turban, the raga (the distinctive pattern of Indian music), arranged marriages, as well as of course the 'strange' way of speaking English – have become representative of what to most people seems a tolerable degree of difference within a larger British identity. It is however, decreasingly appropriate to speak of a homogenous British Asian experience. For example, those of Indian origin, according to government and independent statistics, are the most likely to vote, have considerable savings, or achieve top exam results of all ethnic groups (including white), while Bangladeshis are the least likely.

The identity of Indian and other people in Britain is complicated by a history of colonial relations, and this in its turn is linked with the other major form of response to modern immigration. Since the nineteenth century, certain theories regarding the relations between race, nation, and culture have led to the development of ideas which cast immigration and ethnicity in a very negative light. Influenced by these ideas, much of the modern British response to immigration has been characterised by xenophobia and racism. Racism in modern Britain can take two forms. An older, biological racism tends to be linked with violence and aggression, as

FIGURE 6.2 Mosque in Edinburgh

for example, during the 1960s and 1970s when extreme right-wing elements went on 'Paki-bashing' sprees, and even developed political organisations based on repatriation of immigrants. This form of racism is increasingly rare, although it would be a mistake to underestimate the capacity of certain outmoded 'scientific' discourses of race to feed the cycle of racial hatred inherited from earlier times.

The newer, cultural form of racism is more subtle. It claims that it is unfair to ask people from a particular background to accept the kind of changes in lifestyle necessary for them to become 'real' British citizens. For example, one former politician caused a controversy in the 1990s with his 'cricket test'; Lord Norman Tebbit argued that if people living permanently in Britain support other nations in sporting or other cultural events, then they have not sufficiently adapted themselves to British life, and cannot therefore legitimately be called British. Tebbit used the example of the way in which many black Britons support the West Indies cricket team, but the point was intended to apply to any instance of cultural 'treason'. Indeed, the issue of sporting affiliation has become even more heated since the publication of an article in a prestigious cricketing journal in 1995 which suggested that it would be a mistake to expect any 'ethnic' sportsperson selected to represent Britain, even if born here, to be as committed as a 'real' (that is, white) Briton.

Furthermore, following high-profile investigations into racially motivated attacks, on Damilola Taylor and Stephen Lawrence for example, race relations in Britain reached what some considered a crisis in 2001, when several northern cities were hit by a spate of 'riots'. In Oldham in May, in Burnley in June, and in Bradford in July, clashes between whites and blacks resulted in considerable damage and national fears about Britain's future as a multiethnic commnuity. Reasons for the violent outbursts are open to discussion, but facts suggest some of the inequalities behind them: for example, in Oldham, the infant mortality rate among Muslims is three times higher than that of whites, while life expectancy is lower; adult health is worse and Muslims in the town are three times more likely to be unemployed. Government statistics report that about fifty thousand people in the town experience some of the worst social conditions in the country, and the cotton mills which brought Pakistanis and Bangladeshis to Oldham in the 1950s to 1970s closed down twenty years ago. Perhaps not surprisingly, in a 2001 survey, 19 per cent of Britons cited race relations and immigration as a major concern, where only 3 per cent had said the same in 1996 (the average 2001 figure for other European countries was higher, however, at 21 per cent). In Oldham, a temporary eight-foot-high metal mesh fence was erected in the Hathershaw district, and, while the Home Secretary said there would be no official Belfast-style ring-fencing, some white and Asian communities in the town have asked for more 'peace barriers'.

It does seem clear that Britain's ethnic minorities do not have a straightforward relationship with the state. People from the Commonwealth coming to live in Britain have as a rule identified with it as the 'mother country', and most have sought to become good citizens. Yet, the uncertainty of status, the forms of racism invariably experienced, as well as the very act of displacement from familiar places and practices, means that individuals may wish to preserve, and indeed emphasise, their ethnic identity. Of course, not all ethnic minorities will understand their relationship with the host country and the English language in the same way. Each community brings its own assumptions and aspirations, its own cultural values and beliefs, to the relationship with British identity. When one considers that there are many such ethnic communities in Britain, all experiencing different levels of assimilation and alienation; and when one further considers that different generations will not engage with the available identities in the same ways, then one may begin to appreciate that the question of what is and is not 'British' has become extremely complex in recent years. It now appears, in fact, that the practices, attitudes, beliefs, and values that come together to form any identity are enmeshed in an

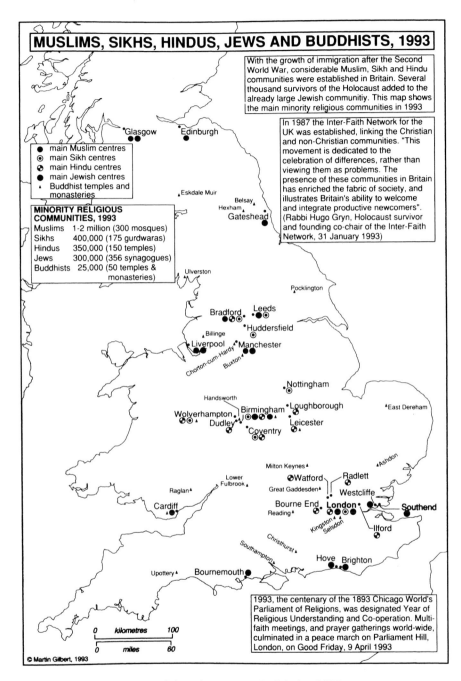

FIGURE 6.3 Distribution of the ethnic group in Britain, 1993
Source: Martin Gilbert, Atlas of British History (Routledge, 1993)

intricate web of similarities and differences, and this web covers every area of modern British life – religion, politics, work, leisure, culture, and education. Nowhere can this complicated situation be seen more clearly than through the subject upon which we have been focusing throughout this chapter – language.

Many British people do not use English as a first language, but speak instead the language of their home country, or of their parents' home country. Chinese people living in Britain, for example, have not traditionally placed a high priority on integration into the host community. In a city such as Liverpool, which has one of the largest Chinese populations in the country (0.4 per cent as against the 0.3 per cent national figure), it is clear that Chinese people make less use of the English language than the city's other ethnic minorities. There are a number of reasons why this might be; the extreme difference between the Chinese and English languages; the hope of many Chinese people eventually to move back to their native country; the wish to preserve a valued cultural heritage; the unwillingness to 'lose face' by speaking English badly. Whatever the reasons, the older Chinese population of Liverpool have maintained a low profile in the social and economic life of the city and as a consequence a high proportion of the community still speak very little English. Chinese children on the other hand, whether immigrants or born in the city, learn to speak the language of their parents (usually Mandarin or Cantonese) at home, but have to learn English for school and for their other interests outside the community. This bilingualism can influence the ways in which the younger Chinese population understand their status in the contemporary life of Liverpool. Familiar both with the traditions of their parents and with the facts of modern British life, the younger people appear to possess greater confidence than their parents and grandparents, and are not afraid of raising the profile of their community. The Chinese New Year has become a major event in the social and cultural life of Liverpool, and street names in the area known as 'Chinatown' are given in English and Chinese. At the same time, these young Chinese people have problems which are different from the ones faced by their parents and different again from the ones faced by the city's other ethnic minorities. Bilingualism is just as likely to bring a sense of being marooned between identities as it is to bring confidence. Third-generation Chinese, having different familial, religious, and cultural values, will accept (or deny) their British identity differently from third-generation West Indians, or Indians, or Irish people. In fact, generalising about such relatively small populations can be dangerous, emphasising once more the political as well as social complexity of issues of ethnicity and language.

One of the most interesting examples of the complexity of modern British ethnicity is illustrated in the language brought by migrants from the Caribbean. People from the West Indies – mostly Jamaica, but also

Trinidad, Guyana, Barbados, the Windward and Leeward Islands – were actively recruited for the British labour market in the years after the war when business was beginning to recover and unemployment was low. When these people came to Britain they brought with them their cultural traditions, the most obvious and important one being their language. But what was this language?

Standard English is the official language of Jamaica and many of the other West Indian islands. But most West Indians speak a version of 'Jamaican Creole', a language developed from the slave culture of the eighteenth and nineteenth centuries. Members of many West African tribes were brought over to the West Indies, and they spoke different languages, so to communicate amongst themselves they developed a form of language known as 'pidgin'. Pidgin drew on the language of the slave-masters – English – but reworked it using the linguistic forms of the numerous West African languages. And this language is basically the same one that has become known as Jamaican Creole (a 'creole' is a 'pidgin' dialect that has become a standard language for a particular community).

Many people would not consider Jamaican Creole to be a distinct language in itself, but merely an exotic form of standard English. This is certainly true at one level, yet, according to linguists and anthropologists, it is possible for West Indian people to derive 90 per cent of their vocabulary from English and still speak a language that is not English. This is because language involves much more than words. Language involves complex physical and mental strategies, verbal styles and techniques, narrative genres and traditions, tones of voice, turn-taking protocols, speech rhythms, and a hundred other things, some of them immensely subtle. As a gesture towards this subtlety, consider this short passage from a poem called 'I Trod', written by the Black British writer Benjamin Zephaniah and published in 1985:

> I trod over de mountain
> I trod over de sea
> one ting I would like to see is
> up pressed people free
> I trod wid I eye peeled . . .
>
> (Benjamin Zephaniah, *The Dread Affair*
> (Arena, 1985), p. 86. Reproduced courtesy
> of The Hutchinson Publishing Group)

This example is interesting in a number of ways. The theme, first of all, is one that is very significant in Caribbean history and one that emerges in much Black British culture – the search for freedom. The poet uses the device of a physical journey over the landscape to represent the quest for a means to remove the spiritual and political scars of slavery. This theme is supported by the language of the poem, in which there is an attempt to reproduce the accents and pronunciations of Jamaican Creole – 'the' becomes 'de', 'thing' becomes 'ting', 'with' becomes 'wid'. Instead of being 'oppressed', these people are 'up pressed', a 'neologism' (a new word invented by the writer) that suggests both the pressure coming down on the people from above, and the people's determination to resist that pressure. This reworking of the language is also a way of linking past and present, as the refusal of standard English is part of the process whereby Black British people resist their 'enslavement' in contemporary Britain. In danger of becoming part of a permanent black British underclass and thereby repeating the cycle of slavery and mastery, Zephaniah celebrates his West Indian identity by emphasising his distinctive speech patterns and rhythms in the face of Anglo-Saxon cultural domination.

The analysis should not stop here, however. The phrase 'I eye' is not typical of Jamaican Creole (in which it would be 'me eye'), but derives from the discourse of Rastafarianism. This religion, which encompasses both a spiritual and a socio-political outlook and which is associated with certain cultural practices such as reggae music, marijuana, and dreadlocks (a hair style), originated in Jamaica and has in recent years become one of the dominant images of West Indian identity. Rastafarians reject words such as 'me', 'my', and 'we' in favour of a single word ('I') which celebrates the unique identity of the individual speaker and his or her unique relationship with Jah (the Rastafarian notion of God). At the same time, Rastafarianism is far from dominant amongst Britain's West Indian population which, typically of the wider British situation with regard to religion, encompasses a range of Christian, Islamic, and atheistic positions. In these few lines, therefore, the poet can be seen as identifying with a very specific group. Analysis of the poem also shows the complex connections between contemporary British society, Caribbean history, and a particular religious system.

Two points should be noted. The first is that, even from the fairly sketchy reading provided here, it is possible to appreciate that Zephaniah's position is not *typical* of Black Britishness, itself a contentious term, but shows instead the diversity of language and identity available to a British person of West Indian ethnicity. The second point is that Jamaican Creole, if not an *actual* separate language, certainly operates as a separate language for those members of the West Indian community who speak it to signal their lack of identity with dominant British culture. If Jamaican Creole is at one end of the spectrum, and standard English is at the other, then a person born in Britain of West Indian parents has potential access to all the variations and nuances of language in between. How the individual from an ethnic community speaks will depend upon that highly complex cultural web mentioned earlier, incorporating different backgrounds, different generations, different levels of assimilation, different desires.

Like all the other languages and dialects mentioned in this chapter, Jamaican Creole has attracted a number of stereotypical images in modern British culture. The West Indian cricket team is the Caribbean cultural image with the highest profile in Britain. Their extended superiority over the 'English' team (which over the years has included 'naturalised' players from all over the Commonwealth, as well as from Scotland and Wales) is, as previously mentioned, a source of pleasure to many Black Britons and of much resentment to many 'real' Britons.

In recent years, other images and role models have helped to reveal the complexities involved in ethnic identity. The Notting Hill street carnival around Ladbroke Grove in London, which began as a local celebration of West Indian culture, is now the biggest event of its kind in Europe, such that in 2001 the authorities argued that it had outgrown its venue and would have to be moved. This cultural festival has in the past seen clashes between Black Britons, organised racists, and the metropolitan police, but more recently it has been peaceful and hugely successful, attracting up to two million people from all over the country and indeed the world, with floats participating in the procession around the three-mile route coming from as far afield as South Africa and Australia. Likewise, the television programme *Desmonds*, about a barber shop owned by a West Indian family, relies for much of its comic effect on the differences in perception

FIGURE 6.4 Notting Hill Carnival 2001

between the older generation, born in the Caribbean and speaking variations of Jamaican Creole, and the children, born in London and speaking English with a typical London accent. Both the street carnival and the television programme confront the confusion which arises from the wide range of identities available; both attempt to offer positive, enabling options rather than insisting on a final decision for or against Britishness.

The same can be said of the enormously popular television series *Goodness Gracious Me*, which parodies cultural stereotypes of the British, Indians, and particularly Indians in Britain. The show, a comedy featuring four British Asian actors, often reverses familiar scenarios, and so celebrated sketches feature a group of rude and loud Indians going for an 'English', and a party of Indian tourists coming to London for its spiritualism and simple, exotic way of life.

Conclusion

What we have seen, then, is that regional accent, as well as dialects and languages such as Gaelic, Scots, and Welsh, challenge the apparent homogeneity of the English language (and the British identity which it supports) from well-established positions within the state. Further, we have seen that although sharing some of the same concerns and strategies, ethnic groups from Asia, from the Caribbean, and from other parts of the world pose a different kind of challenge to British identity. All the issues examined in this chapter have important implications for British identity, and they impact in significant ways throughout the cultural and political life of the country. By way of conclusion, I want to demonstrate this by looking briefly at three areas which are of great importance to British people of whatever background or allegiance – popular music, work, and sport. These areas are examined in greater detail in other parts of this book, but here I wish to focus upon them specifically in relation to the issues of ethnicity and language which have been our concern in this chapter.

Music is one of the principal ways in which ethnic identity is manifested. Ireland for example has a vibrant folk music culture, encompassing strong traditional elements as well as an *avant garde* interested in experiment and innovation. For Irish people living in Britain, or for British people wishing to identify with what they consider to be an 'Irish' way of life, folk music offers a readily accessible means of ethnic identification. In the absence of a Gaelic language, certain distinctive sounds and rhythms come to be associated with Ireland and Irishness, and these effects are invariably reproduced whenever Irish identity is invoked. This close link between identity and cultural practice is, however, always liable to stereotyping, as we have noted with much of the material mentioned so far; the same sounds and rhythms that produce a positive identification for some will suggest a whole range of negative, comic, racist images for others.

Folk music is also very popular and active in Scotland and Wales, where it fulfils slightly different functions while nevertheless continuing to serve as a badge of cultural heritage. The English folk scene, on the other hand, although widespread and successful, tends to attract a more specialist audience, and the music does not play the part in national life that it does in the Celtic countries. One reason for this, perhaps, is that during the period of the rejuvenation of Celtic folk music – roughly since the 1960s – English folk has had to compete with another kind of music in which England has been consistently successful – 'rock'n'roll'. This form of popular music developed in the United States of America in the 1950s, and once again, the fact that the vast majority of songs were in the English language meant that young British people had an advantage when it came to producing rock'n'roll music of their own. There is a widespread belief amongst both English and non-English speakers in fact, that effective rock'n'roll, unlike contemporary dance music, can be produced only through the medium of the English or American language. For example, many of the entries for the Eurovision Song Contest – an annual event attracting huge television audiences across Europe but nevertheless evoking much derision and amusement amongst 'genuine' rock musicians – are now in English, a trend started by the Swedish group Abba in the 1970s. It is certainly true to say that, since the 1960s, British rock musicians have been responsible for some of the most interesting and successful innovations in the genre, though the fragmentation of popular music into myriad styles and fusions has meant that 'rock' has developed a somewhat antiquated image, particularly for those attracted by the dance scene.

Despite legal and voluntary moves towards 'equal opportunities' for all, certain kinds of employment in modern Britain tend to attract certain kinds of people speaking in particular ways. At one level, this is explicable with reference to social class and gender. At another level, however, the way one speaks and the ethnic background with which one identifies have always played a major part in the kinds of work one can expect to find (or not find) in Britain. Certain associations between ethnicity and employment – the Chinese laundry or (food) take-away, the Indian restaurant, the Irish 'navvy' (i.e. building labourer), etc. – have in some cases become so established in popular culture that it can be difficult for individuals from these ethnic communities either to imagine or to be accepted in different employment contexts. Much contemporary popular culture, in fact, turns on the comic exploitation or (more subtly) the dramatic refutation of these stereotypes. The very currency of these images, however, or the desired 'surprise' effect when they are shown to be untrue, points to the fact that most British people still accept them as having some basis in reality.

FIGURE 6.5   Black street vendors selling British flags

A typical example of ethnic employment stereotyping is the association of West Indians with the rail system. Many of the Caribbean people who came to Britain in the 1950s and 1960s were invited specifically to work for British Rail, and this remains an option for second- and third-generation West Indians. At the same time, Black Britons are under represented in almost every other area of employment and especially in the professional sector – medicine, higher education, law, the media, and so

on. Those who have made the breakthrough into higher-paid, more prestigious jobs tend to be haunted by the ambiguities of 'tokenism' and
'positive discrimination' – that is, the racist accusation that they have been
selected especially to give the impression of equality of opportunity rather
than on personal merit.

Whereas Welsh, Scottish, and Irish accents appear to be acceptable
as indicators of certain kinds of 'natural' ethnic qualities, it is very rare to
hear a lawyer or a politician or a media broadcaster speaking Jamaican
Creole. This is a result, as already indicated, of institutional pressure
certainly, but also it seems of personal choice. Black British professionals,
that is, tend as a rule to speak a version of standard English, apparently
because they (or their parents, if it is the language of the home and family)
have decided that this is more suitable to their professional status.

One area in which Black Britons have made a major contribution to
national life in recent years is sport. Indeed in some sports, such as athlet-
ics, boxing, and soccer, people of Afro-Caribbean ethnicity far outstrip their
level as a percentage of the population. The success of people of West Indian
origin in representing Britain in sport has generally not been equalled by
other minority ethnic communities – Indian, Chinese, etc. – and the reasons
for this are not clear. However, while some regard the success of black
athletes as a positive thing – the full identification of people of Afro-
Caribbean origin with Britain – others see it as a sign of the lack of opportunity for Black Britons in other areas of society, as a way of diverting
dangerous social and political tensions into harmless leisure activity, and
as a way of consolidating racist myths about the physical prowess of black
people, as opposed to the supposed mental superiority of Caucasians.

While sport still does much to concentrate national and ethnic identity, the cultural ambiguities upon which ethnicity rely can help to expose
the narrowness of traditional sporting affiliation. Again, Ireland is an interesting case in point. The soccer team representing the Republic of Ireland
has had great success in recent years. Many of the players representing
the country at international level were in fact born in Britain, but claim
Irish citizenship through their immigrant parents or grandparents. A high
percentage of these sportsmen, in fact, are of mixed-race origin, possessing
English, Scottish, and Caribbean ties as well as Irish. This phenomenon has
extended, in a highly popular and accessible way, the possible range of Irish
identity, no longer restricted to the 3.5 million who live in the Republic
itself, but incorporating the huge number of people throughout the world
– more than 70 million according to some estimates – who identify to some
degree with Irishness.

Finishing a chapter on British identity with an example from a non-
British country nicely captures the complexity of the issues we have been
discussing here. The ethnic, racial, and linguistic factors operating in modern

British society make for a highly sensitive, highly nuanced set of possibilities, in which identity is under constant pressure, not only from the society in which one lives but also from the person one believes oneself to be.

 # Exercises

1   Choose a particular regional accent and try to identify some of the stereotypical characteristics that are associated with it. What are the principal differences between British English and American English – vocabulary, grammar, intonation? List some examples.

2   Why do some British people insist on speaking minor languages and dialects, even when they are bilingual? Try to identify some words or phrases from Scots, Welsh, and Gaelic that have entered into the English language and are used regularly in Britain today.

3   What special 'problems' are faced by minority ethnic communities in Britain? What other factors influence *young* British people from minority ethnic backgrounds?

4   Try to obtain a current listing of the British pop music top forty. How many of the singers or groups are British? How many are American, or some other nationality? How many are black?

5   Compose a sentence defining exactly what you understand by the phrase 'equal opportunity'.

6   What is Cockney rhyming slang and do you know any examples? Can you think of any other similar cases of communities constituted through language, speech, or word-play?

 # Reading

Foster, Roy. *Paddy and Mr Punch: Connections in Irish and English History*, Allen Lane, 1993. Series of essays exploring the historical relations between Ireland and England in a scholarly yet readable way.

Gilroy, Paul. *There Ain't No Black in the Union Jack: The Cultural Politics of Race and Nation*, Unwin Hyman, 1987. Influential analysis of race relations in contemporary Britain.

Nairn, Tom. *The Break-up of Britain: Crisis and Neo-nationalism*, Verso, 1981. Somewhat dated, but still a forceful investigation from the left of the unique and precarious condition of modern Britain.

Phillips, Mike. *London Crossings*, Continuum, 2001. Phillips, born in Guyana, but brought up in Britain as a child, offers a portrait of London and the role it played in (re)making black British identities.

Solomos, John. *Race and Racism in Britain*, 2nd edition. Macmillan, 1993. A wide-ranging introduction to the politics of race in Britain.

Sutcliffe, David. *British Black English*, Blackwell, 1982. Very accessible account of the varieties of language spoken by Britain's West Indian population. Includes examples and glossaries.

Cultural Examples

Films

A Clockwork Orange (1971) dir. Stanley Kubrick. Pre-punk alienation of white British youth, manifested in violence and a specialised group language.

Letter to Brezhnev (1985) dir. Chris Barnard. Exploration of regional and national identity during the course of a story in which a Liverpool woman falls in love with a Russian sailor.

My Beautiful Laundrette (1985) dir. Stephen Frears. Sexual and racial tensions between Asian and white Britons in 1980s London.

East Is East (1999) dir. Darren O'Donnell. Comedy about cultural differences as an Asian family, with a white mother, grow up in Lancashire with a stern traditionalist Muslim father.

The Crying Game (1992) dir. Neil Jordan. An exploration of national, political, and sexual identity in Ireland and Britain.

Books

Amit Chaudhuri, *Afternoon Raag* (1993). A highly praised poetic and evocative novel recounting the life and thoughts of an Indian student at Oxford.

James Joyce, *A Portrait of the Artist as a Young Man* (1916). Classic exploration of the tensions between family, nation, religion, and art.

Hugh MacDiarmid, *A Drunk Man Looks at the Thistle* (1926). A poetic plea for a modern Scots language to support a modern Scottish identity.

Colin MacInnes, *Absolute Beginners* (1959). Race relations and riots in 1950s London, as seen through the eyes of a jazz-loving teenager.

Caryl Phillips, *The Final Passage* (1985). Novel about the great emigration in the 1950s from the Caribbean to England, and the life that a young woman, Leila, finds there.

Television programmes

Da Ali G Show. Controversial sketch show in which a Jewish man plays an offensive, ignorant glitzy white streetsmart guy who adopts black hip hop culture.

Rab C. Nesbitt. Comedy with a sharp edge about the adventures and opinions of a working-class Glaswegian.

Goodness Gracious Me. Very successful satirical comedy programme written and performed by four British Asians.

Bandung File. Channel 4 discussion forum for issues of ethnicity in Britain and beyond.

Tales from Pleasure Beach. Drama about the residents of a Welsh seaside town.

Music

Apache (Indian singer whose name puns on the native North American tribe of 'Indians').

Bob Marley (West Indian musician who brought reggae to a worldwide audience).

RunRig (Scottish folk-rock group including many songs in Gaelic).

Clannad (Irish group crossing folk and popular divide, singing many songs in Gaelic and Breton, the Celtic language of Brittany in Northern France).

Roots Manuva (His *Run Come Save Me* (2001) was acclaimed as innovative hip hop expressing the cultural mix of twenty-first century London).

 # Websites

www.askoxford.com
   Guide to English usages, grammar, and expressions

www.netlingo.com
   Guide to internet language words and conventions

jewish.co.uk/
   Guide to Jewish culture and activities in the UK

www.angelfire.com/ga/isbglasgow/
   Website for the Islamic Society of Britain. Good links page

www.scit.wlv.ac.uk/~jphb/american.html
   Differences between UK and US English

www.languagelearn.co.uk/
   Association for Language Learning homepage

www.hecall.qub.ac.uk/studying/ukirelan.html
   Website devoted to the languages of the UK, including Welsh, Cornish, Manx, and Scottish Gaelic and Irish

Chapter 7

Religion and heritage

Edmund Cusick

■ The established church   245

■ Background religion   249

■ Other world religions in Britain   251

■ Religious festivals   255

■ The New Age   258

■ Religious differences: age and sex   262

■ The heritage industry   264

■ Conclusion   268

■ *Exercises*   269

■ *Reading*   270

■ *Cultural examples*   270

■ *Websites*   271

Timeline

1532	Formation of Church of England
1580	Formation of Congregationalists
1652	Formation of Quakers
1739	Formation of Methodists
1760	Board of Deputies of British Jews
1774	First Unitarian Chapel in London
1833	John Keble: Oxford Movement
1843	The Free church splits from Church of Scotland
1850s	Broad Church formed
1880s	Christian Socialism
1942	British Council of Churches (all non-Roman Catholic)
1948	World Council of Churches
1972	United Reformed church (Congregational and Presbyterians)
1978	The London Mosque, Regent's Park
1980	Modern English Church of England service
1988	Lord Chancellor censured by Free Church for attending Roman Catholic funerals
1994	First Church of England woman priest
1995	Hindu Temple, Neasden
	Sheffield rave services condemned
2001	Archbishop Carey: 'Tacit atheism prevails'

THE TIMELINE OPPOSITE provides a quick snapshot of key religious movements, milestones, and changes in the UK over the last five hundred years. Most will be touched upon in this chapter, which will be looking at the importance of public and private religion in the lives of British people and considering the role that notions of 'heritage' have come to play in ideas of national identity in recent years.

A peculiarly British phenomenon is the presence of *established* churches such as the Church of England. These churches have an official constitutional status within the legal and political framework of Britain, and the Christian religion is to some degree woven into every level of British life: government, education, architecture, the arts, broadcasting, and many other areas. In Northern Ireland, religion has the extra political significance of marking the line between Catholic and Protestant paramilitary factions. At a personal level, Christianity may have been encountered in the form of prayers or hymns that were taught at school, or personal acquaintance with a local vicar or a chaplain at a hospital. Most British people feel in some way reassured by the background presence of this religion, even if they do not wish to become actively involved with it. Only in 2001 was a voluntary question on religious affiliation included for the first time on the census form.

Yet, despite the official uniformity provided by an established church, and the shared heritage of, for example, religious music and the Lord's Prayer ('Our father, which art in Heaven'), the religious experiences available in contemporary Britain form a complex and remarkably varied picture. The fact that Britain is commonly assumed to be a Christian country (and a majority of people feel themselves to be 'Christian' in terms of their general principles) is undermined by a number of factors: the rapidly declining levels of people's involvement with the churches to which they nominally belong; the sharp decline in the value which young people attach to Christianity; the growth of a range of New Age religious practices; and the presence of large Hindu, Sikh, and Muslim communities as a result of postwar immigration. All of these changes result in considerable differences between the religious identity of the segments of society and of different generations.

One way in which this 'ingrained' religious identity of British people is communicated is through the physical landscape. The historical evolution of British religion is visible to any visitor. In the countryside, every village will have one or more churches, and even quite small English towns usually have a range of different churches, representing Protestant and Catholic belief, most of which have been present in Britain for two centuries or more, though in larger towns and cities new churches such as those of the Church of Jesus Christ of Latter Day Saints (the Mormons), Jehovah's Witnesses, or Christian Science and Friends' Meeting Houses (Quakers) may also be seen. The visitor will also notice a large range of church buildings which are no longer in use as places of worship. Some lie derelict, while others have been converted to new uses as apartments, restaurants, warehouses, or even night clubs.

Alongside this decline in Christian practice over the last fifty years, particularly in the big cities, there has been a rise in other faiths (see Table 7.1). In addition, in every town high street, bookshops have extensive sections devoted to mythology, witchcraft, palmistry, spiritualism, and related subjects. Off the high street, particularly in seaside, market, or university towns, there are small shops selling incense, crystals, relaxing music, jewellery, and books on magic and meditation. In gross terms, the people who attend the churches are few, elderly, and overwhelmingly female. The people in the New Age shops are young, enquiring, and unbound by any sense of religious duty, motivated rather by their generation's belief in personal freedom. These all indicate Britain's changing religious environment.

Another part of this change is the way in which religious buildings have become a part of what is called 'British heritage'. One obvious example is the *marketing* of a number of great cathedrals which are to be found across the UK, though this is particularly noticeable in medieval cities such as Chester, York, Winchester, and Durham. These buildings are now both religious centres and centres of tourism. A new meaning to the term 'heritage' has arisen – heritage now reflects the intervention of the tourist industry to recreate images and artifacts from Britain's past. The 'heritage industry' has grown rapidly to become one of the fastest developing, and most visible, of Britain's areas of employment and enterprise. It is also one that promotes a particular version of Britain which celebrates continuity, tradition, and conservative values. Partly for this reason, Christianity in Britain is in many ways more of a cultural force than a spiritual one. Table 7.1 indicates that the number of practising Christians is in fact much more in balance with, than exceeding, that of other faiths.

In the 1990s there were, nominally, 27 million Anglicans in Britain. That is, almost two-thirds of the population claimed to belong to the Church of England. However, at the same time the Anglican church had

TABLE 7.1 Attendance at religious ceremonies (total membership in parentheses) (thousands)

Christian denominations	1992	1998
Anglicans	1,808	980 (1,500)
Roman Catholics	2,049	1,230 (8,900)
Presbyterians	1,242	1,010 (1,200)
Church of Scotland	700	600 (700)
Methodists	458	379 (380)
United Reformed Church	148	121 (100)
Baptists	170	277 (300)
Quakers	18	15 (19)
Other faiths		
Muslims	1,200	1,000 (1,100)
Hindus	400	350 (370)
Sikhs	500	400 (420)
Jews	410	285 (350)

Source: Religious Trends No. 2 2000/2001, Christian Research Association, *Whitaker's Almanac*

fewer than two million registered members. Membership signifies active involvement with the church, for example in attending services and offering financial contributions. Between 1960 and 1985, the Church of England's registered membership has halved, while the number who think of themselves as belonging to the church has, in comparison, barely changed. This apparent contradiction between those who choose to think of themselves as Anglicans and those who are actively committed to Anglicanism is perhaps the single most important feature of British Christian life, and is discussed in more detail below.

There are 5 million Catholics in Britain. However on any given Sunday more Catholics than Anglicans will attend a church service – it has been estimated that in Britain 40 per cent of Catholics registered as church members actually attend regularly, as against only 11 per cent of non-Catholics. The north-west of England and the west of Scotland (particularly Liverpool and Glasgow) have had historically, and retain today, a distinctively Roman Catholic heritage. Liverpool is Britain's only Catholic city.

In 2001, pessimistic sound bites on religion were attributed to two senior clergymen, the Anglican Archbishop of Canterbury, Dr George Carey, and Cardinal Cormac Murphy-O'Connor, the Catholic Archbishop of Westminster. Dr Carey, addressing a congregation in the Isle of Man, declared Britain to be a country where 'tacit atheism prevails'. He said that British society concentrated only on the 'here and now' with thoughts of eternity rendered 'irrelevant'. Cardinal Murphy-O'Connor, speaking to a gathering of a hundred priests in Leeds, said, 'Christianity as a background to people's lives and moral decisions and to the Government and to the social life of Britain has almost been vanquished.'

Both statements generated considerable publicity. There were laments about the state of the nation, on the one hand, and complaints about the churches' defeatism on the other. However, both clergymen went on to offer rays of hope. Dr Carey said that despite massive changes religion had survived and there was growth in churches in Africa and the Far East and 'signs of real life' in Europe. Cardinal Murphy-O'Connor said that clergy should use this difficult period in the Church's history 'to change the culture of Catholicism'. He believed the answer for the church could lie in new movements, such as Youth 2000 and New Faith, and the building of small Bible study and prayer groups. He said 'these small communities are the secret for the future of the Church'.

From the 1960s till the present day religious issues in Northern Ireland have been overshadowed by 'the Troubles' – the continuing violence generated by the unresolved political issue of whether Northern Ireland should form part of the UK or of a united Ireland. The religious differences between Protestants and Catholics have thus been exacerbated, as Nationalists want Northern Ireland to be part of a Catholic country (with the South) while Unionists want the province to belong to a Protestant country – that is, the UK. It is often implied by British people that 'the Troubles' are based on religion, but it is probably more accurate to see the conflict as political at root, a stand-off in which the communities have both looked to their differing churches for support. At no time has either church condoned the use of violence in the dispute. As Table 7.2 shows, church membership in Northern Ireland, like attendance, far exceeds that in evidence on the mainland of the UK, and this is the case in both Catholic

TABLE 7.2 Church members by country: thousands of adult population

	1985	*1992*
England	11.6	10.1
Wales	17.0	15.0
Scotland	32.4	29.4
Northern Ireland	81.6	82.7
Total	15.6	14.4

Source: UK *Christian Handbook*, 1994/5, Christian Research Association

and Protestant communities. This is probably largely for political and cultural reasons, as church going is an important way both of establishing solidarity within a community, and of defining its differences with other communities.

Wales has a separate religious tradition in which Methodism and the Congregational church have traditionally played an important part, both churches laying an emphasis on individual devotion and strict adherence to puritanical rules of abstention from worldly behaviour, such as drinking and fornication (sex outside of marriage). 'Chapel' (the word means a small, simple church) has come, in Wales, to represent the ordinary people who embraced nonconformism (a form of Protestantism comparatively extreme in comparison to the Church of England). Welsh chapels are plain, and unadorned, and Welsh nonconformist Christianity has traditionally had no concept of the minister as priest (one with unique spiritual powers and authority to administer sacraments such as the Eucharist, or Holy Communion) but has a strong sense of the prophetic tradition (preachers inspired directly by God). There has been no established church in Wales since 1920 – the Anglican church in Wales is known as 'the Church in Wales'. Nearly all Welsh denominations hold at least some of their services in Welsh, particularly in Welsh-speaking areas. The past devotion of the Welsh (as well as changing population patterns) is evident in the appearance of chapels, many of which are now neglected, in the most remote areas, and the smallest of settlements.

The established church

The Church of England occupies both a political role and a spiritual one. The organisation is referred to as 'the Church of England' when considering its place in the constitution or life of the nation, and as 'the Anglican church' when its spiritual or theological identity is at issue. Because it is the body chosen by, and connected to, the British political system of government, the Church of England is the established church (it differs, however, from the Church of Scotland). It is thus formally tied both to Parliament and to the monarchy.

Partly because of this link, the relation between religious principles and the personal morality of members of the Royal Family is closely observed and, as noted in the introductory chapter, is of continuous interest to the British people and the tabloid press. Though the monarch's religious role no longer includes the 'divine right of Kings' (the idea that the monarch's rule is endorsed by God), people now expect the royals to set personal standards in social and religious institutions such as matrimony. Revelations in the mid-1990s about the adulterous liaisons of both Prince

Charles and Diana, Princess of Wales, compounded by speculation about possible future marriages, matter to many people because the reigning monarch is still the head of the church, the institution which above all others is supposed to offer moral guidance to the country. Likewise, prominent politicians in the UK are still expected to endorse religious belief and to attend church occasionally, while the Church is expected not to get involved in party politics.

The fact that the Church of England has also been known as 'the Tory Party at prayer' has less to do with any identification with the political policies of Conservative governments in the 1980s and the 1990s than with its role as a guardian of the past, and of established views. It is, as British people will say, conservative with a small 'c'. On rare occasions the spiritual and the perceived political function of the church may come into conflict – the memorial service held after the Falklands war aroused anger from many Conservative politicians because of its emphasis on the Christian values of forgiveness and compassion for all in the war, including the relatives of Argentinian forces killed, an attitude not shared by those who felt that the national church should identify itself only with the victorious British forces. The Church of England is, in fact, also represented within the armed forces – every regiment has its chaplain and barracks have their own chapels. It is not unusual to see stained glass windows commemorating British Armed forces (through the flags or insignia of local regiments) or of Royal Air Force squadrons within English churches, and particularly in cathedrals.

The presence of the established church is evident in numerous ways in British life. British coins bear the head of the monarch plus the Latin initials 'F. D.' signifying that the monarch is defender of the faith, a title given to Henry VIII by Pope Leo X in 1521. In 1995, Prince Charles caused some controversy among traditionalists by suggesting that at his coronation he would like to be known as Defender of the Faiths (plural) in recognition that Britain was no longer an exclusively Christian country. He again caused controversy in 1996 when he suggested that money from the 'millennium fund' (a fund of money from the National Lottery which is intended to finance projects to enhance Britain's cultural life and national prestige) should in part be spent on mosques. Despite many moves towards multiculturalism in Britain, sections of the tabloid press reacted with hostility to this suggestion, seeing mosques as a symbol of a foreign and minority religion despite the fact that British Muslims now outnumber adherents of most British Protestant denominations. Meanwhile, even government proposals to reform the House of Lords in 2001 rejected the idea of giving a formal place in the Lords for religions outside the Church of England. Methodists, Presbyterians, Baptists, and Quakers share much the same struggle as Anglicans and Roman Catholics to retain the interest

FIGURE 7.1   Every monarch since William the Conqueror (with the exception of Edward V and Edward VIII) has been crowned in Westminster Abbey, which was built and developed in the thirteenth to sixteenth centuries. Over three hundred people are either buried or memorialised in Westminster Abbey, including 'the Unknown Warrior', whose grave has become a place of pilgrimage, and the figures celebrated at 'Poets' Corner', from Geoffrey Chaucer, Charles Dickens, and Thomas Hardy to Sir John Betjeman

of the population at large. The divisions within Christianity which separated the denominations alienated potential members, and, although they have been addressed by the reconciliatory ecumenical movement, none of the churches is really thriving.

At all levels of society, Britain's churches are involved in its cultural life. Church halls are used for whist drives, jumble sales, play groups, badminton, barn dances, sales of jam by the Women's Institute, and an array of other events for charity and local causes which may be entirely secular. Most of the church's cathedrals hold concerts of classical music, both secular and religious, and may also hold exhibitions of painting. Nearly all British cathedrals have a gift shop, for buying cards, tapes, ornaments, and books, and many also have a 'coffee shop' or café where visitors are encouraged to come and eat. This partly offsets any decline in revenue caused by the fact that marriages may now legally take place in many venues besides a church and a register office. It is perhaps because of this greater flexibility in their use, as well as because of the aesthetic or historical appeal of beautiful buildings and stained glass, that, while churchgoing is in marked decline, attendance at cathedrals (both by tourists and by worshippers) is on the increase. In 1999, Canterbury Cathedral had 1.4 million visitors – more than London Zoo.

Religious tourism for recreation is also very popular, taking the place that pilgrimage for a spiritual purpose held for previous ages, and converging on the same sites. Holy Island (Lindisfarne), for example, which is situated off the Northumbrian coast near Berwick, and which combines a peaceful atmosphere and dramatic setting with the sites of some of the earliest Christian settlements in Britain, receives more than three hundred thousand visitors a year, most of them British. Such spiritual tourism is not always welcome however – such is the demand for property for retreat houses and meditation centres that local people complain of not being able to afford houses on the island, which cost twice as much as they do on the mainland.

Throughout the period between the 1960s and the turn of the new century the church was in a state of change. Conscious of its rapidly diminishing appeal to the population at large, it attempted to change traditions, in some cases hundreds of years old, in order to be more modern and hence attract more worshippers. The decision in 1992 to admit women as priests, in particular, proved controversial and divisive, resulting in many priests leaving the faith to take up holy orders in the Roman Catholic church. Those Church of England priests who were most opposed to women priests may feel at home there but, ironically, many Catholics do not welcome what they see as their male chauvinism, and themselves see the advent of Catholic women priests as both desirable and inevitable.

A further illustration of the shift in the manner of religious expression occurred in 2001 when Tony Blair offered the Americans the redundant

Greenwich Dome to cover the site of Ground Zero, the New York site of the Twin Towers destroyed in the 11 September attack. He was perhaps intending to capitalise on the melding of religious belief with heritage, to cement the Anglo-American 'special relationship', and to bolster the flagging tourist industry. His offer was not taken up.

Background religion

The English capacity for compromise can be seen to have emerged in what we could call 'half belief' or 'passive belief'. While membership of all Christian churches in Britain, and churchgoing, are in steep long-term decline, active Christianity in Britain is not, in general, being replaced by atheism, but rather by a less taxing, and harder to define, 'passive Christianity' (a vague belief in a God, and a vaguer belief in Christ, but a strong adherence to the idea of being Christian). As suggested earlier, the contradiction at the heart of Christianity in Britain is that, while most of the population believe themselves to be in some sense Christian, they have no commitment to, little knowledge of, or belief in, things that the Church regards as central to Christianity. There is in many quarters of the non-churchgoing population an assumption that being English automatically qualifies one for membership of the Church of England and hence confers the right to be considered a Christian. This position is made easier to hold by the Church of England's status as the established church. As the church's rituals of baptism, marriage, and funeral have traditionally been extended to anyone who lives within the parish of a particular church, it has been easy to assume that membership of the church, too, is a right that everyone shares. Thus the English choose the Church of England, but choose to stay away from it – preferring a loose sense of association with it to actually attending its services. Despite this, over all more people still attend church on Sunday than football matches on Saturday. Moreover events such as the 2001 Twin Towers bombings sparked an increase of up to 20 per cent in attendance. Surveys of religious attitudes in Britain regularly reveal a higher percentage of people who claim to be Christian than of people who claim to believe in God, implying a 'cultural Christianity' in which no orthodox spiritual faith in a divine being is necessary, however strange such a concept may be to a traditional believer.

Most British people, it can be said, live in a state of 'popular religion', which, while loosely based on Christianity, would not be recognised as faith by most priests. In moments of crisis, it is the Christian God in some form to whom they will turn in private prayer. Such religion requires no active participation, but may be satisfied for example by listening to radio or television broadcasts. A Sunday service is broadcast nationally every week, while morning radio programmes have 'Thought for the Day' or 'Prayer for the Day' slots – uplifting spiritual thoughts offered to the nation. (For example, the foremost news and current affairs radio programme, 'Today', early morning on Radio 4, has not only a daily interview with a prominent politician but a message from a prominent spiritual leader.) Similarly, *Songs of Praise*, a weekly televised Christian act of worship which focuses on hymn-singing, regularly attracts a greater audience than does *Match of the Day* – the most popular weekly showcase for Britain's national sport, football. The same enjoyment of passive religion

FIGURE 7.2 The Salvation Army hall on Oxford Street is taken over by The Alpha Course: a 'short course' programme of Christian values (mainly for young people disillusioned by the traditionalism of the church), heavily promoted on television by David Frost

is evidenced by the local and national newspapers which carry a weekly column on spiritual decisions written by a pastor. In Scotland, some local papers carry a daily sermon. Across the UK, religious broadcasting, which produces thoughtful programmes of high quality, is surprisingly popular. On an average Sunday in Britain six hours of religious programming will be broadcast by the BBC and independent television companies, and four hours by BBC radio. In general, it is the older generations who watch such programmes. In keeping with British reticence on the subject, religion only occasionally features in television drama. One exception is *Brookside*, a popular soap opera set in Liverpool, whose story lines have included a Catholic priest who leaves the church after an affair with one of his parishioners and one which dealt with a cult of extreme evangelical Christians. On BBC television, *The Vicar of Dibley* is a comedy drama series based around the life of a woman priest in the Church of England, and derives much of its humour from the clash of expectations between the traditional role of a clergyman and the new clergywoman.

Other world religions in Britain

Britain has approximately 1,200,000 Muslims, the majority of whom were born in the UK. Others have arrived from the Indian subcontinent or from African countries. The larger Muslim communities are concentrated in the industrial cities of the Midlands, in London, Bradford, and Strathclyde, and in the textile towns of Yorkshire and Lancashire where in the 1960s the clothing industry attracted workers from overseas. Additionally, immigrant communities who arrived in Britain from colonies and ex-colonies in Asia, West Africa and the Caribbean in the 1950s and 1960s tended to concentrate in particular areas – notably London, Birmingham, Glasgow, and the big industrial towns of northern England – and this has led to large communities of Muslims, Hindus, and Sikhs in these areas. Glasgow, Newcastle, and Leeds have sizeable Muslim populations. Britain's Muslim population is predominately Sunni, with only around twenty-five thousand Shias. For the first generation of Asian settlers, the practice of Islam and the heritage of Asian culture are inextricably intertwined. For their children, who have grown up in Britain, however, Islam is a cultural and religious force in its own right, so that many young Britons of Asian origin may think of themselves as British Muslims, rather than as Asians or as Black Britons. Whereas in the 1980s only a fifth of the Muslims in Britain claimed to practise their religion actively, in the 1990s that figure rose to half.

For this generation the challenge is to continue to find ways to integrate the religious traditions of Islam into contemporary British life and to create a new British Islamic identity. It is a process which involves some difficulty, exacerbated by the fact that, although Britain has laws of blasphemy which could be invoked when Christians were offended by Martin Scorsese's film *The Last Temptation of Christ*, Muslims who objected to Salman Rushdie's novel *The Satanic Verses* had no legal recourse. The Rushdie Affair, as it came to be called, in many ways started abroad. Objections to Rushdie's blasphemy against the Prophet in his book were first voiced in India, and later in Pakistan and, of course, Iran, from where the Ayatollah Khomeini issued his *fatwa*, which Rushdie heard on Valentine's Day 1989. In Britain, the famous organised book burnings began only the month before. The affair raised awareness of Islam in Britain, and several groups emerged into the public eye. For example, the Bradford Council of Mosques attacked Rushdie, while trying to create a political Muslim collective, and the Women Against Fundamentalism group defended him while trying to dislodge stereotypical views of Muslim women. Meanwhile British law did not recognise that any blasphemy had occurred.

In 1996, there was a widespread boycott by Muslims of religious education classes in schools (which, by law, may teach about other religions but must be predominantly Christian). Despite there being state-funded schools offering an education which is distinctively Anglican, Catholic, or Jewish, no state money had by then been awarded to assist in creating a Muslim school. (This situation was not redressed until the year 2000.) The anomaly arose possibly because Islam was still seen as intolerant, or even as a threat, by many conservative Britons, whose folk-memory of Islam was in terms of the medieval Crusades (a word used with a positive emphasis in Britain generally, but which must have adverse connotations for Muslims). Young British Muslims, however, represent an important strand in British identity, feeling themselves to be in the forefront of the development of Islam in Europe. Positive cultural public images have been supplied by the cricketer Imran Khan and Yusuf Islam, the pop singer formerly known as Cat Stevens.

The history of the presence of other faiths and peoples, and their role in public life in Britain, is not widely known. For example, Asian performers are recorded in London in the seventeenth century, and Indian sailors, called Lascars, were living in London at the end of the eighteenth century. England had several Indian professors in the 1800s and a British India Society was established in 1839 (under the influence of the first widely known Indian nationalist, Raja Rammohun Roy), followed by a London Indian Society in 1872. Already by the middle of the nineteenth century there were significant Indian communities in London, Southampton, and Liverpool, though they were smaller than other black communities in Britain. As an indication of this level of cultural presence, it is worth noting that Queen Victoria – who never visited India – asked a Muslim

FIGURE 7.3 Community-built mosque in Hounslow, West London

servant, Abdul Karim, to teach her Hindustani. The founding President of the London Indian Society, Dadabhai Naoroji, also one of the early presidents of the Indian National Congress, was the first Indian elected to the British Parliament, in 1892, when he stood as a Liberal candidate in East Finchley, and another Parsi, Mancherjee Merwanjee Bhownaggree, a merchant from Bombay, was elected Conservative MP for Bethnal Green Northeast in 1895.

There is therefore a long cultural heritage of Asian people and faiths in the UK. This was well demonstrated in 1995, by the opening of the largest Hindu temple outside India, in Neasden in London. This event attracted much media interest since it was the only such structure to be built outside India for a thousand years. It used largely volunteer labour and was paid for entirely by donations from the Hindu community. Now, the majority of Hindus live in Greater London although Birmingham, in the Midlands, has also become a centre of the community. Many British Hindu families came from India and Sri Lanka but considerable numbers also arrived from Uganda and Kenya, when they were expelled by the authorities there in the early 1970s. There are now Hindu temples across the UK in major cities and towns. The Sikh community is also well represented in Britain and is concentrated in particular areas – for example, in Southall and Gravesend in Greater London. Most early postwar migrants, in the 1950s, came from the Jat caste, and were predominantly men. At first they would hold a *diwan* or religious meetings at home, often in all-male households, but soon set up *Gurdwaras* (Sikh temples) for Sunday services. Their families followed from the Punjab in the 1960s and stronger domestic and religious ties were established.

Britain has the second largest Jewish population in Europe. Most Jews live in London, but there are several hundred Jewish congregations in the UK, many Jewish schools, and synagogues serving both the Orthodox faith and the minority Reform group. Fears have been voiced that nowadays half of Jewish men are marrying non-Jewish women and that this will lead to a decline in faith and religious observance.

Finally, the Rastafarian religion has had a sizeable cultural influence in Britain. Rastafarians' philosophy of life was originally based on their adaptation of the Christianity they experienced in the colonial West Indies. They see themselves as Israelites displaced from their homeland, and Babylon is the collective name for all countries of exile outside Africa. Rastafarians have been influential in many cultural ways in Britain. Their 'dreadlocks' hair style is shared by some New Age travellers or Crusties, and they were probably influential in promoting a climate of tolerance towards soft drugs, a major aspect of their religion, in the 1980s. They staked out their territory in urban areas of cities such as Liverpool with graffiti such as 'Toxteth Not Croxteth', meaning that marijuana was welcome in Toxteth, but not the heroin which was available in another district of the city.

Though the religious group is small, millions appreciate the characteristic Rastafarian music, reggae, and particularly that of Bob Marley and the Wailers. Marley's music has been enormously influential, even with many British white punk bands such as The Clash, Stiff Little Fingers, and The Ruts, plus more mainstream groups such as Culture Club and UB40. Among other black British groups displaying Rasta influence are Aswad, Misty in Roots, and Steel Pulse. Also, the critically acclaimed and widely published Rastafarian poets Benjamin Zephaniah and Levi Tafari have raised the profile of Rastafarianism, promoted the interests of ethnic minority groups generally, and contributed to the transformation of British cultural identities.

Religious festivals

One of the most obvious examples of religion in contemporary British life is in the progression of the year through festivals and significant dates. The Anglican church has traditionally divided the year according to a liturgical calendar – basing the year around a number of key religious feasts and thus creating holidays such as Whitsun, named after the feast of the Pentecost which is celebrated on the seventh Sunday after Easter, when the Holy Spirit appeared to the apostles. British life is punctuated by such national holidays, some of which still have a religious meaning, but many of which are now largely secular festivals. An example of the latter is Mother's Day, which is based on Lady's Day (25 March), a celebration of the annunciation to Mary that she was pregnant with Christ, who was to be born nine months later on 25 December. Some public festivals have roots in the pagan religions that held sway in Britain before the arrival of Christianity, lost religions whose customs are being recreated and celebrated by a new generation of 'pagans', who celebrate seasonal events such as the winter and summer solstices (mid-points), by meeting out of doors at ancient sites of worship, most famously at Stonehenge.

The name Easter is derived from the name of the Saxon goddess of spring, Eostre (related to a Mediterranean pagan goddess mentioned in the Bible, Astarte). In some areas, Easter rituals, as well as celebrating the resurrection of Christ, include ceremonies which were once probably part of pagan fertility rites, though now performed in a spirit of secular fun, for example, the rolling of eggs down hills or the eating of pancakes on Shrove Tuesday, at the beginning of Lent, the period of fasting before Easter (observed by few Christians in Britain, in contrast with the month of Ramadan, observed by Muslims). For most non-religious British people Easter is an occasion for the exchange of chocolate, though this chocolate is usually in the shape of an egg or a rabbit (the Easter Bunny), both symbols of fertility. Many British people who never normally go to church will attend a service on Easter morning. The day after Easter Day, Easter Monday, is also a public holiday.

The first of May or May Day is a public holiday introduced by a Labour government. It is a socialist revival of a much more ancient pagan festival of Beltane which is still celebrated by Morris dancers, who dance traditional dances, clad in straw hats and with bells on their ankles, around a Maypole. In places such as Oxford (where there is a tradition of greeting the dawn on May Day morning), Morris dancers are likely to be joined by neo-pagans – young people dressed in the fashions of youth counterculture – ex-army coats, trousers, and boots, dreadlocks, strings of coloured beads or leather thongs worn as bracelets or necklaces, and pierced noses and ears. That such people will share the same celebration as well-heeled middle-class students and conservative middle-aged people points to the deeper rhythms of British life which unite people who otherwise feel themselves to be profoundly different, politically and culturally.

Hallowe'en, on 31 October, is a British festival which now shows many traces of American influence. For example children are now beginning to play 'trick or treat' – that is, to call at houses on Hallowe'en dressed in macabre fancy-dress costumes and ask for sweets. This new and growing fashion, pagan in origin, can be contrasted with the Christian tradition of groups of carol-singers going from door to door at Christmas, singing in exchange for coins or refreshments. Carol-singing is in marked decline. Some people feel uneasy about Hallowe'en. It was originally a pagan festival of remembrance for the end of the old year (according to the pagan calendar) and of communion with the dead (it falls on All Souls' Eve). It is celebrated principally by children, who enjoy the frightening atmosphere created by make-up, masks and costumes on the theme of ghosts, witches, spectres, and skeletons. While in the 1960s and 1970s schools would enthusiastically participate in Hallowe'en, from the 1980s onwards many schools, particularly in Scotland, which had a particularly strong Hallowe'en tradition, banned the celebration, because of pressure from Christian parents who believed the festival was connected with black magic and witchcraft, or because it encouraged children to go out unsupervised, at night.

Guy Fawkes Night (5 November), also known as 'Bonfire Night' or 'Fireworks Night', is another example of how a festival which is now seen as entirely secular can grow from religious origins. While, again, its origins

FIGURE 7.4 Last night of the Proms: young and old share patriotic fervour (© Adam Woolfitt/CORBIS)

lie in pre-Christian pagan customs (a fire festival to welcome the winter), this custom of gathering to light outdoor bonfires, and to burn effigies symbolically representing the old year, was adapted by the Christian state in the seventeenth century to commemorate the defeat of a Catholic plot led by Guy Fawkes (the Gunpowder Plot) to blow up the Houses of Parliament. Like Christmas, Bonfire Night is remarkable in being one of the few customs which actively unite British people. All across the UK, everyone is acutely aware of, if not participating in, festivities typically consisting of a display of fireworks around a bonfire, on which a human effigy of Guy Fawkes is burned.

The role of the traditional churches as part of the British state is most obvious on Armistice Day (the Sunday nearest to 11 November). This day is also known as 'Poppy Day', as many British people, particularly of the older generations, will wear a red paper poppy to show that they remember those who have died fighting for their country. (In the First World War many British soldiers were killed in battle in the wheat fields of Flanders, which had poppies growing in them.) All over the country, ceremonies which combine military drill and Christian ritual are held to remember the war dead, especially those killed in the 1939–45 war. This is principally a time of mourning and of celebration for the generations who have lived through the Second World War, and those who died. However, even many young people, who feel uncomfortable about the solemnity and emphasis on the past of Poppy Day, also feel that some of their sense of identity as British subjects is defined by this day. Even if the themes of patriotism and military service are not those with which they personally identify, the commemoration ceremonies held in schools, churches, and town centres provide an annual reminder of another history of British identity – one which now needs to be negotiated alongside strengthening links with the EU.

For those without significant religious festivals, Christmas (25 December) is without question the single most important event in the British social, religious, and cultural calendar (though it should be noted that in Scotland, where it was not until the 1950s that Christmas Day became a public holiday, the alternative celebration of 'Hogmanay' or New Year has historically been of much greater importance and, in the Highlands of Scotland particularly, remains so). Christmas Day is the one time when people feel the need to re-enact the importance of the family, and most young people who otherwise live elsewhere will still spend that day with their parents. For most British families the Christmas period is the only time, apart from weddings and funerals, when the 'extended family' – including different generations and the children of different branches of the family are gathered together. It is the time when, as John Betjeman put it in his poem 'Christmas', 'girls in slacks remember Dad /

And oafish louts remember Mum'. For many people, this proves to be something of a strain, as British people are not used to sharing their lives so closely with so many other relatives for several days, and this is reflected in statistics for violent domestic crime.

While the Christmas festival, celebrating the birth of Jesus, is of course a religious one, it could be argued that, for most British people, any religious meaning is very slight, and the celebration consists chiefly of drinking and eating (especially Christmas dinner of turkey, roast potatoes, Christmas pudding (a very rich fruitcake), mince pies (sweet fruit pies of mixed dried fruit and brandy), the giving of presents, and the watching of special Christmas programmes on television. Passive religion, however, is more popular at Christmas than at any other time, with many people listening to carol services on the radio, such as that broadcast by the BBC from King's College in Cambridge. For many British people, the Christmas story has sentimental appeal, if only because it reminds them of when they first heard it as children, and it is this, rather than religious faith, which makes the church seem more attractive at Christmas. Generally speaking, public performances of the nativity story of Jesus's birth, which is primarily reserved for children's school plays, take a second place to pantomimes and productions of Dickens's *A Christmas Carol* across the country.

Some Christmas traditions are of fairly recent manufacture. Prince Albert, Queen Victoria's consort, introduced the Christmas tree to Britain from his native Germany. The red uniform and white beard of 'Father Christmas' or 'Santa Claus' are said to have been inspired by a Coca-Cola advertising campaign in only the 1920s. Despite the widespread commercialism, however, most British people do derive some religious meaning from Christmas and, for this one time in the year, will participate in a Christian ceremony. They will also listen to the monarch's only annual talk to the nation, which has an ostensibly religious purpose. It is broadcast on both radio and television and the queen or king asks for God's blessing on the British people. For most of the nation this is a dated occasion devoid of any religious meaning, and indeed of any meaning at all. While in the 1970s up to 27 million people, more than half the population, watched this broadcast, in 1994 this number had fallen to around 15 million, and in 2000 to 11 million. One may only speculate on why 11 million British people watched the broadcast, and what they got out of it. For many it is simply 'a tradition' – part of the Christmas ritual.

The New Age

'New Age' is a broad term devised to describe the renewal of interest in a range of approaches to the spiritual dimension which promote individuals' ability to discover and develop their own spirituality. Whereas Christianity is seen by many as emphasising adherence to a strict moral code (for example through the Ten Commandments, the Bible, confession, or sermons), New Age religions concentrate on developing the spiritual awareness which they believe is present in each person. Their practices have a huge variety in their origin – some being revivals of the pagan magical and religious systems that Christianity replaced in Britain, some being extensions of Eastern meditative and religious practices, and some, such as Yoga and t'ai chi, being concerned with physical exercises. It may be that the presence of an increasingly diverse multiethnic community in Britain has boosted the popularity of some practices. For example, interest has grown in vegetarianism and veganism (large Hindu and other communities have added a considerable market for vegetarian food, which has in turn stimulated British caterers and retailers, and thus aided their popularity) and, while ten years ago vegetarian options on a pub menu were rare, they are now standard. The practice of Chinese medicine, meditation, and yoga is also rapidly increasing in Britain.

The belief in reincarnation, which many young people who have been influenced by paganism adhere to, is one which, while alien to older generations brought up under Christianity, is fundamental to Hinduism for example. Similarly, it is not unusual for young British people involved in the New Age to talk about 'karma', a religious idea of divine cause and effect passed on through different acts and incarnations which they have derived from Hinduism. Other New Age practices have a distinctly European origin, stemming from a revival of interest in Celtic myth and culture, or from new publicity given to old systems of occult knowledge through for example the Kabbalah or palmistry. Hundreds of thousands of people are involved directly in activities such as meditation or astrology (the belief system where people's personalities and destinies are determined by the star signs under which they are born). But more significant is the effect of these beliefs on the overall sense of how British people see themselves and their world. A quarter of British people, for example, claimed in a recent survey regularly to read their horoscope as published in a magazine. Many more will read their horoscope as a form of light-hearted entertainment, but will still hope for good news. Television programmes such as *The Para-normal World of Paul McKenna*, which explores 'inexplicable' phenomena, are also extremely popular. So is Mystic Meg, a television seer formerly on the BBC's weekly National Lottery show who predicted the type of person destined to win the jackpot each week. Also, business people have adopted many alternative spiritual practices, as a cure for stress and as a source of inspiration or energy. Feng shui is also used to create a comfortable working environment for offices. Finally, a small but growing number of people among the professional classes are choosing Buddhism.

FIGURE 7.5 The Globe: Shakespeare's theatre reconstructed by Sam Wanamaker on London's South Bank

The term 'New Age' is used to link all of the above activities, and this grouping has some justification, not least because those who have an interest in one of these practices often also have an interest in others. The term itself is derived from astrology, which holds that every two thousand years the solar system enters a new age. The Piscean age (from the sign of the fish) which started approximately at the birth of Christ was the Christian age (Pisces is seen by astrologers as the sign of self-sacrifice and mass movements), while the new astrological era will be that of Aquarius (Aquarius is the sign of individualism, and hence of any religion which allows individuals freedom).

Some of the increasingly popular practices which have been placed by the media in the New Age category are distinctively religious. For example Wicca (witchcraft, or worship of British forms of the Mother Goddess, often associated with the practice of magic) and Buddhism are religious preoccupations. Interest in oriental medicine, health food, and yoga, however does not require or imply faith. Many facets of the New Age, such as the interest in astrology or in Eastern meditation, are religious in the sense that they involve establishing a link between individuals and a spiritual realm. However, in other ways these activities seem more like hobbies than parts of organised religions because they involve individual study or meditation rather than a formal organisation with its own hierarchy and moral code. New Age groups are thus the antithesis of the highly controlled, brainwashed 'cults' which fascinate newspaper editors in Great Britain (such as followers of the Unification Church, known as 'Moonies').

New Age practices, in the widest sense, are the most important, and most rapidly developing area of religious change across Britain, and must be considered seriously. Aspects of the New Age have permeated very different sections of British society: from business people turning to meditation as a release from the stress of pressurised, urban, executive life, to the Donga tribe – young pagans who have abandoned normal British society and who live, largely, out of doors, and who came to national prominence for their role in actively protesting against the government's appropriation of sites of rare natural value to build new motorways.

In many ways, currents of New Age religion have enabled changes which have occurred in British life between the 1980s and the 1990s to find a religious expression. The rising tide of concern for the environment, for animal welfare and rights (a subject the British think themselves very concerned with, though they have fewer domestic pets *per capita* than for example the Dutch), for conservation, and for green or ecological politics, has helped to create a climate in which religions such as paganism, which celebrate the earth and its wildlife, fulfil a need for many people. A powerful element within the identity of young British people is a sense of identification with the countryside, and a resentment of the loss of countryside to modern building, and in particular of the road-building programme which successive governments have pursued.

Famously, while statistically very few young people seek active involvement in any of the national political parties, and there is generally much cynicism about politics in British life, concern for the landscape is an area for which there is genuine enthusiasm. Many environmental protesters endure poverty and physical hardship to fight new road-building. Such activity earns considerable sympathy from many Britons of all generations. Television coverage of campaigners against the Newbury road bypass and a new runway at Manchester airport turned one young male protester, 'Swampy', into a national hero. Far more young people are involved in such 'single issue' protests than in party politics, as referred to elsewhere in this book. Whereas for previous generations the sense of belonging to a nation may have been expressed through such institutions as the church, the armed forces, or in some cases a university or a public school, many of the young generation find their ideals, and their sense of belonging, in nature and in the land itself.

While Christianity is identified politically with authority, the Establishment, and the older generation, many New Age beliefs, and paganism in particular, are identified with the young and the disaffected.

The most visible adherents are 'New Age Travellers', who, in the hot summers of the 1980s, fought annual battles against the police to reach Stonehenge, Britain's most important ancient site, because they believed that they had both the right and the duty to celebrate the summer solstice, and, in particular, to name their children there. The latter idea offers an example of how quickly an idea essential to identity – the ritual of naming – can become part of British subculture, and how the New Age generates its own 'instant' mythology through which people define themselves.

The British appetite for passive religion, and the commercial forces of tourism show their influence on pagan sites as well as Christian ones. Stonehenge is one of Britain's most popular attractions, receiving 672,000 visitors a year, many of whom are drawn by a vague, but powerful, sense of communion with some other world, or mystic power, which lives on in the imagination of the visitors, if not in the stones themselves. The young New Age pagans who worship at the stones are in a sense a natural extension of British instincts rather than a violation of them, despite their anti-Establishment posture.

Religious differences: age and sex

The decline of Christianity in Britain is not due to individuals' losing their religion, but rather to a process of generational change. A generation which was very religious, at least in terms of church attendance and social attitudes, and which has been the mainstay of church life in England over the last thirty years, is literally dying out, and being replaced by a generation which cares far less for church observance, and for Christianity in general. Christianity is associated for young people with the unfashionable and unnecessary code of restrictive, negative morality of the value systems of their parents or grandparents. Many associate a figure such as the Pope with an authoritarian patriarchal Jehovah and tend to see Christianity, and Catholicism in particular, as a series of prohibitions – 'don't take drugs', 'don't have sex', 'don't get drunk', and 'don't swear'. As such it has very little appeal and has also been seen as male-centred, dictating women's lives: under Catholicism, women cannot be priests, or use contraception, or have an abortion. Attempts by some within the church to integrate elements of 1990s youth culture into worship, including some ideas borrowed from New Age spirituality and others from the 'rave' music scene, have caused problems and controversy. They have been backed by many bishops as an attempt to bridge the enormous cultural gap between the church and young people, yet resisted by many ordinary worshippers who cannot reconcile flashing lights, amplified electronic music, and cinema screens as part of recognisable Christian worship. A visitor to a church service in Britain will be struck by the advanced age of the worshippers: many congregations are largely made up of women in their sixties or seventies, or still older. The chief exceptions to this are evangelical congregations, both within the Church of England and outside it in churches such as the House churches, Baptists, or Pentecostals, which place a strong emphasis on a dramatically emotional conversion experience, and conservative moral values and family structures (for example, no sex except in marriage).

One example of the gulf between the church and society was the church's hostility towards the National Lottery. The church was once again seen as basically prohibitive. While some serious commentators on national life agreed with its reservations about the damaging effects, particularly on poor people, of the compulsion to gamble, and those of extreme wealth on the winners, the week in 1996 when the church raised its strongest objections was also one in which nine out of ten British people bought a lottery ticket for a £40 million jackpot. The church may still try to exercise its role as moral guardian of the nation, but few people take this seriously enough to be guided by it in their own lives. This is even more the case with the young. For them, Christianity is profoundly unfashionable. It is significant that, almost in imitation of the subcultural pagan practice of wearing occult jewellery whose meaning is known only to another 'initiate' of the subculture, Christians have, in Britain, increasingly embraced the symbol

FIGURE 7.6 *Horse Guard and street performer guardsman*

of the fish (an ancient secret sign used when Christianity was itself a minor religion, a cult) rather than the cross, as a badge to identify themselves only to other believers.

Church weddings, despite the aesthetic attraction of historic church buildings and music, are in decline. The comment of one future bride, 'We're not religious at all, we don't believe in God but we want to get married in a church', sums up the confused motives behind many such weddings – the fact that the wedding is a Christian ritual, involving religious vows, is somehow invisible to those used to passive religion. The hit film *Four Weddings and a Funeral* offered an illustration of the lack of religious interest in the church at English and Scottish weddings, which is, paradoxically, matched by the cultural importance to the upper classes of having a church wedding. Christening – the Christian rite of baptism – is now becoming rare.

It should be noted that, while the church is dominated by men, surveys reveal that in groups of every age women are more likely to acknowledge the importance of religious experience than are men. In both New Age groups and Christian churches, it is women who predominate. It may be that British women are more open to spiritual practice and belief than men (a survey conducted for Channel 4 in 1987 found that roughly half of British women believed in astrology, while only a quarter of men shared that belief). It may be that men are simply more reluctant to show religious feeling outwardly. No men's magazines have astrology columns, but almost every woman's magazine has its own named astrologer. Two-thirds of the private clients of leading astrologers are reported to be women.

The heritage industry

A major cultural change in British life from the 1970s through to the present has been that Britons spend more leisure time and money on visiting historical sites and exhibits. It has been argued that the growth in the heritage industry has in some ways filled a gap left in people's lives by the loss of a religious dimension. Reverence for the past could be seen as replacing the religious reverence of previous generations. Britons who, a generation before, might have gone to church now spend their Sunday visiting a stately home or exhibition of local 'heritage' – a modern pilgrimage. The Jorvik Centre in York (the town's modern name is derived from Jorvik, its Viking name) was the first purpose-built centre for heritage tourism. The life-size plastic Vikings of Jorvik have been followed by other exhibition centres showing everything from Oxford scholars to highland Scottish crofters. Such exhibitions use mannequins dressed up in

FIGURE 7.7   Buckingham Palace

historic costume, in restored or imitation historic houses, shops, castles, or factories. They may even be staffed by actors dressed in historic costume. Paradoxically, the increasing secularisation of British life has led to less leisure time on Sunday for many, as in the 1990s shops began to open routinely on Sundays, giving the traditionally quiet Sabbath day more a feel of 'business as usual'.

The attraction of a 'museum culture' does not just extend to the remote past, but applies even to the twentieth century, and to areas of life that have only recently been part of normal life, rather than historical curiosities. In south Wales, for example (where coal mining was until the 1980s the dominant industry, but has now almost disappeared), it is possible to be guided around a redundant coal mine by men who used to work as miners there, but who are now only dressed as miners to show tourists around. While much of this repackaging, particularly in metropolitan areas, might seem to be arranged or created for foreign tourists, in fact most of the visitors to many such attractions are British, being reintroduced to their own past through the professional presentation of a host of corners of its geography and commerce. As justifications for the former 'Greatness' of Great Britain fall away, it could be said that its people turn to the past to find symbols of their identity, and indeed, their importance. Of these, the stately home is one of the most enduring as well as the most successfully marketed to the public.

In some ways the church has benefited from this – the great cathedrals which combine Christian heritage and monuments from the past have never been so popular. In other ways, too, the British could be accused of living in their past. Many films lovingly recreate Edwardian England, particularly those of Merchant and Ivory, who have specialised in finely detailed costume dramas and adaptations of literary classics such as

FIGURE 7.8   Shakespeare's Head Pub at the end of Carnaby Street, London

A Room with a View and *Howards End*. Other films of the 1980s and 1990s, such as *The Remains of the Day* or *A Month in the Country*, and television series such as *Brideshead Revisited* are profitably sold around the world as an image of an ideal Britain, and eagerly consumed by Britons themselves as a kind of national myth. The common elements of the aristocracy, venerable buildings, and English eccentrics occur over and over in such films, offering a picture of a quaint, gentle England.

Fantasies of the Britain of previous generations, particularly of rural Britain, predominate in television drama series such as *Heartbeat*, *All Creatures Great and Small*, *The Darling Buds of May*, and *Brideshead Revisited*, and in advertising – notably for various brands of bread, biscuits, and cakes. Historical settings are also used in some of the numerous 'situation-comedies' which British people watch. *Dad's Army* and *'Allo 'Allo* for example, are set during the Second World War, a time which many in the older generations look back to with nostalgia and pride. The celebrations in 1995 to commemorate the fiftieth anniversary of VE (Victory in Europe) Day were the occasion of a collective nostalgia for the comradeship and certainties of wartime. It should be stressed, however, that children and young people in general know very little about 'the [1939–45] war' – the defining moment in twentieth-century British history, and the flooding of print and broadcast media with images of the war in 1995 made very little impression on them. For example a popular television series, *Goodnight Sweetheart*, with a hero who, by means of time travel, has a double life – one part lived in the wartime 1940s, and one lived in contemporary Britain – appealed only to the old, with their hunger for nostalgia.

Another feature of the British fascination with the past is the re-creation of the world – particularly in rural areas far from London – as a

FIGURE 7.9 Brighton Royal Pavilion: former seaside residence of King George IV, decorated in Chinese taste with an Indian exterior: the architecture reveals one of many influences from Britain's Empire (© Patrick Ward/CORBIS)

series of places defined by some cultural product. Thus one is able to go on an excursion not just to another place but, at least imaginatively, to another time. For example the Lake District is advertised as Wordsworth's home, the Yorkshire Moors as 'Brontë Country' and even towns used for very recent productions – parts of Yorkshire for the televisions series *Heartbeat* (now known as 'Heartbeat Country'), or *Harry Potter* films – have become marketed in this way, and there is a steady demand from the public for such attractions.

The *Harry Potter* film of 2001 forms an interesting glimpse into the way Britain has come to be imagined, and then marketed. Locations for the film include the remote Scottish Highlands at Glen Nevis, buildings such as Oxford's historic Bodleian Library and Alnwick Castle, a preserved steam railway at Goathland, and Gloucester Cathedral. All of these sites, illustrating the recent industry that has grown up around British countryside, history, and nostalgia for the recent past, are already part of 'heritage' Britain. Not on the heritage trail, but more representative of life for the great majority of UK citizens, is the ordinary house where Harry Potter's story begins, filmed in a suburban cul-de sac in Bracknell. The contrast between these two Britains is reflected in road signs. Alongside Britain's real geography, through which one is guided by blue motorway signs and green trunk road signs there, is an alternative network of reddish-brown road signs – indicating the presence of 'heritage' Britain. This may be formed of real places – castles, stately homes, preserved factories – or of invented attractions. For example, in North Wales it is possible to journey through the tunnels of an abandoned mine now converted into 'King Arthur's Labyrinth' – a site with no connections to Arthurian legend, but one where an underground heritage display has been erected. There is an equally disjunctive Dr Who exhibition at Llangollen. In straitened economic times there is a commercial incentive for marketing nostalgia. Tourists, particularly from the USA, appreciate reconstructions whose connections with heritage may be tenuous.

Conclusion

The question of the role that religion plays in establishing British identity is a complex one, and one that reveals great differences between people of different ages in Britain. For a large number of British people over fifty, religion is a quiet and distant but important presence in their lives. It is a touchstone of shared British identity at great national or public occasions and a continuing link with the past, and, although church attendance is in decline, more people go to church in Britain on Sundays than attend football matches on Saturdays. It is also a source of comfort available at times of private or personal tragedy and celebration, such as weddings and funerals, when religion becomes temporarily of far greater importance for all generations.

In England, even many of those who do not believe in Christianity feel a sense of attachment to the Church of England. While they may never attend a church service, they like to know that they are there and would feel robbed if they were taken from them. For a number of people, the Church of England encapsulates in its rituals, liturgies, hymns, and music a distinct cultural expression of Englishness. For that minority of the population who adhere actively and strongly to Christianity, this element of religion as expression of national identity is also there but is probably less important. In Wales and Scotland, membership of the respective communions of the Anglican church serves more to divide them off from their fellow Welsh and Scottish people. Religion becomes an expression of difference or transnationalism, that is, of possible allegiance to Englishness.

For young British people whose parents were born elsewhere in the world, religion – such as Hinduism or Islam – is one important strand of their identity: a key element in the culture that marks their own contribution to Britishness as distinctive and creates a link with another heritage elsewhere. For most people under about thirty, Christianity is associated with a past to which they feel they have little connection. Some will describe themselves as atheists, and many as agnostics, but for those who

FIGURE 7.10 Prince Charles shows his connection with the 'common man' by supping a pint of beer in the traditional male social environment of the pub (© Popperfoto/Reuters)

are interested in spiritual things, the New Age is more likely to attract them. While not part of a formal or organised system, such practices offer people freedom and individuality plus the possibility of exploring spiritual paths for themselves.

Exercises

1   Do you recognise the following phrases? To hide one's light under a bushel, to go the extra mile, to turn the other cheek. What do they mean? How do you feel Christian ideas might be at odds with people's lives in Britain today?

2 Many British commentators try to link a decline in religious practice to a perceived deterioration in morals. Do you think this is a fair connection to make, and what signs or changes in Britain do you think lead people to argue that there has been a worsening of moral standards?

3 What are hot cross buns, Shrove Tuesday pancakes, and Yule logs? When would they be eaten? Remembering that dates such as Valentine's Day (14 February) have a religious background, how would you map out the British calendar in terms of, firstly, Christian festivals, and, secondly, significant dates for all faiths?

4 Where would you locate the following ten World Heritage sites (established by UNESCO) on Figure 1.1: the City of Bath; Blenheim Palace; Canterbury Cathedral; Stonehenge; Westminster Palace; the islands of St Kilda; the Giant's Causeway; Hadrian's Wall; Ironbridge; and the castles and town walls of Caernarfon, Conwy, Beaumaris, and Harlech. Do you know, or can you find out, the natural or cultural significance of each site?

 # Reading

Cashmore, Ellis. *Rastaman: The Rastafarian Movement in England*, Allen and Unwin, 1979. A slightly dated but definitive and widely available review of British Rastafarianism.

Fowler, Peter. *The Past in Contemporary Society: Then, Now*, Routledge, 1992. Examines the extent to which our heritage is still with us in the present.

Parsons, Gerald. *The Growth of Religious Diversity: Britain from 1945*, 2 vols, Open University: Routledge, 1993. Careful and thorough analysis of Britain and religion since the Second World War.

Visram, Rozina. *Ayahs, Lascars, and Princes: The Story of Indians in Britain, 1700–1947*, Pluto, 1986. Reveals the largely unknown heritage and history of Hindus, Muslims, Sikhs, and Parsis from India in the UK.

 # Cultural Examples

Films

Priest (1993) dir. Antonia Bird. A social drama exploring the conflicts between Catholicism and homosexuality in an impoverished Liverpool parish.

No Surrender (1985) dir. Peter Smith. Rival Catholic and Protestant Irish factions collide in a Liverpool club.

Leon the Pig Farmer. (1992) dirs Jean Vadim and Gary Snydor. Young Jewish Londoner moves to rural Yorkshire.

Excalibur (1981) dir. John Boorman. New Age philosophy and Celtic magic projected on to the myth of Arthur's England.

Truly, Madly, Deeply (1991) dir. Anthony Minghella. One woman's private trauma of grief after bereavement.

The Wicker Man (1973) dir. Robin Hardy. A cult movie with a horrifying ending in which a mainland policeman discovers that pagan fertility rituals, including human sacrifice, still dominate the society of a small northern island.

The Lord of the Rings: the Fellowship of the Ring (2001) dir. Peter Jackson. J. R. R. Tolkien's fantasy masterpiece portrays the struggle between good and evil in a quest for the One magic Ring.

Books

Asian Women Writers' Collective, *Flaming Spirit* (1994), ed. Rukshana Ahmad and Rahila Gupta. Religion, identity, and nostalgia for home are common themes in this collection of stories from Asian women across Britain.

David Lodge, *How Far Can You Go?* (1980). Analysis of modern Catholic faith and responsibility in Britain.

Jenny Newman, *Going In* (1995). A British account of entering a French convent and the relationships between the religious and secular worlds.

Salman Rushdie, *The Satanic Verses* (1988). The novel whose portrayal of Islam sparked a major controversy over blasphemy and free speech.

Hanif Kureishi, *The Black Album* (1995). Novel of Anglo-Pakistani youth growing up in London against the backdrop of the Rushdie Affair.

David Hare, *Racing Demon* (1990). David Hare's intelligent and questioning play about two Church of England priests engaging in theological debate and sociological comment in contemporary South London.

Television programmes

Songs of Praise. Perennial Sunday evening favourite in which a congregation and community are visited by the BBC for a weekly service.

Father Ted. Comedy series about three Irish priests and their sometimes less than spiritual lifestyle.

The Vicar of Dibley. Sit-com about a woman vicar written by the author of *Four Weddings and a Funeral*.

Websites

www.church-of-england.org
    Church structure. What it means to be an Anglican, and links

www.unn.ac.uk/societies/islamic/
    Extensive information about the Islamic faith and culture in the UK

www.abm.ndirect.co.uk/
    Simple introduction to Buddhism, beliefs, practices and meditation
www.mysticplanet.com/8diction.htm
    New Age dictionary of terms from 'accupressure' to 'yoga'
www.trinityumc.net/youth/nav.htm
    A cool image of Jesus

Conclusion: Britain towards the future

Peter Childs

■ Europe   276

■ Multiethnic Britain   281

■ New technology   286

■ Conclusion   288

■ *Exercises*   289

■ *Reading*   289

■ *Cultural examples*   289

■ *Websites*   290

I T W A S O B S E R V E D I N Chapter 1 that the very idea of 'Britain' has come under a number of forceful attacks. One of the current features notice-able alongside speculations over the end of Britishness is an increase in discussion of Englishness, spurred on by the rise in Celtic nationalisms over recent years. I say 'increase', because Englishness has always been a substantial topic. Idries Shah noted in *The Guardian* on 21 October 2000 that 'the English are obsessed with themselves. One strongly cherished idea here is that people don't think about themselves [as a nation]. But in my thirty year collection of press cuttings on a diverse range of subjects, those marked "England and the English" . . . are 20 times as numerous as any other category.' However, the fact that Britain is at a crossroads seems to have resulted in a larger batch of publications than usual. Below is a list of just a few of the large number of books that have been published around the Millennium.

Simon Heffer, *Nor Shall My Sword: The Reinvention of England*, Weidenfeld & Nicolson, 1999
Paul Langford, *Englishness Identified: Manners and Character*, 1650–1850, Oxford University Press, 2000
Idries Shah, *The Englishman's Handbook*, Octagon, 2000
Dennis Hardy, *Utopian England: Community Experiments 1900–1945*, E & F. N. Spon, 2000
Roger Scruton, *England: An Elegy*, Chatto, 2000
Maureen Duffy, *England: The Making of the Myth, from Stonehenge to Albert Square*, Fourth Estate, 2001

For many commentators, this contemporary discussion of 'Englishness' emerged from the assaults on 'Britishness' in the 1970s and 1980s by the three-cornered assertions of Celtic nationalism, yet the likelihood of Britain adopting the euro and the changing ethnic mix of the country have also been important factors. Consequently, there appears to be a larger than usual rush to define Englishness because sections of white England increas-ingly feel they have already lost their historical monopoly on Britishness. Perhaps the two most prominent commercial books about this subject in the last few years can indicate the increasing retreat of mainstream media discussions of Britishness to talk of Englishness. The first is Roy Strong's *Story of Britain* (2nd revised edition, London: Pimlico, 1998) and it epitomises the contemporary problem sections of the English have with Britishness.

The first Amazon.co.uk reviewer wrote from Cardiff on 16 October 2000:

> For Britain please read England
>   A very good book about the history of England, but Scotland and Wales get VERY little acknowledgement. At the same time I bought a history on Wales and funnily enough something actually happened there BEFORE 1536 – which is where Wales gets its first mention – 'absorbed into England'.

A second prominent millennial book on national identity is Jeremy Paxman's *The English: A Portrait of a People* (London: Penguin, 1999). The puff on the Amazon website for this book reads:

> What is it about the English? Not the British overall, not the Scots, not the Irish or Welsh, but the English. Why do they seem so unsure of who they are? As Jeremy Paxman remarks in his preface to *The English*, being English 'used to be so easy'. Now, with the Empire gone, with Wales and Scotland moving into more independent postures, with the troubling spectre of a united Europe . . . the English seem to have entered a collective crisis of national identity. Jeremy Paxman has set himself the task of finding just what exactly is going on . . . It is an intriguing investigation, encompassing many aspects of national life and character (such as it is), including the obligatory visit to that baffling phenomenon, the funeral of Princess Diana . . . To him it is a sign that the English are acquiring a new sense of self.

A trend noticeable here is that the recognition of differences between the countries within the (dis)United Kingdom has resulted in attempts to homogenise those within them; to rediscover the English, for example, as though people in England have remained unaltered for decades, or even centuries, despite the changes to their cultural identities brought about by Britain, Europe, the Empire, globalisation, and ethnic migration. In the face of this wave of self-rediscovery, I would want to put forward a comment by Patrick Wright in his important book *On Living in an Old Country*. Considering postwar England, he concludes; 'People live in different worlds even though they share the same locality: *there is no single community or quarter*. What is pleasantly "old" for one person is decayed and broken for another.' Whatever the future holds for the people who live in the British Isles, one thing they cannot move forward to is the past, and perhaps what is required is a new sense not of national identity but of plural imagined communities within and also across nations.

Europe

European union has developed into one of the most important political issues of the present day. Since the Union's conception, Britain has been somewhat slow and reluctant to participate fully, despite the majority perception that European integration is inevitable. It was not until 1 January 1973, following two years of negotiations, that Britain joined the EC. The decision, taken by the then-governing Conservative Party, which is now divided by the issue of European membership more than any other, was not without controversy. A national referendum was called upon the matter in June 1975, and the British populace endorsed EC membership by a two-to-one majority despite considerable opposition from certain quarters. Perhaps the element of EC membership that has caused most dissension between Britain and the EC is the Common Agricultural Policy (CAP). For years this was the central element of the EC budget, commanding 63 per cent of expenditure twenty years ago, such that if the CAP was unfair the redistributional effects of the whole EC budget would also be unfair. Britain argued that, because of the CAP, the value of its contributions far outweighed the value of benefits received, and consequently the EC established two British refunds in the 1980s.

The Maastricht Treaty in 1992 changed the European Community to the European Union, but other main elements of the treaty included further arrangements for economic and monetary union, including adoption of a single currency (then called the Ecu), provisions for an independent European bank, and the development of a common defence and foreign policy. A continued hostility to European integration on the right of British politics led to the 2001 election being fought by the Conservative Party on the platform slogans of 'Keep the Pound' and 'Save the UK from a Federal European Superstate'. The Conservatives lost the election, suggesting that the majority British view on Europe is closer to scepticism than hostility, underlined by the British reluctance to take full advantage of their voting rights in Europe: the European Parliament election of 1999 had a very low turnout of the electorate (like France and Italy, Britain elects 87 of the 626 members). At the start of 2002, while Britain sometimes seems hesitant to participate fully in European initiatives, Tony Blair is decidedly pro-Europe

FIGURE 8.1   Twinning is one of the few long-standing twentieth-century traditions that show a focus on linking British people with the Continent at grassroots level

and it is still true that EU directives apply to Britain as much as anywhere else, while European law ranks above British law in any dispute. Blair has argued that the greatest missed opportunity for Britain occurred when it failed to join the Common Market in 1957, such that rules and precedents had been established by the time of British involvement in 1973. (The present government's 'economic tests', which formally Blair says will decide Britain's European future, are due for completion by June 2003, but there is considerable political pressure to join the single currency before then.)

Some commentators in the media have argued that the level of economic and political integration discussed at present will radically change government and life in Britain. The current process of deregulation which began with the creation of a customs union will have radical consequences for national sovereignty if taken to its conclusion. Subsequent integration, such as adoption of the euro, will mean the sacrifice of certain national economic tools, including control of the interest rate, and a degree of vunerability to economic conditions in other countries. Those who take a negative view of European union argue that the Chancellor should be able to control the British economy from Westminster and that legislation which governs the British populace, concerning the maximum length of the working week for example, should originate only from the British Parliament. However, others maintain that an increased degree of economic stability will be beneficial to industry while closer union will benefit British traders who can exploit EU markets more efficiently.

As Britain under Tony Blair moves closer to inclusion within a single currency – at present the opt-out clause means that Parliament's approval must be sought before such action can be taken – some areas of opposition to European integration have grown more vociferous. Certain members of the Conservative party, so-called Eurosceptics, have tried to split their party into two camps over the subject of Europe, while the 2001 national election again featured members of Sir James Goldsmith's anti-Europe Referendum Party, the sole purpose of which is to call for a public decision on European involvement. Britain's economic success appears to be tied to Europe, yet a reluctance to participate fully is as strong as ever in some quarters.

In 2001, a report from the European Commission warned that public ignorance in Britain of the euro was such that a credible referendum about it could not be held. Only 20 per cent of people felt they were well informed, while 80 per cent of the thousand questioned confessed to a serious lack of knowledge. Almost two-thirds of those questioned said they believed giving up the pound would mean an end to national independence while 60 per cent said they thought the EU could not be trusted with British interests. The academic asked to review the figures in Brussels concluded that views about the euro were based upon 'prejudice and the innate conservatism of British public opinion'. Many of Britain's largest high-street chain stores started to accept euro notes and coins from 1 January 2002, raising the expectation that the currency will become standard in the country before any referendum is held. The phenomenon that this is part of, known to economists as 'Eurocreep', will be of benefit to Europeans shopping in the UK, but it is also expected to change the way the euro is perceived in Britain. Richard Branson's Virgin chain has been one of the most enthusiastic supporters of the shift to a dual currency, and all its tills are now capable of accepting the euro as well as sterling. Vending machine operators have also been quick to make the change, which will cost them about £100 million, though this is only a fraction of the £36 billion the conversion would cost for the whole economy.

Britain's relationship with (the rest of) Europe can be considered in a number of ways, but in general it might be argued that the British have responded positively when the Continent has come to their shores, such as students on the EU's SOCRATES scheme, but have been hostile to legislation which may appear to be imposed at arm's length from Brussels. So, in recent years, the European presence in Britain has been felt most strongly in football, as stars such as Zola (Italian, at Chelsea), Van Nistelrooy

(Dutch, at Manchester United), and Henry (French, at Arsenal) have reversed the trend of the 1970s and 1980s when British footballers such as Kevin Keegan and Gary Lineker went abroad for experience. The recent appointment of Sven-Goran Eriksson, a Swede, to the position of England manager caused a national debate, as it was felt in many quarters that the team had to be led by a countryman, who would understand the importance of football to the English. This attitude seemed to quickly fade away when the team was successful in its first few matches, and the fickle media that questioned Eriksson's appointment began referring to England in a football context as 'Svengland'. Alternatively, Britain has generally been hostile to the ways in which the nation's diet has come under repeated scrutiny by European bureaucrats as they attempt to regulate and standardise agricultural production and markets across the European Union. Rumours concerning legislation over food and drink coming from Europe have become widespread in contemporary folklore, with stories of decrees from Brussels over the size of apples or the straightness of cucumbers fuelling British anti-European feeling. The image of the food mountain, built to stabilise markets and prices, has itself become a powerful symbolic landscape form for Europe. The huge furore around beef and Bovine Spongiform Encephalopathy (a fatal brain disease believed to be passed from infected cattle to humans, where it causes a similarly fatal brain condition called Creutzfeld-Jakob Syndrome Variant), which led to a worldwide ban on British beef in the mid-1990s, also brought out the cultural politics of food production and consumption very starkly – especially so, perhaps, given the association of Britishness with beef (the epitome of this is William Hogarth's eighteenth-century painting *The Gate of Calais*, commonly known as *O the Roast Beef of Old England*, which hangs in the National Gallery). The 'beef crisis' provoked in some Britons the 'patriotic' response of ignoring health warnings and continuing to eat British beef, simultaneously mocking people who were more cautious about their consumption habits. So, in a 2001 United Nations survey of domestic concerns, while for other Europeans 'Beef/BSE' came third in a poll of 'What would you say were the two or three most important problems facing your country today?', for the British it did not figure in the top twelve (the top three were law and order, health, and unemployment).

It is widely understood, however, that food from the Continent has had a pervasive positive impact on British culture. Supermarkets now carry products that would have been hard to find fifteen years ago: rocket, wild mushrooms, Parmigiano-Reggiano, crème fraîche, filo pastry, dry-cured bacon, pancetta, a dozen kinds of rice, of pasta and of olive oil. However, of all people in the West, the British still spend the least part of their monthly income on food, though the middle classes eat out more and more, expecting to be served foods from around the world that they would not have heard of ten years earlier: pad thai, pho, pata negra, sushi, bulgogi, and boutargue. The revolution in British restaurant food has been attributed to the influence of chefs such as the Roux brothers, who opened their restaurant, Le Gavroche, in the early 1970s, and served carefully chosen and prepared 'authentic' French food, as opposed to the imitation fare previously available in London. These were followed by chefs such as Raymond Blanc and Anton Mosimann, and then Nico Ladenis and Marco Pierre White. Arguably, it is this influence that has led to the enormous success of cookery programmes and television chefs in recent years. These are sometimes not professional cooks but those who have simply learnt how to eat well for themselves, such as Nigella Lawson and Sophie Grigson. Many are celebrated because of their personalities rather than their cooking (Ainsley Harriott or Jamie Oliver), while still more are valued simply for educating British people about the basics (Delia Smith). It is cookery books, though, that have changed most, as traditional, 'good English cooking' guides by the likes of Elizabeth David and Jane Grigson were superseded in the 1970s by translations from French originals, and by hundreds of recipe books by chefs such as Blanc and Mosimann which were then emulated by homegrown authors and publications such as the ubiquitous *River Café Cook Book*.

In an *Observer* poll in 2001, Britons were asked which was their favourite European country. The replies placed Spain (26 per cent) over-whelmingly in front, followed by France (13 per cent), Italy (12 per cent), Ireland (11 per cent), and Portugal (8 per cent). These figures were comple-mented by Britons' choice of foreign holiday destinations, recorded in 1999 as: Spain (27 per cent), France (20 per cent), Eire (6 per cent), Italy (4 per cent), and Portugal (4 per cent). These were the top European destinations except for Greece (6 per cent); of non-European countries, only the USA (7 per cent) ranked in the top ten.

Over the last three decades, British people have become decreasingly hostile to and increasingly appreciative of European culture, old rivalries and prejudices themselves passing away with older generations. Among the young, Europe is generally perceived positively and associated with many of the good things in life discussed above, from food to holidays, but the public in general remain deeply divided. On the one hand, polls provide evidence that British people still have a number of fears about European conformity, epitomised by the story in spring 2001 of a grocer prosecuted for selling apples by the old imperial measures of pounds and ounces, which are still preferred by many people over forty. On the other hand, the failure of the Conservative government to gain any headway on Labour in the 2001 elections indicates that its promise to keep British sovereignty and the pound is not the main priority on most people's agenda.

Multiethnic Britain

Statistics about the UK population of the kind given in previous chapters are usually more applicable to some ethnic groups than to others, and this can be for economic as well as cultural reasons (for example, 60 per cent of Bangladeshi and Pakistani Britons are living in poverty, four times the figure for white Britons). So, when discussing language, it is important to realise that while more than half of all sixteen- to twenty-nine-year-old Indians and Pakistanis have English as their main spoken language, this is true of only one-fifth of Bangladeshis in that age bracket. These figures are also contextualised by the fact that nearly half the ethnic minority population is under twenty-four, compared with one-third of the white population. The youth culture of different ethnic groups also varies, such that, for example, young people from ethnic minority backgrounds are a third less likely to use drugs than whites. Similarly, 71 per cent of sixteen- to nineteen-year-olds from ethnic minority groups were in full-time education in 2001, compared with 58 per cent of whites. In terms of gender, women from ethnic minorities hold more educational qualifications than white women, and black African women are twice as likely to be qualified above A-level standard. Again, the proportion of Asian women who have separated or divorced is less than half that recorded among whites, while one in ten white women with children is a single mother, compared with half of Caribbean mothers. Last of these indicators, taken from *The Observer*'s 'Britain Uncovered' survey in March 2001, is the fact that three-quarters of Pakistani and Bangladeshi women are in partnerships by the age of twenty-five, 50 per cent more than white women.

FIGURE 8.2 Britain's ethnic mix is becoming more and more diverse

The rise of multiethnic Britain has seen great changes in areas such as eating and music. Again food in Britain has been revolutionised by exposure to cuisine from around the world. Every market town now has an Indian and a Chinese take-away, and Thai restaurants are becoming nearly as common. This has not been solely because of migrants coming to Britain but also because travel abroad has given the British a taste for such things as baltis and green curry. Celebrity television chefs, such as Ken Hom (Chinese) and Madhur Jaffrey (Indian), have introduced new foods to the domestic diet. It has been said that this is a positive part of the rapid mongrelisation of British culture, such that Robin Cook, who was then Foreign Secretary, said in early 2001 that Chicken Tikka Masala is now the national dish.

In the arts, 'ethnic' and cross-over music particularly have become mainstream in recent years, with an artist such as Nitin Sawhney nominated for the prestigious annual Mercury Music awards. There are now also the annual MOBO awards solely for black artists, and an equivalent ceremony to celebrate the achievements of British Asians in the arts. Since the 1980s Asian musicians in Britain have been experimenting with rap, dub technology, jungle breakbeats, traditional Indian music and rock. In the mid- to late 1990s Anglo-Asian artists with sitars, guitars, and decks, such as Cornershop, Asian Dub Foundation, Fun-da-mental, and Talvin Singh, broke into the pop charts, to be followed by Taz, a British Asian from Coventry, who is a major star in India and whose 2001 hit 'Laila' includes lyrics sung in English, Swahili, and Spanish. Talvin Singh's Anokha played club nights at The Blue Note in London which attracted media stars, and Cornershop's 1997 album *When I was Born for the Seventh Time* became a critical and commercial success (and included the number one single 'Brimful of Asha'). Though the bands vary in their political engagement, Asian Dub Foundation, for example, released their single 'Free Satpal Ram' in 1998 as a protest against the imprisonment of a Birmingham Asian who defended himself against racist attacks. Across the board, Afro-Caribbeans have exerted a decisive stylistic influence on British youth and mainstream cultures as evidenced by the dance appropriation of aspects of Rudeboy, Rasta, hip hop and sound system culture. Soul II Soul perhaps ideally encapsulate the young, black and British cultural awakening of the mid-1980s with their unique synthesis of a black British attitude, music, fashion, and philosophy. Hip hop culture underlines the creative assemblage that defines Afro-Caribbean youth styles in Britain, whether in music (mixing and sampling), dress (arranging assorted fake and real designer labels), or language.

A festival that epitomises the best multicultural aspects of modern Britain is the Edinburgh Mela. This is Scotland's biggest annual multicultural arts festival, and its aim is to celebrate Scotland's diverse cultures.

The festival's roots are in South Asian cultures, and the Edinburgh Mela was originally created by a group of people from Bangladesh, India, and Pakistan, yet the festival intends to reflect the wide diversity of what it means to be Scottish, while also bringing artists from around the world, from the late Nusrat Fateh Ali Khan to Papa Wemba, Bappi Lahiri and Musical Youth. It has become the most significant multicultural event in Scotland, attracting people from all parts of the UK.

A major issue of debate that has often focused on issues of ethnicity in the early years of the new century has been asylum seekers. The Labour government has come under repeated attacks for its scheme of distributing migrants from the ports where they arrive to cities around the country. In late 2001, local authorities in north England and Scotland were increasingly reacting against the scheme: city chiefs in Glasgow were said to be holding an emergency meeting to decide where to house the three busloads of asylum seekers who arrived each week, with almost no prior warning and with misinformation about the nationalities involved. Several councils declared that they could take no more refugee families and stopped providing homes for those who arrived, while others accuse the Home Office of paying self-interested private landlords to house thousands of asylum seekers in slums rather than using accommodation provided by the local authorities. After street violence in Bradford, Stoke, and Burnley, the government suspended plans to send more refugees to these cities, but reports of violence against asylum seekers around the country appear weekly in the newspapers. More than a hundred incidents were reported in Hull alone in the year following the introduction of refugees to the city in the summer of 2000. Many local residents believe that asylum seekers are getting a better deal than they are, but in fact most are subject to a voucher scheme where they are given only a little money for telephone calls or bus fares and have to exchange the vouchers for food at designated stores (the government backed out of the voucher scheme late in 2001). It was also said by the Committee to Defend Asylum Seekers in 2001 that 1,500 applicants for asylum were detained in prisons, while the Home Secretary decided he would deport thirty thousand in that year. The United Nations estimates that there are 37 million refugees across the world, only 0.5 per cent of whom are in Britain. In 1998 there were fewer than four thousand applications for asylum, but this rose to seventy-six thousand in 2000, the highest proportion coming from Iraq (9 per cent), followed by Sri Lanka (8 per cent), the former Yugoslavia, and Afghanistan (7 per cent each). Of these, 21,565 were granted refugee status or exceptional leave to remain by the Home Office (though, by international agreement, asylum seekers are not allowed to seek work).

As a contrast to those voices who see the demise of 'Britishness' in future years, there are those who consider culture, and identity itself, as pluralistic and multi-layered, while recognising the pressures that are currently questioning the limits of Britain. Perhaps most prominently in these quarters, the 'unsettling' of Britain has been detailed by The Parekh Report on *The Future of Multi-Ethnic Britain* in 2000. The report commissioned by the Runnymede Trust sees seven reasons why the idea of Britain is at a turning-point: globalisation, the country's decline as a world power, its role in Europe, devolution, the end of empire, the spread of social pluralism, and postwar migration. The Report's conclusion is that Britain ought to be recognised as the 'community of communities' it has now come to be and, for that matter, always was. Changes in the understanding of British culture and in the transmission of appropriate national stories, signs, and symbols, can follow through from this appreciation of present and past pluralism. The Parekh Report was commissioned in 1997 at a time when debates over British identity were still recovering from the intervention on the subject of Dr Nick Tate, the Conservative government's Chief Curriculum Adviser in the summer of 1995. Tate called for schoolchildren to be taught what it means to be 'British'.

Clearly, Tate's suggestion that school classes should focus on British identity served as a rallying-cry for certain sections of the press to bewail contemporary ignorance about literature, history, and politics. In *The Times* in July 1995 Janet Daley, the philosopher who has recently retired from the BBC's *Moral Maze* programme, took the opportunity to speak out for a generation of children who were being 'culturally disinherited'. Daley argued that the teaching profession was under the sway of a basic Marxist premise: 'that the passing on of culture [is] a kind of political coercion'. Upbraiding those who wanted to overhaul the teaching of a traditional monologic *English* history, she concluded that for these teachers 'National identity was deemed to be a pernicious myth which only served to exclude anyone who was not party to its smug racial and class attitudes.' But, [she argued], all history is a selective version of events and all cultures are prejudiced in their own favour. 'In the end, [pluralism] is the argument not for many cultures but for none.'

The familiar standpoint here is that muticulturalism results in an attentuation of collective identity: that cultural increase means not addition but dilution. Similarly, Andrew Roberts in the *Daily Mail* at the same time in July 1995 argued: 'The liberal believes a man, once stripped of his national and cultural identity, will become Everyman – citizen of the world. The conservative knows that, in fact, he will become bewildered, schizophrenic, unhappy and lonely.' Mistaking plurality for deracination (the erosion of one's ethnic roots), Roberts was actually protesting against the present variety of British identities, opposed to received images of a national past whose people are easier to homogenise. The reactionary stance underlying much of this rhetoric was clearly a nostalgic one which considered itself to be embattled in 1995 and has now moved its territory. Having lost most of the moral high ground, the traditionalist position on national identity has shifted to a different level in the more recent present, resulting in an increase in violence among ethnic groups in some parts of Britain, especially inner-city areas with large migrant or multiracial populations. It is clear that some British people consider a multicultural society to be a threat not just to their ideas of national identity but to their very well-being. The suicide plane attacks on New York and Washington on 11 September 2001 brought cries of support and outrage from the British press and politicians, but it was also apparent that for some British people these extreme terrorist actions were hard to dissociate from their perceptions of Muslims in the UK, and the weeks following the American disaster were marked not just by calls for a greater understanding of religious and cultural differences but also by verbal attacks and acts of violence aimed at Muslim individuals and families.

Literature has provided a number of prominent contemporary examples of multiethnic Britain, from Salman Rushdie's *The Satanic Verses* to the works of Hanif Kureishi. To take one celebrated book, Zadie Smith's debut novel *White Teeth* presents a series of metaphors for the heterogeneity of modern Britain. Her title of course plays with the idea that everyone is the same under the skin, but the novel charts the variety of molars, canines, incisors, root canals, false teeth, dental work, and damage that constitute the history behind different smiles. The commonsensical idea of the uniformity of teeth, which can also be divided into a host of shades from pearly to black, is as much a fiction in the novel as the traditional template of Britishness. The prime examplars of traditional Englishness in *White Teeth* are a family called the Chalfens. The Chalfens are taken to be 'more English than the English' because of their liberal middle-class values, and also their tendency towards empiricism. However, they are in fact third-generation Poles, originally Chalfenovskys: not more English than the English, but as English as anyone else. Smith rings this theme of hybridity and cross-fertilisation through numerous extended metaphors, drawn from horticulture, eugenics, and the weather.

The most prominent person in the novel who considers herself to be 'a stranger in a strange land' is Irie Jones, whose mother is 'from Lambeth (via Jamaica)' and whose father is a white war veteran from Brighton. In the novel's metaphor, Irie sees no reflection of herself in the 'mirror of Englishness'. She turns to her grandmother and Jamaica for a sense of her 'roots' but concludes that the idea of belonging is itself a 'lie'. The other central family of the book, the Iqbals, have come to England from Bangladesh. Their second-generation children spend their teenage years apart, the one in London, the other in Chittagong. Each finds his identity is located elsewhere: Millat, living in London, wishes to be an American gangsta-rapper before he becomes in the words of his father a 'fully paid-up green bow-tie wearing fundamentalist terrorist', while Magid, in Bangladesh, becomes 'a pukka Englishman, white suited, silly wig lawyer'. Their mother, Alsana, expresses the overall view of the novel: 'You go back and back and back and it's still easier to find the right Hoover bag than to find one pure person, one pure faith, on the globe. Do you think anybody is English? Really English? It's a fairy-tale.'

White Teeth's view of race relations, though far from perfect, seems more closely to resemble hopes for Britain's future than observations about its past. The book works politically far more at the level of representation than any kind of confrontation. The novel disseminates a multicultural view of London, where currently over 40 per cent of children are born to at least one black parent. And *White Teeth*, as the novelist Caryl Phillips concluded in his review of the novel, ably dramatises the fact that 'The "mongrel" nation that is Britain is still struggling to find a way to stare into the mirror and accept the ebb and flow of history that has produced this fortuitously diverse condition'. So Smith's horti-multi-cultural view of Britain is best summarised in a passage where she argues that there is, in fact, 'No one more English than the Indian . . . '

New technology

Finally, nothing seems to look to the future more than technology. In the last ten years, a number of machines have materialised in a sizeable number of, if not most, British homes. These include DVD (Digital Versatile Disk) players, which have superseded the video and relegated it to the level of a recorder of television programmes, rather than a device on which to play movies. High-street stores such as Virgin and HMV have given over most of their movie shelf space to DVDs and are selling off films on videotape at bargain prices. Alongside the improved picture quality of DVD, visible on any television, there is the improved sound quality too, which has given birth to the arrival of the Home Cinema System, a set-up of six speakers to convey the aural experience of going to the pictures. As the prices of DVD players has fallen from over £300 to less than £100 in some cases, they have become increasingly de rigueur in middle-class homes, largely because the 'extras' provided on the disks make them worthwhile purchases for people who already have the films on videotape. The music revolution of fifteen years back, when people were persuaded to junk their vinyl collections for CDs, has now happened with film, and is expected to happen again with music in the next few years as Super Audio CDs will supposedly produce better sound quality than CDs, while mini-CDs will store more music, more compactly. Much of this technology, for example WAP phones which give access to the internet, is appealing as much to adults, who traditionally stay in more, as to teenagers, though this is less true of MP3 players, which enable the individual to listen to digital music files downloaded from the internet.

Two other major leisure-time enhancements can also be linked to the television: satellite or cable broadcasting and computer games, both of which have become common in British homes. The race to secure pro-gramme transmission for direct broadcasting by satellite was finally won in 1990 by Rupert Murdoch's Sky, after a series of financial setbacks had forced its sole competitor, British Satellite Broadcasting (BSB), into a merger: since then, the proliferation of extraterrestrial stations in the last ten years has resulted in a vast expansion of (some) viewers' choices, both enhancing television's and decreasing the terrestrial channels' hold on col-lective entertainment, and also an expectation that major events, like some sporting fixtures and movies, will be screened on a pay-per-view basis. While PC games are now an accepted leisure activity even among adults, having lost their 'geeky' image, Playstations, Dreamcast, and Nintendo Gameboys have become firmly established as an aspect of youth culture since 1989. While CD-ROMs, faxes, and pagers now almost seem 'old' tech-nology, the two major changes to professional and private lives have been the rise in sales of mobile telephones and the increased use of the internet.

In 2001, 90 per cent of teenagers under the age of sixteen had a mobile phone, and it is predicted that by 2005 this figure will apply to the entire population, whereas in 1988 the figure stood at 3 per cent. According to research, more than 10 per cent of young teenagers talk for over forty-five minutes every day, while 16 per cent send ten or more text messages a day. Text messaging has become the new email for sending soundbites between children (96 per cent of mobile phone users send them), but also for adults to communicate information or send a brief greeting. Even the Lord's Prayer has now been translated into a text message as part of a scheme to send church services to worshippers on their mobile phones. 'Our Father who art in Heaven' has become 'dad@hvn', and the rest of the prayer now reads: 'urspshl.we want wot u want&urth2b like hvn.giv us food&4giv r sins lyk we 4giv uvaz.don't test us!bcos we kno ur boss, ur tuf&ur cool 4 eva!ok?' The Muslim community has already witnessed the benefits of text messaging believers with their five daily 'calls to prayer' but Christians have had to wait until the launch of the website Ship-of-fools.com. It is reported that the social use of mobile phones now exceeds business use, and knowledge of text message emoticons, such as :-) for happy, is important for the young, for whom messaging is popular partly because it is a new form of communication baffling to many adults. In the third quarter of 2000, 1,648 million text messages were sent, a huge increase from 599 million in the last quarter of the previous year.

After its initial years in which the internet struggled to be taken seriously outside of universities and computer companies, it is now a staple ingredient of British life, the greatest increase in its use now occurring among thirty-five- to forty-four-year-olds. The major internet service providers by far are Freeserve (28 per cent) and AOL (America On Line, 13 per cent). The most visited internet sites are BBC.co.uk and Virgin.net, while Amazon is the largest retail site, by far, in terms of number of visitors (the top products bought on line are books, CDs, holidays, and computer products). By 2001, over 40 per cent of UK households had access to the internet, and this is expected to rise to 90 per cent by 2010, though for many the mode of access may be through a digital television or a mobile phone. Computers have therefore become essential home purchases as much as video recorders (owned by 80 per cent of households) and microwaves (70 per cent). Overall, the speed of technological change has been embraced by the British, who have welcomed new developments such as digital cameras, handheld scanners, GPS (global positioning satellite) systems, and palm organisers, even though according to surveys 50 per cent of people still cannot operate all the features on a video recorder.

Conclusion

The technological revolution has enormously changed people's lives in the home, challenging the idea of the family 'unit' by turning its members into consumers of myriad domestic leisure activities, while postwar migration has greatly altered the ethnic population on the streets, and the rise of the European Union has meant that British people have thought more deeply about their national identities, some wishing to call themselves primarily 'Welsh', 'Irish', 'English', 'Scottish', others 'British', and others 'European', 'Asian', or 'African'. The Britain that the essays in this book have described is composed of various contrasting elements: asylum seekers and moneyed gentry; settled suburban commuters and country farmers; women priests and male nurses; nostalgic OAPs and young ravers – each experiencing a different version and expressing a different view of the country when talking about their relation to Britain. Any of these experiences of being British is a product of individual identity and experience, formed by a range of factors such as employment, gender, region, religion, and education, and each of these alternative views would supply a picture of Britain which can only take a place in a mosaic of opinions. As much as if not more than ever, in the twenty-first century it is wrong to think that there is a single British character or personality, rather than a plurality of cultural identities.

Exercises

1   What do you think are the arguments for and against multiethnic communities?

2   Given that many employers decline to give jobs to people over the age of fifty because they think older people are less likely to keep up with technological developments, to what extent do you feel the proliferation of new technologies adds to a generation gap in society? Are the young's attitudes towards the old different from what they were in the past?

3   Supposedly, the five things that Europeans think of when considering the UK are The Beatles, London, the Royal Family, the BBC, and Shakespeare. To what extent are these things 'British', as opposed to English? What five things that are not English would you list as the most famous aspects to Britain?

4   In this Conclusion, some of the influences of Europe on Britain have been mentioned. What would you consider the main British influences on European countries to be?

Reading

Davey, Kevin. *English Imaginaries*, Lawrence & Wishart, 1998.

Bracewell, Michael, *England is Mine*, 2nd ed. Flamingo 1998.

The Runnymede Trust. *The Future of Multiethnic Britain: The Parekh Report*, Profile, 2000.

Gilroy, Paul. *There Ain't No Black in the Union Jack*, Unwin Hyman, 1987.

Nairn, Tom. *After Britain*, Granta, 2000.

Easthope, Antony. *Englishness and National Culture*, Routledge, 1999.

Wright, Patrick. *On Living in an Old Country*, Verso, 1985.

George, Stephen. *Britain and European Integration Since 1945*, Blackwell, 1991.

Phillips, Mike and Phillips, Trevor. *Windrush: The Irresistible Rise of Multi-racial Britain*, HarperCollins, 1999.

Cultural Examples

Films

Bhaji on the Beach. (1994) dir. Gurinder Chadha. Film, mixing British realist and Indian musical styles, about a group of British Asian women from Birmingham on a day trip to Blackpool. Chadha also directed *Bend it Like Beckham* (2002).

Bladerunner (1982) dir. Ridley Scott. Dystopian sci-fi thriller by British director envisioning an overcrowded, post-industrial, multicultural, cyborg future with dialects that combine English, Spanish, and Japanese (Spanglish).

Trainspotting (1995) dir. Danny Boyle. Shocking and funny tale of heroin addicts in Edinburgh based on novel by Irvine Welsh.

Mike Bassett: England Manager (2001) dir. Steve Barron. Spoof comedy in which Ricky Tomlinson, from television's *The Royle Family*, stars as a pre-Eriksson national football manager who quotes Rudyard Kipling while aiming to take England to the World Cup in Brazil.

Books

Zadie Smith, *White Teeth* (2000). Hugely popular comic novel of multiethnic life in London since 1947.

Victor Headley, *Yardie* (1992). Jamaican gangster pulp fiction set in 1990s Hackney, London. The novel looks at the postwar Afro-Caribbean immigrant experience in conjunction with the transnational drugs economy.

Jeff Noon, *Vurt* (1993). Novel set in a grim, comic Manchester of the future. In a world peopled by vurt, robo and dog beings, gangs escape cops through the use of cyber-technology.

Julian Barnes, *Letters from London, 1990–95* (1995). An assembly of English novelist Barnes's writing for *The New Yorker*, on a range of topics from the fortunes of Margaret Thatcher to the troubles of the Royal Family.

Television programmes

Gas Attack. Channel 4 2001 film, shown on television but also at art cinemas, about an imaginary right-wing anthrax attack on a community of asylum seekers in Glasgow.

East. BBC2 programme which covers important topics and events outside of EuroAmerica, usually from Asia.

Eurotrash. Self-consciously titillating look at the Continent by Antoine de Cannes, previously assisted by Jean-Paul Gaultier. Plays on stereotypes of national identity such as British prudery.

The Kumars at Number 42. Much-lauded parody of mainstream talk shows in which a British Asian family interview well-known celebrities in a studio supposedly adapted from an extension on the back of their house.

 # Websites

www.wired.com/news
> News and analysis of the technologies driving the information age

www.ukmp3guide.co.uk
> A well-known British site for downloading MP3 music files

www.cybertown.com
   A site on which you can live an online life with virtual cash in Cybertown

www.eufactsfigures.com/
   British Eurosceptic site

Glossary

Instead of a set of exercises and questions to end the book, we have noted down the following outlines of keywords. We would like you to use these as starting points for thinking about each of the terms, but also as comprising an elementary glossary to which you may want, perhaps with the aid of a dictionary and other books, to add your own terms and short definitions.

Accent is the inflection given to, and modulation of, speech. It mainly indicates social class and should be distinguished from both *dialect*, which is a combination of accent intonation and local vocabulary and indicates region, and *slang*, which is the use of ungrammatical English among people in the same generational or gender grouping.

Acronyms are examples of compression that are increasingly common in an accelerating culture. Adopted widely in the 1980s to describe new social and cultural phenomena, they included: YUPPIES: 'Young Urban Professionals; DINKIE: 'Dual Income No Kiddies'; NIMBY: people who were in favour of (say) gypsy sites but: 'Not In My Back Yard'. Margaret Thatcher was nicknamed TINA: 'There Is No Alternative'. BOHECA ('Bend Over Here Comes Another') was common in the National Health Service referring to non-stop initiatives and reforms imposed on people.

Consumerism: the idea that consumption, not production is the basis of capitalist society. Hence 'market forces' and 'value for money' can be brought into all aspects of public life. There are three stages of consumerism: goods; services (television entertainment or pizza delivery); and experiences (aerobics programmes or travel).

Do-gooders is a term of abuse for well-meaning, left-leaning liberals. They are seen as sincere but dangerous interferers, rather than as problem-solvers.

Drug culture is an alternative way of life which has produced a range of terminology for drugs. Heroin is 'smack'; cocaine is 'crack'; marijuana or cannabis is 'grass', 'hash [ish]', 'shit', 'slate'. Addicts are 'smack-heads' etc.

The Establishment is a neutral term for the people who are traditionally believed to run Britain – the landed aristocracy, hereditary peers, long-established business interests ('The Beerage'). Alan Clark used it to identify those members of the Conservative Party who represent an old guard, as distinguished from those who currently hold political power in the Party.

Estuary English is a form of speech distinguished from 'Received Pronunciation' or 'proper English'. For example 'regimental' is pronounced 'regimen'au'. 'It'll' becomes 'i'uw'. Identified in 1984, by David Rosewarne, estuary English supplies speakers from different social backgrounds with a means of a camouflaging their origins, whether Cockney or public school. It is commonly used by traders in London's money markets, and a television celebrity like Paul Merton would be considered to speak it.

Gender is a division into masculine and feminine which is socially constructed – as opposed the male/female distinction of sex, which is biologically determined.

Generation X, though an older term, is nowadays used to refer to Douglas Coupland's novel, *Generation X: Tales for an Accelerated Culture*. Loosely, the term defines a group of consumers born between 1964 and 1969. They appear alienated from the values of their affluent parents (Baby Boomers) by their own uncertain prospects, but the difference may be to do with style. They are also known as Busters, or in a later generation, Slackers. They might be said to welcome the internet, quirky advertising, grunge fashion, and the idea of defining themselves.

Grunge was a term used by mid-1980s rock journalists to describe a confrontational form of hard rock music. Despite its overtones of squalor and dirt it has come to describe a particular fashion look – one which is deliberately not smart.

Hegemony, from the Greek word for leadership, refers to a cluster of ideas, practices and connections which enable a small group of people to retain dominance. Formulation of the concept is associated with Antonio Gramsci.

Heritage has overtones of 'inheritance' and is about the transmission of traditional values. It is intended to be a dynamic outgrowth of static 'museum' culture and to indicate concern for the physical and historical environment. Since the 1980s Britain has had a Heritage Secretary. Some see it as just another contender in the struggle between ideologically opposed versions to fix British cultural identity 'officially'. It is thus an aspect of theme-park Britain.

Hybridity, in popular culture usage, denotes the mixing of different styles of fashion, music, or anything else in order to come up with a better synthesis. Within this 'fusion' (now the buzzword) the originals, with their conflicting messages, can sometimes still be detected. So BBC TV's contemporary Jane Austen adaptation might place a more feminist overlay on the original texts (or indeed a message about the slave trade, as in the film of *Mansfield Park* (Patricia Rozema, 1999)).

Jobsworths are people who, when asked to be flexible, protest 'it's more than my job's worth'. They are presumed to be narrowly bureaucratic, unthinking, time-serving employees, who hide within the public service. The use of this disparaging description may indicate that the speaker is part of a new, non-unionised, entrepreneurial Britain.

Laddism is a male culture which may be seen as a reaction to the idea of the caring, sensitive 'new man' produced by the feminist movement. So laddism is characterised by a climate of rough behaviour, excessive drinking ('lager louts') and all-male attendance at soccer matches. Magazines such as *Loaded* and *FHM* cater to it. It is imitated now by women, known as ladettes.

Moral panics are periodic bouts of hysteria, where the media (particularly the tabloid press) whip up national feeling about issues which have existed all along but have lacked the 'oxygen of publicity'. Recent examples would be: chaining of pregnant prisoners; teenage use of the drug Ecstasy, 'social-security scrounging'.

New Age is a broad term devised to describe the renewal of interest from the mid-1980s onwards in a range of approaches to the spiritual dimension which emphasise the individual's ability to discover and develop their own spirituality. The term comes from astrology: every two thousand years the solar system enters a new age, the next one being the age of Aquarius (the sign of individualism). Influences are yoga and t'ai chi. It is associated with alternative culture: the occult, Tarot, astrology and hippy lifestyles. Most visible elements are New Age travellers and the Donga Tribe.

Outing is the practice of publicly declaring someone to be homosexual. It has been used particularly to identify the sexual orientation of e.g. an Anglican bishop who opposes the ordination of homosexual clergy. Its use is controversial within the gay community.

Pagan was originally either a polytheist or someone who doesn't believe in a God at all, but now denotes a New Age movement aiming to recreate links with nature. Its adherents may be interested in: Wicca (see below), the occult, the book of shadows, spells, magic, witchcraft, athames, and myriad rituals. Some pagans believe in the mind-expanding potential of drug use.

Political correctness is a term used to suggest that people are too sensitive about giving offence to oppressed or special interest groups, which include women, gays and ethnic minorities. Language has been purged of many words: housewife; actress; stewardess; chairman. The word 'partner' has become substituted for husband/wife or (gay/lesbian/straight) lover.

Protestant work ethic: the idea that people must take responsibility for their own destinies and therefore not rely on others to support them but must work for themselves to 'justify their experience'. Robinson Crusoe exemplifies a robust self-sufficient practitioner.

Rhyming slang, though originally Cockney, is now incorporated into the language at large. To have a butcher's (hook) is to take a look. The nursery rhyme 'Pop goes the weasel' refers to pawning a suit (a whistle and flute). Slang is often used to avoid obscenity: according to *Chambers Dictionary* a 'berk' (a common English word for a fool) is 'short for Cockney rhyming slang Berkeley Hunt, for cunt', while 'Aris' (used in films such as *Lock, Stock and Two Smoking Barrels*) means 'arse' because it is an abbreviation of 'Aristotle', which rhymes with bottle, and 'bottle and glass' rhymes with 'arse' (see www.bio.nrc.ca/cockney/).

Sound bites are short expressions used by politicians and media commentators to compress ideas into an easily memorable form. The idea is that in a fast-paced modern world, where people have limited concentration spans, ideas have to be got over to them in succinct shorthand. Critics fear that their use leads to the over-simplification of complex arguments. Examples are: Rip-off Britain; spin doctors; Euro-sceptics; dumbing down; cronyism.

Spin doctors are public relations people who manage the flow of information and news so as to cast their corporate or political employers in the best light. They time the release of bad news to coincide with major distracting events, arrange publicity stunts and feed positive information about their clients to the media (Jo Moore, a Labour spin doctor, resigned in 2002 after allegations that she recommended 'burying bad news' on 11 September 2001).

Stakeholder society: the term used to describe Tony Blair's vision of 'active citizenship' in modern Britain.

Subculture refers to both alternative culture and to individual groups operating separately from mainstream society. Often it refers to rival gangs of e.g. mods and rockers, skinheads and bovver boys or punks, but it also refers to groupings of [mainly young] people with gentler outlooks: New Romantics; Goths; Crusties.

Tabloids are sometimes also known as 'red tops'. They include newspapers such as *The Mirror*, the *Daily Star*, *The Sun*. The last named, owned by Rupert Murdoch, is known for its daily nude on page 3. Though despised by highbrows, their political influence is as great as that of the broadsheets, because of their greater circulation.

Theme Park is an American concept, popularised by Disney, based on re-creation of fantasy world. It replaces the previous generation's seaside piers and amusement arcades. Popular British examples are: Alton Towers, Madame Tussaud's and Camelot. The expression 'theme-park Britain' has been applied to attempts to package a slick, plastic, idealised and sanitised version of Britain's past. It is to be sold to foreign and domestic tourists and sustains various hegemonic interests. Traditional version Britain have been seen as engaged in this process. Castle banquets at Ruthin (Wales) and Bunratty (Ireland) are part of it, as are stately homes, and such industrial-archaeology sites as Styal woollen mill or Llechwedd slate mines.

The Third Way is the term used to describe Tony Blair's policies, which purport to carve a political niche between traditional left and right positions. It derives from the theories of the sociologist Anthony Giddens and in particular his book *The Third Way: The Renewal of Social Democracy* (1998).

Upstairs/downstairs represents the idea of Britain as 'two nations': masters and servants. Particularly in Edwardian Britain, servants lived in the basement of houses and owners on the upper floors. This division was reflected in respective power relations. The concept was revived by a popular television series of that name and was in evidence again in 2002 in a new television serial of Galsworthy's *The Forsyte Saga*. Robert Altman's movie *Gosford Park* (2002) observes this social split from a new angle, as did Kazuo Ishiguro's novel *The Remains of the Day* (1989).

Wicca is a revived witchcraft followed by some New Agers. Its practices include herbalism, divination and psychic healing. Partly because of its worship of a 'Great Goddess' it has attracted many feminists looking for alternatives to Christianity and Judaism (the popular image of Wicca was exploited by the cult film *The Wicker Man* (1973)).

Index

accent 50–1, 178–9, 215–16, 235
Acid House 148
adolescence 143–5
age 141–5, 262–4
AIDS 129–30
Alf Garnett 200–1
Alpha course 250
Amélie 24
Americanisation 145
Angles 40
Anglican Church 8, 242–3, 245–9
animals 64
Archers (The) 63–4
art 8, 15
Asian Dub Foundation 282
astrology 259, 264
asylum seekers 283
Atomic Kitten 49
A-Z of Britishness 18–19

Badly Drawn Boy 49
Bannister, Roger 13
Barnes, Julian 11, 19
bars 106
BBC 10, 152, 214, 215
Beatles (The) 10, 55
Beckhams (The) 24–5, 134, 166, 180
Belfast 57–8, 218–19
Bell, Martin 11
Belle and Sebastian 219
Benson, Ross 19
Big Brother 9, 22, 130, 153
Billy Bunter 10
'Blair's Babes' 197

Blair, Tony 22, 65, 80, 81, 83, 117, 170, 181, 197–8, 203–4, 248–9, 276
Bleasdale, Alan 85, 87
Blur 63, 86, 216
boots 164–6
Branson, Richard 26, 182
Brass Eye 128
Bridget Jones' Diary 125
'Britain Uncovered' 17
British beef 279
British Green Party (The) 68
Brookside 9, 87, 91, 251
BSE 279
Buddhism 259
Bulger case 127–8
Burberry 164
Burns, Robert 47
business 26, 182, 186

CAMRA 106
capitalism 89, 182
Cardiff 58–9, 193
Carey, Dr George 243–4
catchphrases/buzzwords 216–17
cathedrals 242, 248
Catholics 243–4
Celts 40
Channel Tunnel 39
'Chapel' 245
Child Support Agency 126–7
Childline 128, 157
children 126–8, 157
Chinese community 224, 228
Christie, Linford 13
Christmas 152, 257–8

Christmas Carol (A) 258
Church in Wales 245
Church of England 245–9
Churchill, Winston 30
city 55–9, 66
Clary, Julian 132
class 30, 179–91
'Clause 28' 130–1
clubs 149–51
Cockneys 48, 178
Common Agricultural Policy 276
Commonwealth (The) 40, 224
comprehensive schools 76–7, 80
computer games 154
Congregationalism 245
Connery, Sean 45
Conservative Party 181, 195–6, 276, 278
consumerism 28
Coogan, Steve 103
'Cool Britannia' 170
Coronation Street 95, 215
countries 40–8
country-city divide 66
countryside 60–7
Countryside Alliance (The) 66, 72
county 52–5
Cowes 8
Crawford, Robert 43
Creed, Martin 8
cricket 8, 97, 225, 231
Crusties 167–9

Daily Telegraph 13
Diana, Princess 22–4, 34, 246
Dickens, Charles 258
disability 68
Disraeli, Benjamin 11
divorce 113, 114, 123–6
Divorce Reform Act (1969) 123
Doc Marten boots 164–6
Dome (Millenium) 12–13
Doyle, Roddy 46
drugs 149, 158–62, 195
dumbing down 27, 166–7

East is East 17
EastEnders 87, 91, 95, 125, 148, 215
Easter 255
eccentricity 17, 18, 19, 163
ecology 68

Ecstasy 149, 160
Eden Project 13
Edinburgh Festival 8, 58
Edinburgh 58, 193
Edinburgh Mela 282–3
education 27, 28, 29, 75–9, 181–2, 284
Education Act (1944) 76
Eisteddfod 47
Eliot, T.S. 3
Emin, Tracey 8
England, England 19–21
English language 213–14
environment 68, 261
Equal Pay Act (1970) 122
Eriksson, Sven-Goran 279
Establishment 177, 261
estuary English 50, 215
ethnic minorities 115, 188, 211, 223–32
ethnicity 15, 146–7, 204, 281
Eton/Harrow 10, 96, 182
EU 43, 277
euro 203, 274, 277–8
Europe 39, 55, 142, 200, 203, 276–81
Evans, Gwynfor 42–3

Factory Act (1848) 113
Fake London 164
Falklands 14, 19, 246
Fall and Rise of Reginald Perrin, The 183–4
family 29, 114–17, 135
fashion 145–51, 155, 163
'Father Christmas' 258
feminism 120–3
Feng Shui 259
festivals 98, 255–8, 282–3
film 47–8, 85–6, 93–5, 96, 125 265–7
food 279–80, 282–3
foot and mouth 64, 193–4
football (soccer) 24–5, 96–7, 278–9
'four nations' 44, 70
Four Weddings and a Funeral 86, 125, 264
Further Education 76

Gaelic 50–1, 217–18
Gardeners' Question Time 64

gay lifestyles 130–2
gender 29, 116, 117–20, 150, 156, 188, 192, 204, 262–4
General Election (1992) 200–2
General Election (1997) 196
General Election (2001) 189, 190, 195–6, 201, 280
Generation X 104, 162
geography 37–9, 40
Geordies 48, 178
Giant's Causeway 52–3
Gladstone, William 4
Glastonbury 98
Glastonbury Festival 8, 169
Gold Blend adverts184, 186–7
Grace, W.G. 13
graffiti 145
grammar schools 76
Guinness 46
Guy Fawkes 256–7

Hague, William 14
Hallowe'en 256
Hamilton, Neil 11
Harry Potter 9, 96, 267
Hay-on-Wye 60–1
Heaney, Seamus 46
Hear'Say 26, 144
Heartbeat 267
Hebdidge, Dick 146
heritage 264–8
heroes 22, 30–1
Hinduja brothers 13
Hindus 241, 253–4, 268
hip hop 282
Hirst, Damien 8
Hoggart, Richard 145
'Hogmanay' 257
holidays 99
Hollyoaks 9
home ownership 191
hooligans 14
Hopkins, Anthony 48
House of Lords 180, 194, 197–8
House of Commons 194
Howards End 266
Hussein, Saddam 14

Ibiza 147
illegitimacy 114
'immigration' 32, 223, 241

individualism 21
institutions 8–9, 193
internet 288

J17 (*Just Seventeen*) 155, 158
Jewish community 254
Jorvik Centre (The) 264

Kelman, James 46
Khan, Imran 252
King Arthur 268
Kureishi, Hanif 9

Labour party 44, 89, 117–18, 196–8
ladettes 156
Lady Chatterley's Lover 128–9
language 16, 50, 122, 213–36
Lara Croft 149
Last Temptation of Christ (The) 252
Lastminute.com 183
'latchkey kids' 120
Lawson, Nigella 280
league tables (school) 80, 81
leisure 29
Lennon, John 30–1
Liberal Democrats 198–9, 201
Lindisfarne 248
literature 9, 19–20, 46, 92, 184–5, 285–6
Livingstone, Ken 56
'Loadsamoney' 186
Lodge, David 85, 99
Lord of the Rings (The) 96
Lord's Prayer (The) 242, 287
Lucozade 149

Maastricht Treaty 276
MacArthur, Ellen 26
MacGregor, Ewan 48
Madonna 47
magazines 93–4, 134, 144, 155, 158
magazines 154–5
Major, John 21, 84
Manic Street Preachers 220
Margaret, Princess 12
Marley, Bob 254
Marr, Andrew 41
marriage 115, 123–6, 264
Match of the Day 250
May Day 256
McDonald's 5, 105, 144

McLuhan, Marshall 5
media celebrities 25
Merchant/Ivory 86, 128, 265
Methodism 245
Milosevic, Slobodan 14
Milton Keynes 60–1
Mormons 242
Morris dancers 256
Mother's Day 255
Mugabe, Robert 14
multiculturalism 56, 281–6
Murphy-O'Connor, Cardinal 244
museums 56–7, 72, 99
music 24–5, 56, 86, 144, 159–62,
    183–4, 217, 219–20, 232–4, 254,
    282–3
Muslims 77, 88, 224, 226, 251–3
Mystic Meg 259

Nairn, Tom 41
National Curriculum 79, 177
National Lottery 87, 101–3, 178, 259,
    263
National Parks 53–5
nationalism 47, 55, 199, 244, 274–5
nationality 43–4
Neeson, Liam 48
New Age 163, 167, 242, 258, 260–1,
    268
New Age Travellers 262
newspapers 32, 93, 214
No Logo 28
Northern Ireland Assembly 37
north–south divide 49–50
Notting Hill 125
Notting Hill Carnival 8, 231

Observer 10, 17
Oliver, Jamie 25, 134, 280
Open University 78–9
Orwell, George 80, 101,187
OutRage 131, 132
Oxbridge 78, 83, 182

pantomime 95
*Para-Normal World of Paul McKenna
    (The)* 259
Parekh Report (The) 284
parenting 114, 120, 126–8
parliament 193–4
patriotism 41–3, 279

patron saints 44–5
Plaid Cymru 47, 200
Planet of the Apes 166
political parties 195–9
politics 11–12, 30, 37, 58, 117, 177–8,
    192–203, 221–2, 246
Pop Stars 26–7
Pop Idol 27
pop music 158–60
'Poppy Day' 257
popular culture 9, 248
population 40, 114
Portillo, Michael 132, 196
Postmodernism 15
Prince Charles 246, 269
Private Eye 28, 187
public schools 77, 79, 183
pubs 92–3, 105–6, 133, 149–50

Quakers 243
Queen Mother 12

Rab C. Nesbit 219
racism 225–6
radio 63, 68
Rastafarians 254
raves 148–9
reality television 27–8, 153
'redbricks' 78
Redgrave, Steve 22
Redwood, John 41
reggae 149, 254
region 29, 48–52
religion 5, 12, 89, 119, 245–63
Remains of the Day, (The) 266
rhyming slang 217
'rich list' 16, 180
riots 190, 226
Roddick, Anita 26, 123, 182
Room with a View (A) 266
Roux brothers 280
royalty 12, 20, 22, 92, 116, 194, 245
rugby 11, 58–9, 97
'Rule Britannia' 13
Russell, Willy 86

S4C 52
'Salatariat', (The) 185
Satanic Verses (The) 56, 252, 285
Saturday Night and Sunday Morning
    84–5, 188

Sawyer, Miranda 17
Saxons 40
Scargill, Arthur 189
school 9–10, 75–8, 79–83
Scorsese, Martin 252
Scots 219–21
Scottish Nationalist Party 45, 55, 199
Scottish Parliament 37
Scouse(rs) 48, 178, 215–16
Servius, Septimus 5
Sex Discrimination Act (1975) 122
Sexual Offences Act (1967) 129–30
sexuality 128–33, 157
Shakespeare, William 10, 30–1, 55, 215
shopping 15
Simpsons (The) 104
Smith, Zadie 9, 285–6
Smith, Paul 163
SOCRATES 278
Songs of Praise 250
Spitting Image 117, 201
sport 13–14, 22, 24–5, 58–9, 96–8, 133, 225, 235, 278–9
Stevens, Cat 252
Stonehenge 169, 262
subcultures 145–53
subjects of conversation 4
Sullivan, Andrew 41–2
Sun, (The) 13
Sunday Times, (The) 10
Swampy 261
symbols and emblems 44–5

Tafari, Levi 254
T'ai Chi 259
Tate, Dr Nick 284–5
Taylor, Richard 11
Taz 282
Tebbitt, Lord Norman 225
technology 286–8
'teenager' 144
television 9, 21, 22, 52, 80, 85, 90–2, 103–5, 123, 128, 148, 151–6, 191, 215, 217, 232, 250–1
Terence Higgins Trust 129

texting 287
Thatcher, Margaret 11, 14, 83, 117, 135, 177, 188, 193, 196
Thomas, R.S. 4, 42
Thought for the Day 250
Today 250
town 59–61
trade unions 189–90, 197
Trafford Centre 15

'underclass' 190
unemployment 87–90, 187, 191
Union Jack Flag 46, 69
university 78–9

vegetarianism 259
Vicar of Dibley (The) 251
video 127
village 61–4
voting 199–203

Warhol, Andy 153
Wax, Ruby 16, 103
Wazir, Burhan 17
Weakest Link (The) 22
weather 67
wedding cost 114
Welsh Assembly 37, 44
Welsh language 50, 221–2
West Indians 225, 228–9, 231, 234
Westminster, Duke of 17, 180
Westwood, Vivienne 163
Wicca 260
women priests 119, 248
Women's Institute (The) 133
Wood, Victoria 103
work 29, 75, 83–90, 120–3, 183, 185

xenophobia 14–16

Yoga 259
youth 29, 143–5

Zeitgeists 146
Zephaniah, Benjamin 9, 229–30, 254